STUDY GUIDE
TO ACCOMPANY
Hilton:
MANAGERIAL ACCOUNTING

Item 6024

XL - White

L - Ash

Item

5141

5089

STUDY GUIDE
TO ACCOMPANY
Hilton: MANAGERIAL ACCOUNTING
SECOND EDITION

by ROLAND A. MINCH
SUNY at Albany

McGRAW-HILL, INC.

New York St. Louis San Francisco Auckland Bogotá Caracas
Lisbon London Madrid Mexico City Milan Montreal New Delhi
San Juan Singapore Sydney Tokyo Toronto

STUDY GUIDE to accompany Hilton:
MANAGERIAL ACCOUNTING

6 7 8 9 0 MAL MAL 9 0 9 8 7 6 5

ISBN 0-07-028994-8

This book was set in Times Roman by Ann Eisner/Paula Martin.
The editors were Johanna Schmid, Judy Howarth, and Ira C. Roberts;
the production supervisor was Louise Karam.
The cover was designed by Wanda Lubelska.
Malloy Lithographing, Inc., was printer and binder.

CONTENTS

Preface

This study guide is designed to assist you in understanding the content of the text *Managerial Accounting,* second edition, by Ronald W. Hilton. It is intended to be a supplement to this text which will help you organize and evaluate your study effort in managerial accounting.

Each chapter of the study guide begins with an overview and a set of learning objectives of that chapter. The main points and key terms of the chapter are outlined and summarized in the order in which they appear in the text. For each chapter there is a variety of true-false, fill-in-the-blank, multiple-choice, and problem-type questions, together with the answers to these questions. These questions cover the major topics of the chapter and will give you an opportunity to test your understanding of the chapter material.

While there are several ways that you can make use of this study guide, the following approach may be helpful to you.

1. Start with the text itself and read the learning objectives to get an idea of what the chapter is about.
2. Read the chapter of the text with care, possibly highlighting those portions that appear important. As you read the chapter, try to keep in mind the learning objectives for the chapter. Work the text exercises and problems that have been assigned by the instructor.
3. Use the study guide to refresh yourself on the learning objectives. Then carefully go through the chapter outline in the study guide to assure yourself that you have assimilated the main points and key terms of the chapter. If there are any items that you do not understand, go back to the text and study them again.
4. Evaluate your comprehension of the chapter by doing the self-test questions and exercises that are in the study guide. Don't refer to the answers to these questions and exercises until you have tried them on your own. When you are finished, check your performance by comparing your answers with those given in the study guide.

However you decide to use this study guide, do not let it take the place of reading the text material and doing the text questions, exercises, and problems assigned by your instructor. Use this study guide as a supplementary tool to help in your understanding of the text; it is the author's hope that you will find this study guide to be valuable to you.

Roland A. Minch

STUDY GUIDE
TO ACCOMPANY
Hilton:
MANAGERIAL ACCOUNTING

Chapter 1

Managerial Accounting: An Overview

CHAPTER OVERVIEW AND LEARNING OBJECTIVES

In this chapter you will learn what the broad picture of managerial accounting is like. It will help you to see how managerial accounting is related to accounting in general and the management of organizations in general and how it differs from other areas of accounting. After finishing this chapter, you should understand:

1. The four key management processes that aid organizations in reaching their goals
2. Four objectives of the work done in managerial accounting
3. The main differences between managerial and financial accounting
4. The nature of the work done by an organization's controller, treasurer, and internal auditor
5. The major contemporary themes in managerial accounting
6. The work of various professional organizations in the field of managerial accounting, as well as the certification process and ethical standards used in managerial accounting

AN OUTLINE FOR CHAPTER STUDY

A. All organizations have a set of goals. Management needs various kinds of information to pursue these goals. In particular, managers rely on managerial-accounting information to plan and control the activities of an organization. Examples of organizational goals are: profitability, growth, product quality, and environmental responsibility.

B. The task of the management of an organization is to ensure that the goals of the organization are realized. In order to do this, managers conduct four fundamental activities:

1. Make decisions about alternative choices of action.
2. Plan the financial and operational activities of the organization.
3. Run the organization on a day-to-day basis.
4. Control the operations of the organization so that the goals are achieved.

C. Managerial-accounting work consists of the following four activities:

1. Give managers information needed for decision making and planning.
2. Help managers in directing and controlling operations.
3. Motivate managers and other employees to direct their efforts toward achieving the goals of an organization.
4. Measure the performance of subunits, managers, and other employees of an organization.

D. In managerial accounting the focus is on the needs of managers within the organization. In financial accounting the emphasis is on reporting to parties outside the organization. Both managerial accounting and financial accounting use data from an organization's basic accounting system. There is *no* regulation of managerial-accounting work, whereas financial-accounting work must conform to generally accepted accounting principles and is regulated by the Financial Accounting Standards Board (FASB) and the Securities and Exchange Commission (SEC).

E. A cost-accounting system is used to accumulate cost data for both managerial- and financial-accounting purposes.

F. Understanding an organization's structure will help one to comprehend the role of an accountant in that organization.

1. Line managers are directly involved in the specific operation of the organization.
2. Staff managers supervise activities that support the mission of the organization and are indirectly involved in the operations of the organization.

G. The controller of an organization is the chief managerial and financial accountant. The treasurer of an organization is mainly responsible for safeguarding the organization's assets and raising capital. An internal auditor of an organization reviews the accounting procedures, records, and reports to test the effectiveness of the organization's accounting system.

H. Managerial accounting has the following key themes:

1. Providing information to managers to help facilitate decision making and to influence these decisions.
2. Understanding human behavior and reaction of managers to information provided them in order to be effective in providing managerial-accounting information.
3. Evaluating costs and benefits of providing information for management. The cost of providing managerial-accounting information may exceed the benefits derived from that information.
4. Adapting information provided managers to rapidly changing and varied business environments. This information must be relevant to the following environments:

   a. Service organizations as well as manufacturing organizations need managerial-accounting information. In service organizations, services are usually consumed as they are produced; service organizations are more labor-intensive than manufacturing firms.
   b. In today's business environment a firm must strive for excellence in product quality and service due to intense international competition.
   c. New high-tech industries which employ just-in-time production systems have emerged. These systems use a "pull" approach to controlling manufacturing.
   d. There is greater emphasis on product quality and the need for tracking the cost of quality.
   e. Modern manufacturing processes are conducted by computer-controlled machines. This is commonly referred to as computer-integrated manufacturing.
   f. Automated production systems generate more diverse products with shorter life cycles.

I. The goals of a cost management system are to:

1. Measure the cost of resources used in performing the significant activities of an organization
2. Eliminate those costs that add no value to the product or services generated by the organization
3. Ascertain the efficiency and effectiveness of the major activities of the organization
4. Identify new activities that can improve the future performance of the organization

J. A system is an integrated structure designed to achieve a stated purpose. It is made up of:

1. Inputs, which are data entered into the system
2. A process, which is the set of activities performed to achieve the stated purpose
3. Outputs, which are the information provided by the system and available to the user of the system

K. The majority of businesses today employ computers in virtually all functions that involve data. Computer information systems consist of:

1. Hardware—input and output devices together with a central processing unit
2. Software—programs which provide instructions for the computer

3. Data—numbers and words stored or manipulated by the computer
4. Humans—the people who operate and maintain the system

L. The data maintained and manipulated by a computer information system constitute a database. The software used to manage the database is called a database-management system.

M. A computer-based system designed to help managers make certain types of decisions is called a decision-support system. It includes access to a database and pertinent methods of utilizing the database to provide results about the database that are useful in making certain decisions.

N. The set of linked, value-creating activities ranging from obtaining raw materials to the delivery of products is called the value chain of an organization. Managers must understand the entire value chain in which their organization participates. It is important to understand the costs incurred in creating value in each link in the value chain; the cost-causing factors are called cost drivers. Managing these cost relationships to the organization's advantage is called strategic cost management. The theory of constraints refers to an approach where management seeks to discover the most cost-effective means of relaxing those constraints that prevent the organization from reaching a higher level of achievement.

O. Primary professional organizations that relate to the work of managerial accountants are:

1. Institute of Management Accountants (IMA) in the United States. This organization sponsors the Certified Management Accountant (CMA) program.
2. Society of Management Accountants of Canada. This organization sponsors the Registered Industrial Accountant (RIA) program.
3. Institute of Chartered Management Accountants in Great Britain.
4. Institute of Chartered Accountants in Australia.

P. The Institute of Management Accountants has developed ethical standards for managerial accountants that pertain to the following areas:

1. Competence
2. Confidentiality
3. Integrity
4. Objectivity

KEY TERMS

Activity accounting 15
Activity-based costing (ABC) 15
Attention-directing function 6
Certified Management Accountant (CMA) 20
Computer information system (CIS) 17
Controller (or comptroller) 9
Controlling 5
Cost-accounting system 7
Cost driver 18
Cost management system 15
Database management system 17
Decision making 4
Decision support system 17
Directing operations 5
Financial accounting 7
Internal auditor 10
Just-in-time (JIT) production system 13
Line positions 8
Managerial accounting 3
Non-value-added costs 15
Planning 5
Staff positions 9
Strategic cost management 18
System 15
Treasurer 10
Value chain 18

SELF-EVALUATION QUESTIONS AND ANSWERS

True-False Questions

_____ 1. Managers rely on managerial-accounting information to prepare financial statements.

_____ 2. A chief purpose of managerial accounting is to motivate managers toward achieving the goals of the organization.

_____ 3. Production-cost data are used exclusively for managerial-accounting purposes.

_____ 4. In order to understand the role of a managerial accountant in an organization, it is necessary to know the structure of that organization.

_____ 5. Making a managerial decision means choosing among the alternative goals of the organization.

_____ 6. Planning involves developing a detailed financial and operational description of past operations.

_____ 7. A main purpose of managerial accounting is to motivate managers to direct their efforts toward achieving the goals of an organization.

_____ 8. A means of motivating people toward an organization's goals is to measure their performance in achieving those goals.

_____ 9. In some organizations, internal auditors make a broad performance evaluation of middle management.

_____ 10. The effectiveness of a managerial accountant in providing information does not depend on his or her understanding of human behavior.

_____ 11. Information is a commodity.

_____ 12. The main difference between service and manufacturing organizations is that in service organizations most services are consumed as they are generated.

_____ 13. An implication of the just-in-time inventory philosophy is the need to deemphasize product quality.

_____ 14. A system is made up of a set of inputs, a process, and a set of outputs.

_____ 15. Today most businesses rely on computers for virtually all functions that involve data.

_____ 16. The Institute of Management Accountants sponsors the Certified Management Accountant (CMA) program.

_____ 17. Recognizing important cost relationships among activities in a value chain and managing those relationships to the firm's advantage is known as optimal cost management.

Fill-in-the-Blank Questions

1. In pursuing the goals of an organization, managers need _______________.
2. The system which accumulates cost data for use in both managerial accounting and financial accounting is called a(n) _______________ system.
3. Ensuring that the organization operates in the intended manner and achieves its goals means that management is engaged in _______________.
4. The focus of _______________ accounting is on the needs of managers within the organization.
5. _______________ managers are directly involved in the specific operations of an organization.
6. In many organizations the _______________ is the chief managerial and financial accountant.
7. A(n) _______________ system is a fully automated, computer-controlled production process.
8. In _______________ accounting the emphasis is on reporting to parties outside the organization.
9. Managers in _______________ positions supervise activities that support the goals of the organization.
10. The _______________ of an organization is responsible for safeguarding its assets.
11. A(n) _______________ is an integrated structure designed to achieve a stated purpose.
12. A(n) _______________ system is software designed to allow a computer information system to make the most efficient use of its database.
13. A(n) _______________ system is a computer-based system that is designed to assist managers in making certain kinds of decisions.
14. The _______________ of the organization is the set of linked, value-creating activities ranging from getting raw materials to the delivery of products.

Multiple-Choice Questions

_____ 1. Which of the following would *not* typically be a goal of an organization?
(a) Profitability
(b) Product quality
(c) Cost maximization
(d) Market diversification

_____ 2. In pursuing an organization's goals, which of the following is *not* a basic activity of managers?
(a) Decision making
(b) Financial reporting to stockholders

(c) Directing operations
(d) Controlling

_____ 3. Which of the following is true of financial accounting?
(a) Users of its information are primarily outside the organization.
(b) It is not regulated by outside agencies.
(c) Only a small portion of its data is drawn from the organization's basic accounting system.
(d) Its reports are seldom based on historical transaction data.

_____ 4. The controller of an organization
(a) supervises the accounting department.
(b) prepares all reports for external parties.
(c) is responsible for preparing reports for internal users.
(d) does all of the above.

_____ 5. The objectives of a cost-management system do *not* include
(a) measuring the cost of resources used in performing significant activities.
(b) eliminating the non-value-added costs.
(c) eliminating the need for financial reporting.
(d) determining the effectiveness and efficiency of all major organizational activities.

_____ 6. Which of the following is *not* a component of a computer information system?
(a) Hardware
(b) Software
(c) Data
(d) Work station desk and chair

_____ 7. Which of the following is an area of concern in the ethical standards set forth by the Institute of Management Accountants?
(a) Confidentiality
(b) Integrity
(c) Objectivity
(d) All of the above

Exercise

1.1 Carter's Home Products, Inc. (CHP) has in inventory a significant number of health care items that are relatively obsolete and now have a market value well below the amount paid for these items originally. The external auditors observed this and recommended to the chief executive officer of CHP that provision should be made in the accounting records for the reduction of any obsolete inventories to their net realizable values.

The controller, who reports directly to the chief executive officer and is eligible for a bonus plan tied to corporate profits, was aware of the obsolete inventory and its market value declining below original cost long before the external auditors arrived, but he failed to appraise the chief executive officer of this matter and did nothing to adjust recorded inventory values.

Required:

Write a concise paragraph explaining any actions the controller should have taken and any ethical problems associated with the controller's behavior.

Solution Space for Exercise 1.1:

____

____

____

____

Answers to True-False Questions

1. F Managers rely on financial-accounting information to prepare financial statements.
2. T
3. F These data are also used for financial-accounting purposes.
4. T
5. F Managerial decisions are made by choosing among the alternative courses of action available to the manager.
6. F Planning pertains to future operations, not past operations.
7. T
8. T
9. T
10. F Understanding human behavior is an important factor in contributing to the effectiveness of a managerial accountant in providing information.
11. T
12. T
13. F The just-in-time philosophy implies that product quality must be emphasized.
14. T
15. T
16. T
17. F This is known as strategic cost management, not optimal cost management.

Answers to Fill-in-the-Blank Questions

1. information
2. cost-accounting
3. control
4. managerial
5. Line
6. controller
7. computer-integrated manufacturing
8. financial
9. staff
10. treasurer
11. system
12. database-management
13. decision-support
14. value chain

Answers to Multiple-Choice Questions

1. **(c)** An organization would most likely be interested in cost minimization.
2. **(b)** Financial reporting to stockholders is primarily an activity of financial accountants.
3. **(a)** Financial accounting is regulated by the FASB and the SEC. The major portion of its data comes from the basic accounting system, and its reports are based chiefly on historical transaction data.
4. **(d)** The controller's work involves each of the items indicated in choices (a), (b), and (c).
5. **(c)** A cost-management system seeks to improve the quality of financial reporting.
6. **(d)** A computer information system does not need a desk or a chair to make it function.
7. **(d)** Each of the items in (a), (b), and (c) is of concern in the ethical standards of the IMA.

Solution to Exercise

1.1 The controller's lack of action concerning the overstatement of inventory does not comply with generally accepted accounting principles. The controller had an ethical obligation to communicate the information to the chief executive officer in a timely manner. The controller's behavior of not reducing the value of inventory was apparently for the purpose of keeping expenses down so that profit would increase and hence his bonus would increase. This self-serving motive is clearly suspect.

Chapter 2

Basic Cost Terms and Concepts

CHAPTER OVERVIEW AND LEARNING OBJECTIVES

This chapter deals with the variety of ways in which costs can be described. Since costs are used for several different purposes in accounting, it is necessary to become acquainted with cost terminology and how it is used in practice. The material is straightforward and should give you no difficulty. When you have finished this chapter, you should understand:

1. The meaning of the phrase "different costs for different purposes"
2. The nature of variable and fixed costs, both in total and on a unit-cost basis
3. The concept of a cost driver and its importance
4. The difference between direct and indirect costs and between controllable and uncontrollable costs
5. The difference between product costs, period costs, and expenses
6. The various functional-area costs, such as merchandise, marketing, administrative, research, and development, and the three types of manufacturing costs
7. The role of costs in an income statement and a balance sheet for merchandising, manufacturing, and service industry organizations
8. How to prepare a schedule of cost of goods manufactured, a schedule of cost of goods sold, and a manufacturing income statement
9. The meaning of other costs, including opportunity costs, out-of-pocket costs, sunk costs, differential costs, marginal costs, and average costs
10. The behavior people demonstrate when dealing with opportunity costs and sunk costs

AN OUTLINE FOR CHAPTER STUDY

A. The meaning of the term "cost" depends on the context in which it is used. Adjectives are attached to the word "cost" to describe the type of cost that pertains to a particular situation. Thus, we use different costs in accounting depending on the particular purposes these cost descriptions are supposed to serve. The use of these different types of costs enables managerial accountants to give the proper cost data to managers.

B. An important way of classifying costs in an organization is according to whether they are variable or fixed. The following are important points about fixed and variable costs:

   1. Both fixed and variable costs depend on the notion of an "activity" or a "cost driver." An activity is a measure of an organization's output of products or services. Activities that cause costs are called cost drivers.

2. A variable cost in total changes in direct proportion to the cost driver. While the total variable cost changes in direct proportion to the cost driver, the variable cost per unit of the cost driver does not change; it is constant.
3. A fixed cost in total does not change as the level of the cost driver varies. However, if the total fixed cost is divided by a specified level of the cost driver, we say that the fixed cost is unitized. Dividing the total fixed cost by various specified levels of the cost driver gives different units fixed costs. Thus, fixed costs change as levels of the cost driver vary.

C. When identifying cost drivers, the extent to which a cost or pool of costs varies with the cost driver should be considered. The greater the correlation between the cost and the cost driver, the better will be the understanding of cost behavior. There is a trade-off between the cost of measuring cost drivers and the quality of the cost information obtained. As the number of cost drivers used to explain cost behavior increases, the accuracy of the cost information increases, but so does the cost of getting that information.

D. Responsibility accounting is a type of accounting in which costs are traced to the work center where they are incurred. Such costs that can be traced to specific work centers are called direct costs. If a cost cannot be traced to a specific work center, it is called an indirect cost. An important goal of a cost management system is to trace as many costs as possible to the activities that cause these costs.

E. A controllable cost is a cost that a manager can control or significantly influence the level of. Those costs that managers cannot influence in a significant way are called uncontrollable costs. Some costs may be controllable in the short run but not in the long run.

F. Manufacturing costs are the same as production costs. They are classified as direct material, direct labor, and overhead.

1. Direct-material costs are the costs of raw materials that are directly incorporated into and directly traceable to the finished product.
2. Direct-labor costs are the salaries, wages, and fringe benefits of personnel who work directly on the product being made.
3. Manufacturing overhead (sometimes called factory overhead) refers to all other costs of production that are not direct material or direct labor. The following points about these overhead costs should be noted:

   a. Indirect-material costs are those costs of materials needed for production that are not an integral part of the finished product.
   b. Indirect-labor costs are the costs of personnel who are needed for the production process but who do not work directly on the finished product.
   c. Other types of overhead costs include depreciation of plant and equipment, utilities, and the costs of service departments. A service department offers support to the manufacturing process but does not work directly on the manufacturing of products.
   d. Overtime premiums and idle-time costs are examples of manufacturing-overhead costs. Overtime premiums are wages paid to personnel who work beyond regularly scheduled hours. Idle-time costs refer to the costs of employees' time that is not spent productively on the manufacturing process; this idle time could result from equipment breakdowns.

4. Conversion costs refer to the combination of both direct-labor and manufacturing-overhead costs. Prime costs refer to the combination of direct-material and direct-labor costs.
5. The relative proportion of an organization's fixed and variable costs is known as the organization's cost structure. In today's manufacturing environment, many cost structures are moving toward a greater proportion of fixed costs.

G. In service and nonprofit organizations, services are consumed as they are generated. The process of recording and classifying costs in these types of organizations is important for the same kinds of reasons as it is in manufacturing organizations.

H. Nonmanufacturing costs are all the other costs of an organization besides the costs of production.

1. Merchandising costs are the costs of acquiring merchandise for sale in a retail or wholesale organization.

2. Marketing costs are made up of selling costs and distribution costs. Selling costs are the costs of getting orders for sales, which include sales commissions and advertising. Distribution costs consist of the costs of storing, handling, and shipping goods.
3. Administrative costs are the costs of running the organization as a whole; they include the salaries of top management.
4. Research and development costs refer to the cost of creating and developing new goods and services.

I. The timing with which costs are recognized in the accounting system is very important.

1. An expense is a cost that is incurred or an asset that is used up or sold for the purpose of generating revenue.
2. A product cost (or inventoriable cost) is the cost assigned to products that were either purchased or made to be sold.
3. A period cost is a cost that is recognized as an expense in the period in which that cost was incurred. Research and development, marketing, and administrative costs are period costs.
4. When product costs are expensed, they are called the costs of goods sold.

J. In service organizations, the costs of generating services are known as operating expenses; they are period costs.

K. There are three types of inventories (which are assets) in manufacturing organizations:

1. Raw-materials inventory includes all materials acquired before they are used in production.
2. Work-in-process inventory consists of all costs of products that are partially completed as of a given balance sheet date.
3. Finished-goods inventory is made up of all costs of products that are completed and ready for sale.

The formula that describes the behavior of raw-materials inventory is as follows:

Beginning inventory of raw materials	+	Purchases of raw materials	−	Ending inventory of raw materials	=	Cost of raw materials used

The formula for cost of goods manufactured is:

Beginning inventory of work in process	+	Total manufacturing overhead	−	Ending inventory of work in process	=	Cost of goods manufactured

The formula for cost of goods sold is:

Beginning inventory of finished goods	+	Cost of goods manufactured	−	Ending inventory of finished goods	=	Cost of goods sold

You should relate these formulas to Exhibit 2-9 in the text.

L. Very often managerial accountants use concepts from economics to classify costs. These costs are useful to managers in making decisions.

1. An opportunity cost measures the economic benefit that is forgone when one choice of action is taken, thus precluding an alternate choice of action.
2. An out-of-pocket cost is a cost that involves the payment of cash or other assets when that cost is incurred.
3. A sunk cost is a historical cost—one that is history; it was incurred in the past and cannot be changed by future action.
4. A differential cost (or incremental cost) is the amount by which the cost differs under two alternative actions.
5. A marginal cost is the cost incurred when one additional unit is made.
6. The average cost per unit is the total cost divided by the quantity of units related to that total cost.

M. One of the key tasks of the managerial accountant is to apply the cost concepts and classification to each situation in the most appropriate way. The benefits of measuring and classifying costs must be weighed against the cost of doing this work. It is possible that managers will receive more cost data than they can utilize effectively; this is known as information overload.

KEY TERMS

Activity 30
Administrative costs 39
Average cost per unit 49
Controllable cost 35
Conversion costs 37
Cost drivers 30
Cost of goods sold 39
Cost structure 37
Differential cost 48
Direct cost 34
Direct-labor cost 36
Direct material 36
Distribution costs 39
Expense 39
Finished goods 43
Fixed cost 31
Idle time 37
Incremental costs 48
Indirect cost 34
Indirect labor 36
Indirect material 36
Information overload 50
Inventoriable cost 39
Inventoriable goods 39
Manufacturing costs 35
Manufacturing overhead 36
Marginal cost 48
Marketing costs 39
Merchandise costs 39
Operating expenses 41
Opportunity cost 45
Out-of-pocket costs 45
Overtime premium 36
Period costs 39
Prime costs 37
Product cost 39
Raw material 42
Research and development (R & D) costs 39
Schedule of cost of goods manufactured 44
Schedule of cost of goods sold 44
Selling costs 39
Service departments 36
Service industry firm 37
Sunk costs 47
Variable cost 30
Work in process 42

SELF-EVALUATION QUESTIONS AND ANSWERS

True-False Questions

____ **1.** Cost data classified in one way for a given purpose may be inappropriate for other purposes.

____ **2.** If the unit variable cost is $45 to make one unit of product, then the total variable cost to make 100 units is $4,500.

____ **3.** Costs that are not directly traceable to a particular department are known as uncontrollable costs.

____ **4.** An important objective of a cost management system is to trace as many costs as possible directly to activities that caused those costs.

____ **5.** Raw materials that are consumed in making a product and are physically added to the finished product are known as direct materials.

____ **6.** The total fixed costs during the period to make 5,000 units is $35,000. Based on these data, the unit fixed cost is $7.

____ **7.** Activities that are caused by the incurrence of cost are called cost drivers.

____ **8.** Costs that are controllable in the long run are also controllable in the short run.

____ **9.** If a product cost is neither direct labor nor direct materials, then it must be manufacturing overhead.

____ **10.** Direct-material cost plus conversion cost is known as prime cost.

____ **11.** Merchandising cost and marketing cost both refer to the same type of cost.

____ **12.** The cost of developing new products and services is known as marketing cost.

____ **13.** Period costs are recognized as expenses during the time period in which they are incurred.

____ **14.** Overtime premiums are part of direct-labor costs.

____ **15.** Operating expenses are period costs.

____ **16.** Work-in-process inventory includes the cost of products that have been completed and are ready for sale.

____ **17.** Total cost divided by the quantity of units related to that total cost is the marginal cost per unit.

____ **18.** As the number of cost drivers increases, the accuracy of the cost information goes down.

Fill-in-the-Blank Questions

1. The measure of an organization's output of products or services is known as activity.
2. variable cost per unit does not change as the level of the cost driver varies.
3. Tracing costs to particular work centers is known as responsibility accounting.
4. The cost of salaries, wages, and fringe benefits of personnel who do not work directly on the product but who are needed for the production process is called indirect labor cost.
5. Direct labor plus manufacturing overhead make up conversion costs.
6. The relative proportion of an organization's fixed and variable costs is called the cost structure of the organization.
7. Total variable cost changes in direct proportion to the level of the cost driver.
8. A cost that can be traced to a particular work center is known as a(n) direct cost.
9. When an asset is used up or sold for the purposes of generating revenue, the cost incurred is called a(n) expense.
10. A(n) inventoriable cost is the same as a product cost.
11. All materials acquired to be used in production constitute raw materials inventory.
12. Out of pocket costs are those costs that require the payment of cash or other assets as the result of their incurrence.
13. Sunk costs are those costs that have been incurred in the past.
14. Finished goods inventory is made up of all goods completed and ready for sale.
15. A(n) opportunity cost is the economic benefit forgone when one action is chosen over an alternative course of action.
16. The cost incurred to make one additional unit is known as the marginal cost.

Multiple-Choice Questions

b 1. Which of the following is correct? As the level of a cost driver varies,
   - (a) unit variable costs change.
   - (b) total variable costs change.
   - (c) fixed cost in total changes.
   - (d) unit fixed cost does not change.

d 2. Which of the following are manufacturing costs: I, direct materials; II, indirect labor; III, depreciation on plant and equipment?
   - (a) Only I
   - (b) Only I and II
   - (c) Only II and III
   - (d) I, II, and III

c 3. Marketing costs do *not* include
   - (a) sales commissions.
   - (b) shipping costs.
   - (c) the president's salary.
   - (d) advertising costs.

c 4. Consider the following two statements:
   - I. Beginning inventory of finished goods, plus cost of goods manufactured, less the cost of goods sold equals the ending inventory of finished goods.
   - II. Beginning inventory of finished goods, plus the cost of goods manufactured, less ending inventory of finished goods equals the cost of goods sold.

   Which is (are) true?
   - (a) Only I
   - (b) Only II
   - (c) Both I and II
   - (d) Neither I nor II

a 5. The cost of goods manufactured does *not* include
  (a) the cost of distributing the goods from the warehouse during the period.
  (b) direct-labor costs incurred during the period.
  (c) manufacturing-overhead costs incurred during the period.
  (d) the cost of direct materials used in production during the period.

b 6. The total cost to produce 500 units of finished product is $75,000. This total cost is made up of $60,000 variable cost and $15,000 fixed cost. Which of the following is true?
  (a) The average cost per unit is $120.
  (b) The unit fixed cost is $30.
  (c) The variable cost per unit is the same as the average cost per unit.
  (d) The variable cost per unit is $150.

Exercises

2.1 Smokey Mountain Furniture Company makes wooden lawn furniture in its Hicksville Division. Several costs incurred by this division are listed below:

1. Salaries of workers who cut the wood to form chair arms and legs
2. Electricity used in the Assembly Department
3. Salary of the sales manager
4. Oil used to lubricate the cutting machines
5. Wood used to make the furniture
6. Property taxes on the plant
7. Depreciation on the word processing equipment in the division manager's office
8. Fringe benefits for the workers who assemble the furniture
9. Paint for chairs used in the Finishing Department
10. Sandpaper used in the Finishing Department
11. Overtime premiums paid to Assembly Department workers
12. Fire insurance on the furniture warehouse
13. Salaries of janitors in the plant
14. Fringe benefits of the general office workers
15. Repairs made to the cutting machines
16. Shipping costs for sending furniture to retail outlets
17. Billing costs for furniture sold
18. Cartons used to ship the finished furniture
19. Travel expenses of salespeople
20. Cost to ship lumber to the Hicksville plant

Required:

Classify these costs according to the following categories:

(a) Product
(b) Period
(c) Administrative
(d) Marketing
(e) Manufacturing
(f) Direct Material
(g) Direct labor
(h) Manufacturing overhead

Solution Space for Exercise 2.1:

1. a, e, g
2. a, e, h
3. b, d
4. a, e, h
5. a, e, f
6. a, e, h
7. b, c,
8. a, e, h
9. a, e, f
10. a, e, h

11. a, e, h

12. b, d

13. a, e, h

14. b, c

15. a, e, h

16. b, d,

17. b, c

18. a, e, f

19. b, d,

20. a, e, f

2.2 The Taber Company makes and sells clay pottery. The following cost data were recorded for 19x2:

1.	Direct materials used in production	$482,000
2.	Salaries of salespersons	67,000 ✓
3.	Property taxes on factory building	8,000
4.	General office salaries	105,000
5.	Factory supervision	50,000
6.	Depreciation on general office equipment	6,000
7.	Wages paid for direct labor	291,000
8.	Factory utilities	34,000
9.	Advertising expense	93,000 ✓
10.	Miscellaneous administrative expenses	17,000 ✓
11.	Depreciation on factory plant and equipment	85,000
12.	Fringe benefits for direct laborers	73,000

There were no beginning or ending inventories, except for an ending finished-goods inventory of $83,000.

Required:

Compute the following costs for 19x2:

(a) Total conversion costs
(b) Total prime costs
(c) Total costs of goods manufactured
(d) Total cost of goods sold
(e) Total marketing costs
(f) Total administrative costs
(g) Total period costs

a 8,000
50,000
34,000
85,000
73,000

Solution Space for Exercise 2.2:

(a) Overhead 250,000 + Dir Labor 291,000 = 541,000

(b) 482,000 + 291,000 + 73,000 = 846,000

C = 482,000
250,000 (overhead)
291,000 (labor)

(c) 482,000 + 250,000 + 291,000 = 1,023,000

(d) 0 + 1,023,000 − 83,000 = 940,000

(e) 67,000 + 93,000 = 160,000 (Sales salaries & advertising)

(f) 105,000 + 6,000 + 17,000 = 128,000

(g) 160,000 + 128,000 (Admin & Marketing Costs

2.3 The cost of the electricity at the Helman Company each month is $400 plus $.02 for each kilowatt-hour used. During the month of March the company used 8,000 kilowatt-hours.

Required:

(a) Find the total variable cost of electricity for March.
(b) Find the unit fixed cost of electricity for March.
(c) Find the average cost of electricity per kilowatt-hour for March.

Solution Space for Exercise 2.3:

(a) $160.00

(b) $.05

(c) $.07

2.4 Given the following set of data:

Beginning inventory, raw materials		$15,000
Ending inventory, raw materials		$10,000
Purchases of raw materials	85,000	?
Direct materials used	90,000	?
Direct labor		$175,000
Manufacturing overhead	—	$112,000
Total manufacturing costs		$377,000
Beginning inventory, work in process	28,000	?
Ending inventory, work in process		$16,000
Cost of goods manufactured		$389,000
Beginning inventory, finished goods	73,000	?
Cost of goods available for sale		$462,000
Ending inventory, finished goods		$61,000
Cost of goods sold	401,000	?
Sales		$741,000
Gross margin	340,000	?
Selling and administrative expenses	197,000	?
Income before taxes		$143,000
Income tax expense	45,000	?
Net income		$98,000

Required:

Find the missing amounts in the given set of data.

Solution Space for Exercise 2.4:

Beg Inventory Raw Materials	15000
Ending Inven. Raw Materials	10,000

Answers to True-False Questions

1. T
2. T
3. F These costs are called indirect costs.
4. T
5. T
6. T
7. F Activities that cause cost are called cost drivers.
8. F Costs that are controllable in the long run may be uncontrollable in the short run.
9. T
10. F Prime cost is direct-material cost plus direct-labor cost.
11. F Merchandising cost is the cost of acquiring goods for sale, whereas marketing costs are the costs of selling and distributing goods.
12. F These costs are called research and development costs.
13. T
14. F Overhead premiums are part of manufacturing overhead.
15. T
16. F Work-in process inventory includes only the cost of partially completed products.
17. F Total cost divided by the corresponding quantity of units is called average cost. Marginal cost is the cost to make one extra unit.
18. F The accuracy of the cost information goes up.

Answers to Fill-in-the-Blank Questions

1. activity
2. Variable
3. responsibility
4. indirect-labor
5. conversion
6. cost structure
7. variable
8. direct
9. expense
10. inventoriable
11. raw-materials
12. Out-of-pocket
13. Sunk
14. Finished-goods
15. opportunity
16. marginal

Answers to Multiple-Choice Questions

1. **(b)** When the cost driver level varies, unit variable costs and total fixed costs remain constant, whereas unit fixed cost changes.
2. **(d)** All three of these costs are manufacturing costs.
3. **(c)** The president's salary is an administrative expense.
4. **(c)** Both statements are true.
5. **(a)** The costs of distributing goods from the warehouse are marketing costs.
6. **(b)** Unit fixed cost = $15,000/500 = $30. Note that average cost per unit = $75,000/500 = $150; variable cost per unit = $60,000/500 = $120.

Solutions to Exercises

2.1

1.	a, e, g	**11.**	a, e, h
2.	a, e, h	**12.**	b, d
3.	b, d	**13.**	a, e, h
4.	a, e, h	**14.**	b, c
5.	a, e, f	**15.**	a, e, h
6.	a, e, h	**16.**	b, d
7.	b, c	**17.**	b, c
8.	a, e, g	**18.**	a, e, f
9.	a, e, f	**19.**	b, d
10.	a, e, h	**20.**	a, e, f

2.2 **(a)** $541,000 = $8,000 + $50,000 + $291,000 + $34,000 + $85,000 + $73,000

(b) $846,000 = $482,000 + $291,000 + $73,000

(c) $1,023,000 = $482,000 + $8,000 + $50,000 + $291,000 + $34,000 + $85,000 + $73,000

(d) $940,000 = $1,023,000 − $83,000

(e) $160,000 = $67,000 + $93,000

(f) $128,000 = $105,000 + $6,000 + $17,000

(g) $288,000 = $160,000 + $128,000

2.3 **(a)** $160 = 8,000 × $.02

(b) $.05 = $400/8,000

(c) $.07 = ($400 + $160)/8,000

2.4	Beginning inventory, raw materials	$15,000
(1)	Add: Raw-materials purchases	$85,000
	Raw materials available for use	$100,000
	Less: Ending inventory, raw materials	$10,000
(2)	Raw materials used	$90,000
	Direct labor	$175,000
	Manufacturing overhead	$112,000
	Total manufacturing costs	$377,000
(3)	Add: Beginning inventory, work in process	$28,000
	Subtotal	$405,000
	Less: Ending inventory, work in process	$16,000
	Cost of goods manufactured	$389,000
(4)	Add: Beginning inventory, finished goods	$73,000
	Cost of goods available for sale	$462,000
	Less: Ending inventory, finished goods	$61,000
(5)	Cost of goods sold	$401,000
	Sales	$741,000
	Less: Cost of goods sold	$401,000
(6)	Gross margin	$340,000
(7)	Less: Selling and administrative expenses	$197,000
	Income before taxes	$143,000
(8)	Income tax expenses	$45,000
	Net income	$98,000

Note: The missing amounts can be calculated as follows in the order indicated:

(8) 143,000 – 98,000 = 45,000
(5) 462,000 – 61,000 = 401,000
(6) 741,000 – 401,000 = 340,000
(7) 340,000 – 143,000 = 197,000
(4) 462,000 – 389,000 = 73,000
(3) 389,000 + 16,000 – 377,000 = 28,000
(2) 377,000 – 112,000 – 175,000 = 90,000
(1) 90,000 + 10,000 – 15,000 = 85,000

Chapter 3

Job-Order Costing Systems

CHAPTER OVERVIEW AND LEARNING OBJECTIVES

This chapter begins your study of product-costing systems. It will extend through the next two chapters. In this chapter the focus is on job-order costing, which is appropriate for those organizations that make products or render services that are different from customer to customer. These products or services are "specialized" to meet customer needs. When you have finished this chapter, you should understand:

1. The role of product and service costing in various types of organizations
2. The flow of costs through the manufacturing accounts that are used in product costing
3. The difference between job-order and process costing
4. How to compute predetermined overhead rates and their use in a job-order costing system
5. How to prepare journal entries that record the costs of production in a job-order costing system
6. How to prepare a schedule of cost of goods manufactured, a schedule of cost of goods sold, and an income statement for a manufacturer
7. The cost-benefit issues of accuracy versus timeliness of information in accounting for overhead.
8. The two-stage allocation process used to compute departmental overhead rates.
9. How to diagram and describe the two-stage allocation process used in activity-based costing
10. Project-costing methods used in service and nonprofit organizations

AN OUTLINE FOR CHAPTER STUDY

A. The purpose of product-costing systems is to accumulate the costs incurred in production and to assign these costs to the finished products made by the organization.

   1. The product costs in a manufacturing organization are used in financial accounting to value inventory and to compute the cost of goods sold; they are used in managerial accounting for planning, control, and decision making.
   2. In merchandising companies, where products are sold but not made, product costing consists of keeping track of the costs of buying and transporting the merchandise for sale.
   3. In service and nonprofit organizations, product (service) costing involves the accumulation of the cost of services that are rendered by the organization.

B. In manufacturing firms, the flow of costs through the manufacturing accounts proceeds according to these steps:

1. As production takes place, the costs of direct materials, direct labor, and manufacturing overhead are added to Work-in-Process Inventory. Work in process is partially completed inventory.
2. When products are completed, their product costs are transferred from Work-in-Process Inventory to Finished-Goods Inventory.
3. When the products are sold, the product costs in Finished-Goods Inventory are transferred to Cost of Goods Sold; these product costs in Cost of Goods Sold become an expense in the period when the products are sold.

C. Job-order costing is employed by organizations whose products are made in distinct batches that are significantly different from one another; each batch is called a job or job order. The costs of production are accumulated by each job. On the other hand, process costing is used by organizations that make large numbers of identical units; in process costing, costs of production are accumulated for a large number of units and these costs are then averaged over all the units.

D. In job-order costing, all manufacturing costs associated with a particular job are accumulated on a document called a job-cost sheet; this job-cost sheet is a subsidiary-ledger account. The totality of all these subsidiary-ledger accounts of jobs that are partially completed constitutes Work-in-Process Inventory. A job-cost sheet consists of all the direct materials, direct labor, and manufacturing overhead assigned to the job.

1. The direct-material costs are those costs of raw materials that are added to the job. The materials that are to be used in the job are listed on a material-requisition form. (This form is an example of a source document which is the basis of an accounting entry.) If raw materials are routinely used in production, they are often listed on a bill of materials; this form gives all the materials needed to make a product. In scheduling the use of raw materials in production, an operations-management tool known as material-requirements planning (MRP) is often employed.
2. Direct-labor costs are assigned to jobs based on time tickets filled out by employees; these time tickets record the time a worker spends on each job.
3. Manufacturing overhead is a heterogeneous pool of indirect production costs. These costs are assigned to jobs in steps.

   a. These overhead costs are first assigned to department overhead centers; this step is called cost distribution.
   b. Next the overhead costs of service departments (departments such as energy and management-information systems which support the departments that make the products) are allocated to the production departments. This step is called service-department cost allocation.
   c. Third, the overhead costs accumulated in the production departments are assigned to the jobs. This step is called overhead application.

E. Manufacturing overhead can be applied to jobs on the basis of actual costs or estimated costs. However, actual costs may not be available in a timely manner. Consequently, overhead costs are often applied to jobs by using predetermined overhead rates. Predetermined overhead rates are developed using an estimate of manufacturing-overhead cost for the forthcoming period and an estimated cost-driver level for this period. These rates are computed as follows:

$$\text{Predetermined overhead rate} = \frac{\text{Budgeted manufacturing-overhead cost}}{\text{Budgeted level of the cost driver}}$$

F. The specific journal entries to record the costs of production in job-order costing and other related entries are as follows (debits are in the left-hand column and credits are in the right-hand column):

		Debit	Credit
1.	Raw-Material Inventory	$$$	
	Accounts Payable		$$$
	To record the purchase of direct materials.		
2.	Work-in-Process Inventory	$$$	
	Raw-Material Inventory		$$$
	To record the use of direct materials in production.		

		Debit	Credit
3.	Manufacturing Overhead	$$$	
	Manufacturing-Supplies Inventory		$$$
	To record the addition of indirect materials to overhead.		
4.	Work-in-Process Inventory	$$$	
	Wages Payable		$$$
	To record the use of direct labor in production.		
5.	Manufacturing Overhead	$$$	
	Wages Payable		$$$
	To record the addition of indirect labor to overhead.		
6.	Manufacturing Overhead	$$$	
	Various Accounts		$$$
	To record the addition of other overhead costs to the overhead account.		
7.	Work-in-Process Inventory	$$$	
	Manufacturing Overhead		$$$
	To record the application of overhead to production.		
8.	Finished-Goods Inventory	$$$	
	Work-in-Process Inventory		$$$
	To record the transfer of completed jobs to finished goods.		
9.	Cost of Goods Sold	$$$	
	Finished Goods		$$$
	To record the cost of goods sold during the period.		
10.	Accounts Receivable	$$$	
	Sales Revenue		$$$
	To record the jobs sold on credit during the period.		
11.	Selling and Administrative Expense	$$$	
	Various Accounts		$$$
	To record the period selling and administrative expenses.		
12.	Cost of Goods Sold	$$$	
	Manufacturing Overhead		$$$
	To record the disposition of underapplied overhead for the period. (*Note:* If overhead was overapplied for the period, Cost of Goods Sold would be credited and Manufacturing Overhead would be debited.)		

G. When manufacturing overhead is applied to jobs on the basis of predetermined overhead rates, the overhead applied during the period is usually different from the total overhead costs incurred during the period. If the applied overhead exceeds the incurred overhead, then we have overapplied manufacturing overhead; if applied overhead for the period is less than the overhead incurred for the period, we have underapplied overhead for the period. Journal entry 12 in the previous section represents the simplest way of disposing of this overapplied or underapplied overhead. A more involved, but also more accurate, procedure for disposing of overapplied or underapplied overhead is called proration; this method allocates overapplied or underapplied overhead to Work-in-Process Inventory, Finished Goods Inventory, and Cost of Goods Sold on the basis of the current period's applied overhead remaining in these accounts.

H. A schedule of cost of goods manufactured shows the production costs incurred during the period and the changes that occur in Work-in-Process Inventory over the period.

I. Job-order costing can be either actual costing or normal costing. In actual costing an actual overhead rate is used to assign manufacturing overhead to jobs. This rate is defined as:

$$\text{Actual overhead rate} = \frac{\text{Actual manufacturing for the period}}{\text{Actual period level of the cost driver}}$$

This rate is computed at the end of the period. Actual costing is more accurate but usually untimely. On the other hand, accountants often prefer to use predetermined overhead rates for applying manufacturing overhead to jobs that are computed over a long period of time; this approach is called normal costing. Normal costing results in smoothing out overhead rates over time, thus eliminating the effects of fluctuating actual overhead rates.

J. Manufacturing firms can use either a single plantwide predetermined overhead rate or multiple departmental predetermined overhead rates. The use of multiple overhead rates (one for each production department) is more complicated and costly to use, but it is both more accurate and more useful for decision making. In any event, these predetermined overhead rates should be based on cost drivers that correlate with the incurrence of manufacturing-overhead costs. In today's production systems there is a trend away from using direct labor as a cost driver in developing overhead rates. Today some firms use throughput time as a cost driver for overhead rates; throughput time is the average time needed to convert raw materials into finished products ready for shipment. Most modern manufacturers use multiple cost drivers for overhead application.

K. When a firm uses departmental overhead rates, overhead costs are assigned to production jobs in two stages. In the first stage all manufacturing overhead is assigned to production departments (such as fabricating and assembly). In this stage the costs of service departments (such as maintenance and energy supply) are first allocated to the production departments; thus, in this stage all production departments wind up with both their own assigned overhead costs and the overhead costs that have been allocated to them from the service departments. In the second stage the overhead costs accumulated in each production department are allocated to production jobs on the basis of appropriate cost drivers.

L. The use of activity-based costing (ABC) provides even more accurate product costing than the method described in the previous section, even though the allocations in ABC are similar to those described in the previous section. This is so because ABC puts the focus on many manufacturing activities and not just departments. In ABC, overhead costs are first assigned to the most significant activities of the production process. This is stage one. For each activity cost pool an appropriate cost driver is determined. Then in stage two the overhead costs are allocated to production jobs on the basis of the levels of the cost drivers. That is, in stage two each production job is allocated activity-overhead costs on the basis of the amount of activity (as measured by the level of the cost driver) used by that job.

M. Project costing consists of accumulating the costs of services rendered for each individual customer or client. These accumulated costs include any direct materials used, professional labor used, and overhead costs related to the rendering of services. The overhead costs are applied on the basis of overhead rates, such as:

$$\frac{\text{Budgeted overhead costs for the period}}{\text{Budgeted direct professional labor costs for the period}}$$

KEY TERMS

SELF-EVALUATION QUESTIONS AND ANSWERS

True-False Questions

___ **1.** Work-in-Process Inventory is partially completed inventory.

___ **2.** In job-order costing the costs assigned to each job are averaged over the units of production in a job to get an average cost per unit.

___ **3.** Manufacturing overhead is a homogeneous pool of indirect production costs.

___ **4.** In financial accounting, product costs are needed for planning and cost control and to provide managers with data for decision making.

___ **5.** A document, such as a material-requisition form, which is used as the basis for an accounting entry is called a source document.

___ **6.** In job-order costing the predetermined overhead rate is used to apply manufacturing overhead costs to service departments.

___ **7.** The journal entry to record the use of direct materials in production includes a debit to Work-in-Process Inventory.

___ **8.** The journal entry to record the application of manufacturing overhead to Work-in-Process Inventory includes a credit to Manufacturing Overhead.

___ **9.** In managerial accounting, product costs are needed to value inventory on the balance sheet and to compute cost-of-goods-sold expense on the income statement.

___ **10.** The journal entry to record the moving of completed products from Work-in-Process Inventory to Finished-Goods Inventory consists of a debit to Work-in-Process Inventory and a credit to Finished-Goods Inventory.

___ **11.** Procedures similar to those used in job-order costing are also used in many service organizations.

___ **12.** A time ticket is a form that records the length of time needed to manufacture a product.

___ **13.** The journal entry to record the usage of indirect materials in production includes a debit to Work-in-Process Inventory.

___ **14.** If actual overhead is more than applied overhead, the difference is called underapplied overhead.

___ **15.** A schedule of cost of goods sold shows the cost of goods sold during an accounting period and details the changes in Work-in-Process Inventory during the period.

___ **16.** If an actual overhead rate is used in job-order costing, it can be computed only at the end of the accounting period.

___ **17.** When direct materials and direct labor are added to Work-in-Process Inventory at their actual amounts and overhead is applied to Work-in-Process Inventory based on a predetermined overhead rate, this product-costing system is called actual costing.

___ **18.** There should be a correlation between the incurrence of overhead costs and use of the chosen cost driver for overhead application.

___ **19.** When multiple cost drivers and overhead rates instead of a single plantwide rate are used in overhead application, the resulting product-cost information is more accurate and more useful for decision making.

___ **20.** Job-order costing is not used in nonmanufacturing organizations.

___ **21.** Greater accuracy in product costs can be achieved with activity-based costing than with just the use of departmental overhead rates.

Fill-in-the-Blank Questions

1. When finished products are sold, the journal entry to remove these products from Finished-Goods Inventory consists of a(n) ___ to Cost of Goods Sold and a(n) ___ to Finished-Goods Inventory.
2. ___ costing is used in organizations where goods are produced in distinct batches and there are significant differences among the batches.

3. In a job-order costing system, the cost of direct materials, direct labor, and manufacturing overhead are the ___inputs___ to this product-costing system.

4. ___MRP___ is an operations-management tool that assists managers in scheduling production in each stage of the manufacturing process.

5. The first step in assigning manufacturing overhead costs to jobs is called Cost distribution

6. The second step in assigning manufacturing overhead costs to jobs is through a process called service dept Cost allocation

7. The third step in assigning manufacturing overhead costs to jobs consists of applying the overhead costs accumulated in a production department to the ___jobs___ that department has worked on.

8. The subsidiary-ledger account assigned to each job in job-order costing is a document called a(n) job cost sheet

9. A(n) ___bill of Materials___ lists all the materials needed to make a product that is produced routinely.

10. The left-hand side of the Manufacturing Overhead Account is used to accumulate ___actual___ manufacturing overhead costs as they are incurred throughout the accounting period.

11. If actual overhead is less than applied overhead, the difference is called ___overapplied___ overhead.

12. When underapplied or overapplied overhead is allocated among Work-in-Process Inventory, Finished-Goods Inventory, and Cost of Goods Sold, the process is called ___proration___.

13. A schedule of ___COGM___ shows the manufacturing costs incurred during an accounting period and the change in Work-in-Process Inventory.

14. If an overhead rate is computed over a long period of time to smooth out fluctuations in this rate, we call this a(n) ___normalized___ overhead rate.

15. ___Through-put___ is the average amount of time needed to convert raw materials into finished goods ready to be shipped to customers.

16. ___Overhead applic___ is the process of assigning manufacturing overhead costs to production jobs.

Multiple-Choice Questions

___b___ 1. When direct materials are used in production,
   (a) Work-in-Process Inventory is credited.
   (b) Work-in-Process Inventory is debited.
   (c) Direct-Materials Inventory is debited.
   (d) Finished-Goods Inventory is debited.

___a___ 2. In the application of manufacturing overhead, the predetermined overhead rate is computed as the estimated manufacturing overhead cost
   (a) divided by the estimated amount of the cost driver.
   (b) multiplied by the estimated amount of the cost driver.
   (c) divided by the actual amount of the cost driver.
   (d) multiplied by the actual amount of the cost driver.

___d___ 3. Suppose the predetermined overhead rate is $5 per machine hour. If Job K31 required 10 machine hours, then the overhead applied to Job K31 is
   (a) $2.
   (b) $5.
   (c) $15.
   (d) $50.

___a___ 4. The journal entry to record the use of indirect labor in production includes a
   (a) debit to Manufacturing Overhead.
   (b) credit to Manufacturing Overhead.
   (c) debit to Work-in-Process Inventory.
   (d) credit to Work-in-Process Inventory.

d 5. The journal entry to record the transfer of job costs from Work-in-Process Inventory to Finished-Goods Inventory includes a
(a) debit to Cost of Goods Sold.
(b) credit to Finished-Goods Inventory.
(c) debit to Work-in-Process Inventory.
(d) credit to Work-in-Process Inventory.

d 6. The journal entries to record the sale of products made for a particular job order include a
(a) credit to Finished-Goods Inventory.
(b) credit to Accounts Receivable.
(c) credit to Cost of Goods Sold.
(d) debit to Sales Revenue.

Exercises

3.1 The accounting records of Bramer Company showed the following recorded amounts as of December 31, 19x3:

Plant utilities	$ 78,000 ✓
Raw-materials inventory, 12/31/x2	51,600
Work-in-process inventory, 12/31/x3	72,000
Plant supervision	75,000 ✓
Direct-labor cost incurred	336,000
Finished-goods inventory, 12/31/x3	130,800
Purchase of raw materials	168,000
Finished-goods inventory, 12/31/x2	144,000
Work-in-process inventory, 12/31/x2	78,000
Other manufacturing overhead	12,000
Selling and administrative expenses	187,100
Indirect-labor cost incurred	60,000
Raw-materials inventory, 12/31/x3	31,200
Indirect materials used	42,000
Depreciation on plant and equipment	54,000
Sales revenue	1,342,000

Required:

Prepare for 19x3:

(a) A schedule of cost of goods manufactured
(b) A schedule of cost of goods sold
(c) An income statement

Solution Space for Exercise 3.1:

(a)

THE BRAMER COMPANY
Schedule of Cost of Goods Manufactured
For the Year Ended December 31, 19x3

Raw Materials Inventory 12/31/x2	51,600	
Plus: Purch of Raw Materials	168,000	
Minus: Raw Mat. Inv 12/31/x3	(31,200)	
Raw Materials Used		188,400

Direct Labor		336,000
Mfg Overhead		
Plant Utilities	78,000	
Plant Supervision	75,000	
Other Overhead	12,000	
Depreciation	54,000	
Indirect labor	60,000	
Indirect Material	42,000	
Total Manuf Overhead		321,000
Total Manuf. Costs		845,400
Plus WIP Inventory 12/31/X2		78,000
Sub Total		923,400
Minus WIP Inv. 12/31/X3		(72,000)
Costs of Goods Manufactured		851,400

(b)

THE BRAMER COMPANY
Schedule of Cost of Goods Sold
For the Year Ended December 31, 19x3

Finished Goods Inventory 12/31/x2	144,000
Plus: Cost of Goods Manuf.	851,400
Subtotal	995,400
Minus: Fin. Goods Inventory 12/31/x3	(130,800)
Cost of Goods Sold	864,600

(c)

THE BRAMER COMPANY
Income Statement
For the Year Ended December 31, 19x3

Sales Revenue	1,342,000
Less COGS	(864,600)
Gross Margin	477,400
Selling + Admin Expenses	(187,100)
Income before taxes	290,300

3.2 The Standard Furniture Company makes and sells customized computer furniture and uses job-order costing. The following events occurred during the month of September:

1. Lumber costing $135,000 was purchased on account.
2. Various indirect-material supplies costing $4,800 were used in production.
3. Utility bills for plant operations totaling $9,000 were received, but not paid.
4. Lumber and other direct materials amounting to $95,000 were used in production.
5. Depreciation on the plant and production equipment amounted to $12,000 for the month.
6. Direct labor of $30,000 for 2,500 direct-labor hours was used in production and paid for in cash.
7. Indirect labor of $4,000 was used in production and paid for in cash.
8. Manufacturing overhead was applied to jobs on the basis of $12.80 per direct-labor hour.
9. Furniture completed and transferred to finished goods amounted to $123,000.
10. The cost of furniture sold amounted to $105,900.

Required:

Prepare journal entries to record the events described above.

Solution Space for Exercise 3.2:

1.

Raw Materials Inventory	135,000	
Accts Payable		135,000

2.

Manuf Overhead	4800	
Indirect Supplies		4800

3.

Manuf. Overhead	9000	
Accts Payable		9000

4.

WIP Inventory	95,000	
Raw Materials Inventory		95,000

5.

Manuf. Overhead		
Accum. Depreciation		

6.

WIP Inventory	30,000	
Cash		30,000

7.

Manuf. Overhead	4000	
Cash		4000

8.

WIP Inventory	32,000	
Manuf Overhead		32,000

9.

Finished Goods Inv.	123000	
WIP Inventory		123,000

10.

COGS	105,900	
Finished Goods Inv		105,900

3.3 The Matthews Company makes and sells lamps and lighting fixtures. The following data are for their operations in 19x5.

Budgeted machine hours	12,000
Budgeted direct-labor hours	18,000
Budgeted manufacturing overhead	$375,000
Budgeted direct-labor rate	$12
Actual direct-labor hours	17,000
Actual machine hours	10,000
Actual direct-labor rate	$13.50
Actual manufacturing overhead	$394,000

Required:

(a) Compute the predetermined overhead rate for 19x5 using each of the following cost drivers
 (1) Direct-labor hours
 (2) Direct-labor cost
 (3) Machine hours

(b) For each cost driver given in part (a), compute the underapplied or overapplied overhead for 19x5.

Solution Space for Exercise 3.3:

(a) (1) 375,000 ÷ 18000 = 20.83/ DLH

(2) $12.00 x 18,000 = $216,000 375000 ÷ 216,000 = 1.74

(3) 375,000 ÷ 12000 = 31.25/ MH

(b) (1) 17,000 X 20.83 = 354,110

394,000 − 354,110 = 39,890 Underapplied

(2) 17000 X 13.50 = 229,500 Labor $ X 1.74 (costdriver) = 399,330

394,000 - 399,330 = $ 8330 overapplied

(3) 10,000 X 31.25 = 312,500

394,000 - 312,500 = 81,500 underapplied

3.4 The Johnson Company is a privately held company that makes compressors. It has been the customary practice at Johnson to classify a significant amount of manufacturing-overhead expenses as administrative expenses. This has had the effect of keeping the inventory value of the compressors low while increasing period expenses, thus giving Johnson a lower period income tax. Harry Scholz, the head accountant, knows that this practice has been going on for some time and has told the president that this is not a proper accounting practice. The president's consistent response is "Let things stay the way they are."

Required:

Write a paragraph or two explaining what Harry Scholz's professional ethical obligations are in this situation and what further action Harry should take.

Solution Space for Exercise 3.4:

Answers to True-False Questions

1. T
2. T
3. F Manufacturing overhead is a heterogeneous pool of indirect costs.
4. F In managerial accounting, product costs are needed for planning, cost control, and decision making.
5. T
6. F The predetermined overhead rate is used to apply overhead costs to products.
7. T
8. T
9. F In financial accounting, product costs are needed to value inventory and to compute the cost-of-goods-sold expense.
10. F This entry consists of a debit to Finished-Goods Inventory and a credit to Work-in-Process Inventory.
11. T
12. F A time ticket is a record of the time a worker spends on a job.
13. F This journal entry includes a debit to Manufacturing Overhead, not Work-in-Process Inventory.
14. T
15. F A schedule of cost of goods sold details the changes in Finished-Goods Inventory, as well as the cost of goods sold during the period.
16. T
17. F This costing system is called normal costing.
18. T
19. T
20. F It is used by various nonmanufacturing organizations.
21. T

Answers to Fill-in-the-Blank Questions

1. debit, credit
2. Job-order
3. inputs
4. Material-requirements planning (MRP)
5. cost distribution (cost allocation)
6. service-department cost allocation
7. jobs
8. job-cost sheet
9. bill of materials
10. actual
11. overapplied
12. proration
13. cost of goods manufactured
14. normalized
15. Throughput time
16. Overhead application

Answers to Multiple-Choice Questions

1. (b) To record direct materials used in production, Work-in-Process Inventory is debited and Raw-Materials Inventory is credited.
2. (a) For the rate to be a predetermined rate, we must divide by the estimated or planned amount of the cost driver.
3. (d) $50 = $5 × 10.
4. (a) This entry consists of a debit to Manufacturing Overhead and a credit to Wages Payable.
5. (d) This entry consists of a debit to Finished-Goods Inventory and a credit to Work-in-Process Inventory.
6. (a) The two entries to record the credit sale of products made are: (1) a debit to Cost of Goods Sold and a credit to Finished Goods Inventory and (2) a debit to Accounts Receivable and a credit to Sales Revenue.

Solutions to Exercises

3.1 (a)

THE BRAMER COMPANY
Schedule of Cost of Goods Manufactured
For the Year Ended December 31, 19x3

Direct material:		
Raw-materials inventory, 1/1/x3	$ 51,600	
Add: 19x3 purchase of raw materials	168,000	
Raw materials available for use	219,600	
Less: Raw-materials inventory, 12/31/x3	31,200	
Raw materials used in production		$188,400
Direct labor		336,000
Manufacturing overhead:		
Plant utilities	$ 78,000	
Plant supervision	75,000	
Indirect labor	60,000	
Indirect materials	42,000	
Depreciation on plant and equipment	54,000	
Other manufacturing overhead	12,000	
		321,000
Total manufacturing costs		$845,400
Add: Work-in-process inventory, 1/1/x3		78,000
Subtotal		$923,400
Less: Work-in-process inventory, 12/31/x3		72,000
Cost of goods manufactured		$851,400

(b)

THE BRAMER COMPANY
Schedule of Cost of Goods Sold
For the Year Ended December 31, 19x3

Finished goods inventory, 1/1/x3	$144,000
Add: Cost of goods manufactured	851,400
Cost of goods available for sale	$995,400
Finished-goods inventory, 12/31/x3	130,800
Cost of goods sold	$864,600

(c)

THE BRAMER COMPANY
Income Statement
For the Year Ended December 31, 19x3

Sales revenue	$1,342,000
Less: Cost of goods sold	864,600
Gross margin	$ 477,400
Selling and administrative expenses	187,100
Net income before taxes	$ 290,300

3.2

1.	Raw Materials	$135,000	
	Accounts Payable		$135,000
2.	Manufacturing Overhead	4,800	
	Manufacturing Supplies Inventory		4,800
3.	Manufacturing Overhead	9,000	
	Accounts Payable		9,000

4.	Work-in-Process Inventory	95,000	
	Raw-Materials Inventory		95,000
5.	Manufacturing Overhead	12,000	
	Accumulated Depreciation: Plant & Equipment		12,000
6.	Work-in-Process Inventory	30,000	
	Cash		30,000
7.	Manufacturing Overhead	4,000	
	Cash		4,000
8.	Work-in-Process Inventory	32,000	
	Manufacturing Overhead		32,000
9.	Finished-Goods Inventory	123,000	
	Work-in-Process Inventory		123,000
10.	Cost of Goods Sold	105,900	
	Finished-Goods Inventory		105,900

3.3 **(a)** (1) \$375,000/18,000 DLH = \$20.83/DLH
(2) \$375,000/\$216,000 = 1.74
(3) \$375,000/12,000 MH = \$31.25/MH

(b) (1) Applied overhead: 17,000 DLH × \$20.83/DLH = \$354,110
Underapplied overhead: \$394,000 – \$354,110 = \$39,890
(2) Applied overhead: 17,000 DLH × \$13.50 × 1.74 = \$399,330
Overapplied overhead: \$399,330 – \$394,000 = \$5,330
(3) Applied overhead: 10,000 MH × \$31.25/MH = \$312,500
Underapplied overhead: \$394,000 – \$312,500 = \$81,500

3.4 Accountants have a professional responsibility to comply with generally accepted accounting principles (GAAP). In this case the manufacturing-overhead expenses should be classified as such and work their way through the inventory accounts, eventually reaching the cost of goods sold.

Apparently Scholz did repeatedly inform the president that the company's present practice is wrong according to GAAP, but was he sufficiently objective and complete about the way he informed the president? Scholz's own competence and reputation are at stake. Perhaps the best course of action at this point is for Scholz to go back to the president and lay out in clear and complete terms the consequences of continuing this wrong accounting practice; if this fails, Scholz should consider employment elsewhere.

Chapter **4**

Process-Costing and Hybrid Product-Costing Systems

CHAPTER OVERVIEW AND LEARNING OBJECTIVES

This chapter continues the discussion of product-costing systems. In this chapter you will learn about the nature of process-costing and other hybrid product-costing systems. When you have finished this chapter, you should understand:

1. The similarities and differences between job-order costing and process costing
2. How to prepare journal entries for process costing when there is a sequence of production departments
3. How to account for equivalent units in both weighted-average and FIFO process costing
4. How to compute the cost per equivalent unit under both weighted-average and FIFO process costing
5. The analysis of total production costs for a department under the weighted-average and FIFO methods
6. The nature of operation costing and how it is a hybrid between job-order costing and process costing

AN OUTLINE FOR CHAPTER STUDY

A. Both job-order costing and process costing have the same objective—the assignment of manufacturing costs to units of product. Also, both costing systems have the same flow of costs through the manufacturing accounts. Job-order costing is used in those production environments where dissimilar batches of units are made, whereas process costing is employed in repetitive production situations where large numbers of similar products are made in a continuous flow.

B. Consider the use of process costing for a production process that consists of working first on units in Department A and then on units in Department B; we say that these production departments are sequenced.

   1. In this case the flow of production costs goes first through Department A. Then all production costs accumulated in Department A are transferred to Department B; these product costs are called transferred-in costs. Transferred-in costs are then combined with the production costs of Department B. Finally, the combined production costs are transferred to Finished-Goods Inventory when the units are completed. When the completed units are sold, the product costs are added to cost of goods sold. Notice that in process costing costs are accumulated by department.

2. The journal entries for the production process would be as follows:

		Debit	Credit
a.	Work-in-Process Inventory, Dept. A	$$$	
	Raw-Materials Inventory		$$$
	Wages Payable		$$$
	Manufacturing Overhead		$$$
	To record the use of direct materials and labor and the application of overhead in Department A.		
b.	Work-in-Process Inventory, Dept. B	$$$	
	Work-in-Process Inventory, Dept. A		$$$
	To record the transfer of production costs from Department A to Department B.		
c.	Work-in-Process Inventory, Dept. B	$$$	
	Raw-Materials Inventory		$$$
	Wages Payable		$$$
	Manufacturing Overhead		$$$
	To record the use of direct materials and labor and the application of overhead in Department B.		
d.	Finished-Goods Inventory	$$$	
	Work-in-Process Inventory, Dept. B		$$$
	To record the transfer of completed units to finished goods from Department B.		
e.	Cost of Goods Sold	$$$	
	Finished-Goods Inventory		$$$
	To record the cost of units sold during the period.		

C. Equivalent units in process costing are a measure of partially completed units stated in terms of completed units. For example, we say that 300 units that are 40 percent completed are equivalent to 120 units ($300 \times .4$) fully complete. The main point of process costing is that direct-material costs and conversion costs are assigned to equivalent units instead of physical units. Equivalent units are computed for direct-material cost and, separately, equivalent units are computed for conversion costs. In the production process, direct materials are most likely to be added at specific points in time (for example, at the beginning of the process); on the other hand, conversion costs are usually incurred continuously or uniformly throughout the process.

D. The main document in a process-costing system is the department production report. This report shows the following:

1. An analysis of the physical flow of units
2. The calculation of material equivalent units and the calculation of conversion equivalent units
3. The cost per equivalent unit for materials and the cost per equivalent unit for conversion
4. The production costs that are to be transferred out, either to Finished-Goods Inventory or to the next department in the production sequence, and the costs that remain in Work-in-Process Inventory for the given department.

E. The flow of costs and their corresponding equivalent units in process costing is based on one of two possible flow assumptions: the weighted-average method or the first-in, first-out (FIFO) method. The weighted-average method is most widely used in practice, probably because of its simplicity. However, the FIFO method is preferred for purposes of cost control and performance evaluation.

F. Under the weighted-average method, the following steps are used:

1. Analyze the physical flow of units according to the formula:

Physical units in beginning Work-in-Process Inventory + Physical units started during the period = Physical units completed and transferred out during the period + Physical units in ending Work-in-Process Inventory

2. Compute the equivalent units separately for each of direct materials and conversion as follows:

Equivalent units of activity in the units completed and transferred out	+	Equivalent units of activity in ending Work-in-Process Inventory	=	Total equivalent units of activity

It should be noted that the number of equivalent units computed here makes no distinction as to whether the activity occurred in the current period or in the previous period.

3. Compute the unit costs separately for each of direct materials and conversion. The direct-material cost per equivalent unit is the sum of the direct-material cost in beginning Work-in-Process Inventory and direct-material cost for the current period divided by the total material equivalent units computed in step 2. The conversion cost per equivalent unit is the sum of the conversion cost in beginning Work-in-Process Inventory and the conversion cost for the current period divided by the total conversion equivalent units computed in step 2.
4. Analyze the total costs of direct materials and conversion to determine what portion of these costs is transferred out and what portion remains in ending Work-in-Process Inventory. The portion that is transferred out is computed as the number of units transferred out times the total cost (direct material plus conversion) per equivalent unit from step 3. The portion that remains in ending Work-in-Process Inventory is obtained by adding the following two costs:

   a. The material equivalent units in ending Work-in-Process Inventory times the cost per equivalent unit of direct material

   b. The conversion equivalent units in ending Work-in-Process Inventory times the cost per equivalent unit of conversion

   Notice that the unit costs used to determine the production costs that are transferred out and those that remain in ending Work-in-Process Inventory are based on combining both current-period and previous-period costs and on equivalent units from both the current period and the previous period. Thus, the unit costs are a weighted average of the previous-period (as reflected in beginning Work-in-Process Inventory) and the current-period costs.

G. The FIFO method does not mix the production costs of the previous period with those of the current period in determining the unit costs used to compute those production costs to be transferred out and those that are to remain in ending Work-in-Process Inventory. The following steps are used in this method:

1. Analyze the physical flow of units in the same manner as under the weighted-average method as described in Section F.
2. Calculate the equivalent units by subtracting from the equivalent units computed under the weighted-average method those equivalent units in beginning Work-in-Process Inventory.
3. Compute the unit costs as follows:

   a. The cost per equivalent unit for direct materials is the direct-material cost for the current period only divided by the material equivalent units determined in step 2.

   b. The cost per equivalent unit for conversion is the conversion cost for the current period only divided by the conversion equivalent units determined in step 2.

4. Analyze the total costs as follows:

   a. The production costs that are transferred out consist of all costs in beginning Work-in-Process Inventory plus the current-period costs to finish the beginning Work-in-Process Inventory plus the cost of producing units that were both started and completed in the current period.

   b. The production costs that remain in ending Work-in-Process Inventory are computed in the same manner as was done in Sections F.4.a and F.4.b.

   Notice that the unit costs under the FIFO method are based only on current production costs and current equivalent units.

H. The difference between the weighted-average and FIFO methods becomes less significant in a just-in-time (JIT) production environment. This is because under the JIT philosophy all inventories are kept at very low levels.

I. A process-costing system can use either actual costing or normal costing. The normal-costing approach uses predetermined overhead rates; in actual costing, the actual cost of manufacturing overhead is included in Work-in-Process Inventory. In both actual and normal costing, the actual costs of direct materials and direct labor are included in Work-in-Process Inventory. In normal process costing, conversion costs have to be separated into direct labor and manufacturing overhead if a cost driver other than direct labor is used for manufacturing overhead.

J. Hybrid product costing involves some of the characteristics of both job-order costing and process costing. A particular type of hybrid product costing is operation costing. Under operation costing, direct-material costs are accumulated by job order or batch as in job-order costing, and conversion costs are accumulated by department as in process costing.

K. (Appendix) When there are sequential production departments in process costing, the first department in the sequence does not have any transferred-in costs. However, all the remaining departments in the sequence will have transferred-in costs. The transferred-in costs for a department are assigned to the units transferred in from the previous department in the sequence. Transferred-in costs in process costing are given the same kind of treatment as direct-material costs, whereby the materials are added at the beginning of the process in a department.

KEY TERMS

Batch manufacturing 155
Departmental production report 138
Equivalent units 137
FIFO (first-in, first-out) method 138
Hybrid product-costing system 155
Operation costing 156
Process-costing system 134
Repetitive production 134
Transferred-in costs 135
Weighted-average method 138

SELF-EVALUATION QUESTIONS AND ANSWERS

True-False Questions

_____ 1. The ultimate purpose of process costing is to assign production costs to units of output.

_____ 2. In process costing, as products are produced, the manufacturing costs are accumulated in the Finished-Goods Inventory account.

_____ 3. The most significant feature of process costing is that direct-material costs and conversion costs are assigned to equivalent units instead of physical units.

_____ 4. The department production report for a department summarizes the flow of production quantities through the department.

_____ 5. Nine hundred physical units that are 20 percent completed correspond to 720 equivalent units.

_____ 6. In calculating equivalent units of activity under the weighted-average method, no distinction is made as to whether the activity occurred in the current period or in the previous period.

_____ 7. The total cost per equivalent unit is the sum of the cost per equivalent unit of direct materials and the cost per equivalent unit of conversion.

_____ 8. The FIFO method mixes costs from two or more accounting periods.

_____ 9. Process costing is used where relatively small numbers of products are made in distinct batches that are significantly different from one another.

_____ 10. The flow of costs through the manufacturing accounts is the same in process costing as it is in job-costing.

_____ 11. In preparing a department production report, either the FIFO method or the LIFO method may be used.

_____ 12. The cost per equivalent unit for conversion under the FIFO method is obtained by dividing current-period conversion costs by current-period conversion equivalent units.

_____ 13. In FIFO process costing, all the production costs in beginning Work-in-Process Inventory of a department are transferred out of that department in the current period.

_____ 14. If there is no beginning Work-in-Process Inventory in a department, then the costs transferred out of that department during the period are the same under the FIFO method as under the weighted-average method.

_____ **15.** The weighted average of process costing is more widely used in practice than is FIFO.

_____ **16.** Normal costing can be used with process costing, but actual costing cannot.

_____ **17.** If some driver other than direct labor is used for applying manufacturing overhead in a process-costing system, then overhead costs are accounted for separately from direct-labor costs in the process-costing computations.

_____ **18.** The weighted-average method is superior to the FIFO method for purposes of cost control and performance evaluation.

_____ **19.** In operation costing, conversion costs are accumulated by batch or job order.

_____ **20.** (Appendix) Transferred-in costs in process costing are given the same type of treatment as are direct-material costs, whereby the materials are added at the beginning of the process.

Fill-in-the-Blank Questions

1. In sequential production departments, the manufacturing costs of the first department that are passed to the second department are called _______________ costs.
2. In process costing, costs are accumulated by _______________; in job-order costing, costs are accumulated by _______________.
3. The term _______________ is used in process costing to refer to the amount of manufacturing activity that has been applied to a batch of physical units.
4. The department production report for a department shows the amount of production cost transferred out of the department's _______________ account during the period.
5. Under the weighted-average method, the cost of goods completed and transferred out of a department is the product of the number of units transferred out and _______________.
6. The cost per equivalent unit for direct materials under the FIFO method is obtained by dividing current-period direct materials cost by current-period _______________.
7. The main document in a process-costing system is the _______________ report.
8. If a predetermined overhead rate is used in a process-costing system, then this process-costing system is also a(n) _______________ costing system.
9. _______________ and _______________ costing are the polar extremes of product costing.
10. _______________ operations have features of both job-order costing and process-costing environments.
11. _______________ costing is used when conversion activities are common across product lines, but the direct materials used in these products differ significantly.
12. (Appendix) In a sequential production process involving two departments, the second department in the sequence has three cost elements; they are _______________, _______________, and conversion costs.

Multiple-Choice Questions

_____ **1.** In a two-department sequential production process, A is the first department and B is the second. When partially completed goods are moved from A to B, the journal entry to record the transfer of production costs from A to B includes a

(a) debit to Work-in-Process Inventory, Dept. A.
(b) debit to Work-in-Process Inventory, Dept. B.
(c) credit to Work-in-Process Inventory, Dept. B.
(d) debit to Finished-Goods Inventory.

_____ **2.** If 600 physical units are 80 percent complete with respect to direct materials and 30 percent complete with respect to conversion, consider the following two statements:

I. There are 180 conversion equivalent units.
II. There are 120 material equivalent units.

Which is (are) true?

(a) Only I
(b) Only II
(c) Both I and II
(d) Neither I nor II

_____ **3.** Preparing a production department report does *not* involve which of the following steps?
(a) Analysis of physical flow units
(b) Calculation of equivalent units
(c) Computation of costs per equivalent unit
(d) Preparation of the journal entry to account for the flow of costs

_____ **4.** If beginning inventory of work in process has 3,000 physical units, 7,000 physical units were started during the period, and 8,000 physical units were completed and transferred out during the period, then the physical units in ending Work-in-Process Inventory amount to
(a) 12,000.
(b) 2,000.
(c) 4,000.
(d) 5,000.

_____ **5.** Consider the following two statements:
I. In operation costing, direct-material costs are accumulated by department.
II. In operation costing, conversion costs are accumulated by job order or batch.
Which is (are) true?
(a) Only I
(b) Only II
(c) Both I and II
(d) Neither I nor II

Exercises

4.1 The Fraiser Company uses process costing and had the following data for the month of May:

Work-in-process inventory, May 1	3,000 units
Direct materials	100% complete
Conversion	40% complete
Finished and transferred out in May	78,000 units
Work-in-process inventory, May 31	5,000 units
Direct materials	100% complete
Conversion	70% complete

Required:

(a) Using the weighted-average method, compute the equivalent units of direct material and conversion for May.
(b) Do part (a) using the FIFO method.

Solution Space for Exercise 4.1:

(a)

(b)

4.2 The Rockwell Company makes latex paint and uses process costing. The following data are for the Mixing Department for the month of April:

Work in process, Apr. 1	5,000 gal.
Direct materials	$ 22,000
Conversion	14,000
Costs incurred during April	
Direct materials	148,000
Conversion	350,000

The equivalent units (gallons) of activity for April were:

	Weighted Average		FIFO	
	Materials	**Conver.**	**Materials**	**Conver.**
Beginning work in process	5,000	5,000	0	3,500
Started and completed	35,000	35,000	35,000	35,000
Ending work in process	2,000	1,000	2,000	1,000
Total equivalent units	42,000	41,000	37,000	39,500

Units completed and transferred out in April: 40,000 gal.

Required:

(a) Use the weighted-average method to compute:
 (1) The cost of goods completed and transferred out during April
 (2) The cost of work-in-process inventory on April 30
(b) Do part (a) again using the FIFO method.

Solution Space for Exercise 4.2:

(a)

(b)

4.3 The Kettler Company makes women's purses and uses operation costing. These purses are made of either leather or plastic. Both types of purses receive the same operations in the Cutting Department and the Assembly Department. However, only the leather purses receive a special type of stainproofing in the Treatment Department. During June there were two batches started and finished, and there were no beginning or ending work-in-process inventories. Batch L consisted of 4,000 leather purses, and batch P consisted of 6,000 plastic purses. Costs incurred were as follows:

Direct-material costs:	
Batch L	$40,000
Batch P	24,000
Conversion costs:	
Cutting Department	$30,000
Assembly Department	45,000
Treatment Department	8,000

Required:

Compute each of the following:

(a) The conversion cost per unit in the Cutting Department
(b) The conversion cost per unit in the Assembly Department
(c) The conversion cost per unit in the Treatment Department
(d) The product cost of a leather purse
(e) The product cost of a plastic purse

Solution Space for Exercise 4.3:

(a) ______________________________

(b) ______________________________

(c) ______________________________

(d) ______________________________

____

____

____

____

____

(e) ______________________________

____

____

____

____

____

Total costs accounted for:
$517,110 + $16,860 = $533,970 (error due to rounding)

4.3 (a) $30,000/(4,000 + 6,000) = $3.00
(b) $45,000/(4,000 + 6,000) = $4.50
(c) $8,000/4,000 = $2.00
(d)

Direct-material cost per unit: $40,000/4,000 =	$10,00
Conversion cost per unit: $3.00 + $4.50 + $2.00 =	9.50
Total production cost per unit	$19.50

(e)

Direct-material cost per unit: $24,000/6,000 =	$ 4.00
Conversion cost per unit: $3.00 + $4.50 =	7.50
Total production cost per unit	$11.50

4.4

THE FITZ COMPANY
Production Report—Assembly Department
Weighted-Average Method
For the Month of July

	Physical Units	Percent of Completion in Conversion	Equivalent Units Dir. Mat.	Equivalent Units Conversion
Work in process, July 1	18,000	50%		
Units started during July	37,000 (1)			
Total units to account for	55,000			
Completed and transferred out, July	43,000 (2)	100%	43,000	43,000
Work in process, July 31	12,000 (3)	25%	12,000	3,000
Total units accounted for	55,000			
Total equivalent units			55,000	46,000 (4)

	Dir. Mat.	Conversion	Total
Work in process, July 1	$ 90,000	$ 19,800 (5)	$109,800
Costs incurred in July	218,000 (6)	90,600	308,600
Total costs to account for	$308,000	$110,400	$418,400
Equivalent units	55,000	46,000	
Cost per equivalent unit	$5.60	$2.40 (7)	$8.00
Cost of goods completed and transferred out, July			$344,000 (8)
Costs remaining, July 31 work in process			
Direct material		$ 67,200 (9)	
Conversion		7,200	74,400
Total costs accounted for			$418,400

The numbers in parentheses in the above production report refer to the missing data and can be calculated as follows in the given sequence:

(9) 74,400 – 7,200 = 67,200
(8) 418,400 – 74,400 = 344,000
(7) 8.00 – 5.60 = 2.40
(6) 308,600 – 90,600 = 218,000
(5) 109,800 – 90,000 = 19,800
(4) (19,800 + 90,600)/2.40 = 46,000
(3) 67,200/5.60 = 12,000
(2) 55,000 – 12,000 = 43,000
(1) 55,000 – 18,000 = 37,000

Chapter 5

Cost Management Systems for the New Manufacturing Environment

CHAPTER OVERVIEW AND LEARNING OBJECTIVES

This chapter provides a contrast between traditional product-costing systems and modern high-tech production-costing systems. The contemporary cost issues and emerging costing methods are surveyed by means of a real-world type of example. The Aerotech Example will show you how activity-based costing can improve the accuracy of product costing. After completing this chapter, you should understand:

1. The main differences between a traditional production process and an automated, computer-assisted manufacturing environment.
2. How to compute product costs under a traditional, volume-based costing system and an activity-based costing system.
3. The operation of an activity-based costing system, including the two-stage procedure for cost assignment, the identification of activity cost pools and the choice of cost drivers.
4. How traditional, volume-based costing systems tend to distort product costs.
5. Issues related to activity-based costing such as activity-based management, criteria for selecting cost drivers, transaction costing, and hints that a new system is needed.
6. The key features of a cost management system, including the elimination of non-value-added costs.
7. The eight important features of just-in-time inventory and production management systems.
8. How to prepare journal entries to record costs under backflush costing in a just-in-time environment.

AN OUTLINE FOR CHAPTER STUDY

A. Traditional volume-based costing systems typically accumulate product cost as the sum of actual direct-material cost, actual direct-labor cost, and applied manufacturing-overhead cost. In the past the usual volume of activity was labor hours. Very often manufacturing overhead was applied using only a single overhead rate.

B. An alternative to traditional volume-based costing that is being widely accepted is activity-based costing (ABC), which uses a two-stage procedure to assign overhead costs to products. After assigning overhead costs to activity cost pools in stage one, appropriate cost drivers are identified for each pool. Then, in stage two, the overhead costs are allocated from the activity cost pools to each product line based on the amount of cost driver used by the product line. To understand this process, it would be wise to study Exhibit 5-10 in the text carefully.

C. Two factors that work against using traditional volume-based costing and in favor of ABC are that many production activities are not unit-level activities, and firms often manufacture a diverse set of products. For example, some overhead costs are related to production batches instead of units of product. Also, when a firm makes many different products, these products often consume activities in very different proportions. When characteristics like these are present, volume-based costing methods tend to distort product costs.

D. There are other factors and conditions that help make ABC systems important today. The pressure of foreign competition is forcing manufacturers to have a better understanding of their cost structures. Labor is becoming a much smaller component of total production costs. Movement toward ABC systems is made possible because of the availability of sophisticated real-time information systems. The use of activity-based costing to improve operations is called activity-based management. By identifying the cost of activities, managers can try to reduce or eliminate unnecessary costs.

E. A cost driver is an event or condition that results in the incurrence of costs. In choosing cost drivers, three factors should be present.

1. There is a correlation between the consumption of an activity and the consumption of the cost driver. The higher the degree of correlation, the more accurate is the cost assignment.
2. It should be cost-effective to measure the cost driver.
3. The use of the cost driver should have beneficial behavioral effects.

F. Other issues pertaining to an ABC system are as follows:

1. The costs in an activity cost pool should be consumed in essentially the same proportion by each product line.
2. Often transactions provide a readily measurable gauge of the activity of a segment or department. In this situation, activity cost is assigned to product lines on the basis of the number of transactions generated by each product.
3. The design and implementation of an ABC system require a large amount of information from all facets of a firm's operations. Putting an ABC system into place involves personnel from a variety of functional areas within the firm.
4. In an ABC system an effort is made to account for as many costs as possible as direct costs of production.

G. Examples of conditions which give hints that management should consider implementing an ABC system are:

1. Line managers don't believe the product costs reported by the accounting system.
2. Marketing personnel refuse to use reported product costs in pricing decisions.
3. Product-line profit margins are hard to explain.
4. Sales are increasing, but profits are decreasing.
5. Direct labor is a small portion of total production costs.
6. Competitors' high-volume products seem to be priced unrealistically low.

H. A cost management system is a management planning and control system that has the following objectives:

1. To measure the cost of resources used in performing an organization's significant activities
2. To identify and eliminate non-value-added costs
3. To determine the efficiency and effectiveness of all major activities performed by the organization
4. To identify and evaluate new activities that can improve the future performance of the organization

I. Non-value-added costs are those costs that can be eliminated without reducing product quality, performance, or value. The inefficient or unnecessary use of time in the production process is often a cause of non-value-added costs. Production time is usually spent in the following ways:

1. Process time is the time during which a product is undergoing conversion activity. In general, process time is usually a value-added activity, but inefficiencies of operations and unnecessary process operations add no value to the cost of a product.
2. Inspection time is the time used to ensure product quality by examining the product for defects. If product quality can be improved, inspection time may possibly be reduced.

3. Move time is the time spent moving raw materials, work in process, or finished goods. If unnecessary move time can be eliminated, then so can the non-value-added costs of this unnecessary time.
4. Waiting time is the time raw materials or work in process spend waiting for the next operation. If production can be scheduled so that production queues do not build up, then work-in-process inventories can be virtually eliminated. Maintaining work-in-process inventories that are unnecessary adds no value to the product.
5. Storage time is the time during which materials and products are held in stock before further processing or shipment to customers. Eliminating unnecessary inventories will eliminate storage time; such storage time adds no value to the products.

J. A just-in-time (JIT) production system is an inventory and manufacturing control system in which no materials are bought and no products are made until they are required. A goal of a JIT production system is to reduce inventories as much as possible at every stage of production. The JIT philosophy of production has the following key characteristics:

1. A smooth and uniform production rate is achieved.
2. A "pull" method of production, in which goods at each production stage are made only as they are needed at the next stage, is used. Nothing is manufactured at any stage until its need is signaled from the subsequent process by a Kanban (a card showing the number and type of parts needed).
3. The purchase of materials and the manufacture of products are done in small lot sizes.
4. The setup of production equipment is quick and inexpensive.
5. Raw materials and finished products have high quality. Many firms that use JIT also have a total quality control (TQC) program.
6. Preventive maintenance of equipment is used.
7. An atmosphere of teamwork is maintained to improve the production system.
8. Production equipment is flexible, and workers are multiskilled. High-tech production machines are often grouped in cells by production technology, so machine operators need to know how to operate several machines; this is called group technology.

K. In JIT, materials and parts are purchased from outside vendors only as they are required, thus avoiding costly buildup of material inventories. Key features of JIT purchasing include:

1. Only a few suppliers are used.
2. Long-term contracts are negotiated with suppliers.
3. Materials and parts are delivered in small lot sizes immediately as they are needed (hence the idea of "just in time").
4. Inspection of delivered materials and parts is minimal.
5. Payments for purchases are made for a group of purchases instead of for each delivery.

L. Some new terminology has emerged to describe today's production environment. These new terms are as follows:

1. A computer-numerically-controlled (CNC) machine is a stand-alone machine controlled by a computer via a numerical, machine-readable code.
2. A computer-aided manufacturing (CAM) system is a production process in which computers are used to help control production equipment.
3. A computer-aided design (CAD) system is computer software used by engineers in designing a product.
4. An automated material-handling system (AMHS) is a system in which computer-controlled machines automatically move materials and products from one production stage to another.
5. A flexible manufacturing system (FMS) is an integrated system of computer-controlled machines and automated material-handling equipment which can make a variety of technologically similar products.
6. An FMS cell is a specific grouping of machines and personnel within a flexible manufacturing system.
7. A computer-integrated manufacturing (CIM) system is a system in which virtually all facets of the production process are done by computer-controlled machines and automated material-handling equipment. The entire system is an integrated network that is centrally controlled by a computer.

8. Off-line quality control refers to activities during the product design and engineering phases that will improve the manufacturability of the product, reduce manufacturing costs, and ensure high quality.
9. A production process that is accomplished mainly by machines rather than manual labor is said to be capital-intensive; if it is accomplished largely by manual labor, it is said to be labor-intensive.
10. The strategy of target costing refers to the attempt to design a product so that it can be sold at the market price.

M. Backflush costing is a costing method for tracking the flow of costs through a JIT production system. Examples of the basic journal entries to record events related to production are as follows:

		Debit	Credit
1.	Raw and In-Process Inventory	$$$	
	Accounts Payable		$$$
	To record the purchase of raw materials.		
2.	Finished-Goods Inventory	$$$	
	Raw and In-Process Inventory		$$$
	To record the transfer of raw materials to finished goods.		
3.	Cost of Goods Sold	$$$	
	Finished Goods Inventory		$$$
	To record the cost of raw materials in products sold.		
4.	Cost of Goods Sold	$$$	
	Conversion Costs		$$$
	To record total applied conversion costs.		
5.	Raw and In-Process Inventory	$$$	
	Finished-Goods Inventory	$$$	
	Cost of Goods Sold		$$$
	To record conversion costs applicable to period-ending inventories.		

Notice that raw-material purchase costs are added to an account (Raw and In-Process Inventory) that is different from the traditional Raw-Materials Inventory. Also, note that conversion costs are added to Cost of Goods Sold instead of a Work-in-Process Inventory account. The term "backflush" comes from the fact that entries to record production costs are delayed until the goods are finished or sold. At that point these costs are "flushed" out of the accounting system.

N. The costs and benefits of investing in advanced manufacturing systems must be analyzed quantitatively and qualitatively over the entire life of the equipment being considered. With complex equipment and rapidly changing technology, costs and benefits may be difficult to predict. The investment can be justified only if the benefits exceed the costs involved.

KEY TERMS

Activity accounting 209
Activity-based costing (ABC) system 197
Activity-based management 209
Activity cost pool 197
Automated material-handling system (AMHS) 221
Backflush costing 227
Batch-level activity 197
CAD/CAM system 221
Capital-intensive 225
Computer-aided design (CAD) system 221
Computer-aided manufacturing (CAM) system 221
Computer-integrated manufacturing (CIM) system 221
Computer-numerically-controlled (CNC) machines 221
Consumption ratio 208
Cost driver 208
Cost management system (CMS) 210
Facility (or general-operations) level activity 198
Flexible manufacturing system (FMS) 221
FMS cell 221
Homogeneous cost pool 211
Inspection time 216
Just-in-time (JIT) inventory and production-management system 218
Just-in-time (JIT) purchasing 220
Labor-intensive 225
Move time 216
Non-value-added costs 215
Pool rate 199
Process time 216
Product life-cycle costing 230

SELF-EVALUATION QUESTIONS AND ANSWERS

True-False Questions

____ **1.** Traditional product-costing systems are volume-based costing systems.

____ **2.** The use of multiple overhead rates in the application of manufacturing overhead usually results in more accurate product-cost data than does a single overhead rate.

____ **3.** In activity-based costing, a single cost driver is used for all manufacturing overhead costs.

____ **4.** It would be unreasonable to assume that packing and shipping costs are driven by the number of production runs to be packed.

____ **5.** The pressure of foreign competition is forcing U.S. manufacturers to strive for better understanding of their cost structures.

____ **6.** Transactions provide a readily measurable gauge of the activity in a department.

____ **7.** In ABC costing an effort is made to account for as few costs as possible as direct costs of production.

____ **8.** A strategic analysis identifies the activities by which an organization creates a valuable product or service.

____ **9.** The amount of time that raw materials or work in process spend waiting for the next operation is called move time.

____ **10.** A possible cost driver of engineering costs is the number of engineering change orders.

____ **11.** A possible cost driver of receiving and inspection costs is the number of shipments received and inspected.

____ **12.** Nowadays, direct labor is becoming a much larger portion of total production costs than in the past.

____ **13.** The cost structures of many manufacturers have changed significantly over the past decade.

____ **14.** In an activity-based costing system, only those cost drivers that are related to the bulk of costs need to be identified and tracked.

____ **15.** In an activity-based costing system, the costs of activities are assigned to product lines on the basis of the amount of cost driver consumed by each product.

____ **16.** The goal of JIT production is to build up inventories as much as possible for future use.

____ **17.** Under JIT costing, raw-material purchases are recorded directly in the Raw-Materials Inventory account.

____ **18.** In JIT costing, conversion costs are initially applied directly to Cost of Goods Sold.

____ **19.** Any analysis of an investment in advanced manufacturing systems must consider the costs and benefits of the equipment over the entire life of the equipment.

____ **20.** In stage two of an ABC system, overhead costs are assigned to activity cost pools.

Fill-in-the-Blank Questions

1. A(n) ________________ is an event or activity that results in the incurrence of costs.
2. ________________ is the collection of financial or operational performance information about significant activities in an organization.
3. ________________ is a broad-based, managerial-accounting analysis that supports strategic management decisions.
4. The time during which a product is undergoing conversion activity is called ________________.
5. The time during which materials, partially completed products, or finished goods are held in stock before further processing or shipments to customers is called ________________.

6. A(n) ________________ production system is a comprehensive inventory and manufacturing control system in which no materials are purchased and no products are made until they are needed.
7. The approach of grouping machines into cells that produce a variety of items requiring similar production technology is called ________________.
8. A(n) ________________ machine is a stand-alone machine controlled by a computer via a numerical, machine-readable code.
9. The amount of time spent moving raw materials, work in process, or finished goods between operations is called ________________.
10. Any production process in which computers are used to help control production equipment is called a(n) ________________ system.
11. If a production process is accomplished largely by machines instead of manual labor, it is said to be ________________.
12. Computer software used by engineers in designing a product is called a(n) ________________ system.
13. The strategy of attempting to design a product so that it can be sold for its market price is called ________________.
14. Computer-controlled equipment that automatically moves materials and products from one production stage to another is called a(n) ________________ system.
15. An integrated system of computer-controlled machines and automated material-handling equipment that is capable of making a variety of technologically similar products is called a(n) ________________ system.
16. A production process that is accomplished by computer-controlled machines and automated material-handling equipment and in which the entire production system is an integrated network controlled by a central computer is called a(n) ________________ system.
17. ________________ costing is the accumulation of costs for activities that occur over the entire life cycle of a product.
18. The ________________ is the proportion of an activity consumed by a product.

Multiple-Choice Questions

____ 1. Consider the following two statements about activity accounting:

I. It attempts to assign the costs of significant activities to the products that caused those costs to be incurred.

II. It seeks to identify the costs of activities so that managers can attempt to reduce or eliminate unnecessary costs.

Which is (are) true?

(a) Only I
(b) Only II
(c) Both I and II
(d) Neither I nor II

____ 2. Which of the following are cost drivers, as measured in terms of transactions?

(a) Number of material moves
(b) Number of units reworked
(c) Number of vendors
(d) All of the above

____ 3. Which of the following is *not* an objective of a cost management system?

(a) Measuring the cost of resources used in performing the organization's significant activities
(b) Identifying and creating non-value-added costs
(c) Determining the effectiveness and efficiency of all major activities performed by the organization
(d) Identifying and evaluating new activities that can improve the future performance of the organization

b 4. Which of the following is *not* a key feature of the JIT philosophy?
   (a) A smooth, uniform production rate
   (b) A "push" method of coordinating the steps of a production process
   (c) The purchase of materials and the making of products in small lot sizes
   (d) High quality levels for materials and products

a 5. Which of the following is *not* a key characteristic of the JIT philosophy?
   (a) Single-skilled employees and flexible facilities
   (b) Effective preventive maintenance of equipment
   (c) Quick and inexpensive setups of production equipment
   (d) An atmosphere of teamwork to improve the production system

Exercises

5.1 Mosher Abrasives, Inc., has two production departments, I and II, with the following overhead budget data for the forthcoming year:

	Total	Production Dept. I	Production Dept. II
Depreciation of equipment	$110,000	$20,000	$90,000
Occupancy costs	$ 30,000	$10,000	$20,000
Energy costs	$ 14,000	$ 6,000	$ 8,000
Machine hours	12,500	4,500	8,000
Direct-labor hours	15,000	10,500	4,500

154,000

The company makes two products, *A* and *B*, for sale. The production times per unit needed for these products are as follows:

	Labor Time		Machine Time	
	Dept. I	Dept. II	Dept. I	Dept. II
Product *A*	1.5	0.5	0.4	0.6
Product *B*	0.6	0.4	0.5	1.0

Required:

(a) Find a single overhead rate based on direct-labor hours.
(b) How much overhead will be assigned to product *A* per unit and to product *B* per unit if the overhead rate in part (a) is used?
(c) Find two overhead rates, one for Department I based on direct-labor hours and another for Department II based on machine hours.
(d) How much overhead will be assigned to product *A* per unit and to product *B* per unit if the overhead rates found in part (c) are used?
(e) Explain why the unit costs of overhead for each product in parts (b) and (d) are different.

Solution Space for Exercise 5.1:

(a) 154,000 / 15,000 = 10.27 lab Hr

(b) 2 X 10.27 = 20.54 per unit

1.0 X 10.27 = 10.27 per unit

(c) $36,000 / 10,500 = $3.43 / DLH

$118,000 / 8000 = $14.75 / MH

(d)

(e)

5.2 Vosburgh Heating and Plumbing Products, Inc., uses just-in-time costing. The following events occurred in October:

(a) Raw material costing $215,000 was bought on account.
(b) Finished goods with raw-material costs of $73,000 were completed.
(c) Goods with raw-material costs of $38,000 were sold.
(d) Conversion costs of $136,000 were applied.
(e) On October 31 the conversion costs remaining in inventory were estimated to be $44,000 in work in process and $17,000 in finished goods.

Required:

Prepare the journal entries needed to record the above events.

Solution Space for Exercise 5.2:

(a)

(b)

(c)

(d)

(e)

5.3 The Duncan Company makes and sells three products, *A*, *B*, and *C*. The company uses activity-based costing. The following budget data for overhead for next year are available:

	Total	Product *A*	Product *B*	Product *C*
Units to be made and sold		12,000	8,000	3,000
Manufacturing overhead costs:				
Engineering	$500,000	30%	50%	20%
Receiving and Inspection	180,000	40%	30%	30%
Material handling	430,000	50%	30%	20%
Machining	960,000	60%	20%	20%
Packing	120,000	50%	20%	30%

The above percentages represent the proportion of transaction items for each overhead item that pertains to each product. The cost drivers for the overhead items are as follows:

Engineering—number of change orders
Receiving and inspection—number of inspections
Material handling—raw-material costs
Machining—machine hours
Packing—number of shipments made

Required:

Find the total overhead costs assigned to each product on a per-unit basis.

Solution Space for Exercise 5.3:

From engineering:

From receiving and inspection:

From material handling:

From machining:

____

____

____

From packing:

____

____

____

Product	Total Overhead per Unit
A	______________
B	______________
C	______________

5.4 The Hanson Manufacturing Company has recently installed new computerized devices to help monitor the quality of the output of their production processes. These devices, which are operated by three technically trained computer specialists, have replaced 15 quality control personnel, who were regarded as direct labor. The operating costs of these new computerized devices, including the salaries of the computer specialists, have been included in manufacturing overhead. Hanson presently uses a plantwide manufacturing overhead rate based on direct labor dollars.

The president of Hanson was told how efficiently the new computer devices are working but was amazed when she found out there is a twofold increase in the manufacturing overhead rate compared to what it used to be. The data that led to her amazement are as follows:

	After the Devices	Before the Devices
Annual budgeted overhead	$2,700,000	$1,728,000
Annual budgeted direct labor	750,000	960,000
Budgeted overhead rate	360%	180%

The president complained, "This information is absurd, and something must be done about it!"

Required:

Explain the basis of the dilemma presented in the scenario above and how activity-based costing could help to address the issues and concerns expressed by the president of Hanson.

Solution Space for Exercise 5.4:

____

____

____

Answers to True-False Questions

1. T
2. T
3. F In activity-based costing, each cost pool for manufacturing overhead has its own cost driver.
4. F It is reasonable to assume that there is a causal relationship between the number of production runs and packing and shipping costs.
5. T
6. T
7. F An effort is made to account for as many costs as possible as direct costs of production.
8. T
9. F This is called waiting time.
10. T
11. T
12. F Labor is now a much smaller portion of total production costs than in the past.
13. T
14. T
15. T
16. F Quite the contrary! The goal of JIT is to reduce inventories as much as possible.
17. F They are recorded in the Raw and In-Process Inventory account.
18. T
19. T
20. F This is done in stage one of an ABC system.

Answers to Fill-in-the-Blank Questions

1. cost driver
2. Activity accounting
3. Strategic cost analysis
4. process time
5. storage time
6. just-in-time
7. group technology
8. computer-numerically-controlled
9. move time
10. computer-aided manufacturing
11. capital-intensive
12. computer-aided design
13. target costing
14. automated material-handling
15. flexible manufacturing system
16. computer-integrated manufacturing
17. Product life cycle
18. consumption ratio

Answers to Multiple-Choice Questions

1. **(c)**
2. **(d)** They are all cost drivers as measured in terms of transactions.
3. **(b)** The objective is to eliminate non-value-added costs.
4. **(b)** The method of coordinating the steps of a production process is a "pull" method.
5. **(a)** Employees need to be multiskilled.

Solutions to Exercises

5.1 **(a)** $154,000/15,000 DLH = $10.27/DLH

(b) To product *A:* 2 DLH × $10.27/DLH = $20.54/unit
To product *B:* 1 DLH × $10.27/DLH = $10.27/unit

(c) For Department I: $36,000/10,500 DLH = $3.43/DLH
For Department II: $118,000/8,000 MH = $14.75/MH

(d) To product *A:*
1.5 DLH × $3.43/DLH + 0.6 MH × $14.75/MH = $14.00/unit
To product *B:*
0.6 DLH × $3.43/DLH + 1.0 MH × $14.75/MH = $16.81/unit

(e) The unit costs of overhead for product *A* in parts (b) and (d) are different because each is based on a different set of cost drivers. The same statement applies to product *B*.

5.2

		Debit	Credit
a.	Raw and In-Process Inventory	215,000	
	Accounts Payable		215,000
b.	Finished-Goods Inventory	73,000	
	Raw and In-Process Inventory		73,000
c.	Cost of Goods Sold	38,000	
	Finished-Goods Inventory		38,000
d.	Cost of Goods Sold	136,000	
	Conversion Costs		136,000
e.	Raw and In-Process Inventory	44,000	
	Finished-Goods Inventory	17,000	
	Cost of Goods Sold		61,000

5.3 Engineering:

To A: \$500,000 × .3/12,000 = \$12.50
To B: \$500,000 × .5/8,000 = \$31.25
To C: \$500,000 × .2/3,000 = \$33.33

Receiving and inspection:

To A: \$180,000 × .4/12,000 = \$ 6.00
To B: \$180,000 × .3/8,000 = \$ 6.75
To C: \$180,000 × .3/3,000 = \$18.00

Material handling:

To A: \$430,000 × .5/12,000 = \$17.92
To B: \$430,000 × .3/8,000 = \$16.13
To C: \$430,000 × .2/3,000 = \$28.67

Machining:

To A: \$960,000 × .6/12,000 = \$48.00
To B: \$960,000 × .2/8,000 = \$24.00
To C: \$960,000 × .2/3,000 = \$64.00

Packing:

To A: \$120,000 × .5/12,000 = \$ 5.00
To B: \$120,000 × .2/8,000 = \$ 3.00
To C: \$120,000 × .3/3,000 = \$12.00

Total overhead per unit of product A is
\$12.50 + \$6.00 + \$17.92 + \$48.00 + \$5.00 = \$89.42

Total overhead per unit of product B is
\$31.25 + \$6.75 + \$16.13 + \$24.00 + \$3.00 = \$81.13

Total overhead per unit of product C is
\$33.33 + \$18.00 + \$28.67 + \$64.00 + \$12.00 = \$156.00

5.4 The data that amazed the president of Hanson resulted from the fact that when 15 direct laborers were replaced by computerized devices the budgeted annual direct labor costs went down, while budgeted manufacturing overhead went up. Manufacturing overhead went up because of the salaries of the computer specialists and the depreciation expense related to the new devices.

Activity-based costing (ABC) seeks to account for manufacturing overhead costs by forming homogeneous cost pools and then ascertaining appropriate cost drivers for those cost pools. If Hanson used this costing approach, it would be able to track its overhead costs with much more accuracy than with its present plantwide rate method. Also, the ABC approach would help Hanson identify those production activities that add no value to the products it makes; by highlighting the non-value-added activities, management will be encouraged to reduce these non-value-added costs of production.

Chapter 6

Cost Behavior and Estimation

CHAPTER OVERVIEW AND LEARNING OBJECTIVES

This chapter shows the various methods that accountants use to analyze the behavior of costs. The concepts of fixed and variable costs studied in Chapter 2 are central in analyzing cost behavior. After finishing this chapter, you should understand:

1. The relationships among cost estimation, cost behavior, and cost prediction.
2. The behavior of six types of costs: variable, step-variable, fixed, step-fixed, semivariable (or mixed), and curvilinear
3. The significance of the relevant range in using a cost-behavior pattern to predict cost
4. Four methods of cost estimation: account classification, visual fit, high-low, and least-squares regression
5. The nature of other approaches to cost estimation: multiple regression, engineering, and work measurement
6. Some problems often encountered in collecting data for cost estimation

AN OUTLINE FOR CHAPTER STUDY

A. Cost behavior is the relationship between cost and activity and is relevant to managerial planning, control, and decision making. Cost prediction is a forecast of cost at a specific level of activity; it is an important part of the planning process. Cost estimation is the process of determining how a particular cost behaves. The term "cost function" refers to the patterns a cost tends to exhibit.

B. Cost behavior is described by the following six types:

1. A variable cost changes in total in direct proportion to a change in the cost driver (or activity level) associated with that cost. The variable cost per unit remains unchanged as the cost-driver level changes.
2. A step-variable cost is a cost that increases in small steps, but not continuously. If these steps are small enough, a step-variable cost can be approximated by a variable-cost function without any significant loss in accuracy.
3. A fixed cost remains unchanged in total as the level of the associated cost driver changes. However, the fixed cost per unit does change as the level of the cost driver varies. It is preferable in cost analysis to work with total fixed cost rather than fixed cost per unit.
4. A cost that remains fixed over a wide range of activity but jumps to a different amount for activity levels outside that range is called a step-fixed cost.

5. A semivariable (or mixed) cost has both fixed and variable elements. The slope of the total semivariable cost line is the variable cost per unit of the cost driver.
6. A curvilinear cost-behavior pattern has a graph that is a curve. It could exhibit decreasing marginal costs or increasing marginal costs. (Recall that a marginal cost is the cost of generating the next unit). Sometimes a semivariable cost-behavior pattern is used to approximate a curvilinear cost.

These types of cost behavior are of concern to management only over the organization's relevant range—the range of activity within which management expects the organization to operate.

C. An engineered cost is a cost based on the physical design of a product; an example is the cost of direct materials used in making a product. A committed cost is a cost that management is going to incur based on its organizational ownership or use of facilities and its organizational structure; these costs can be changed only through relatively major decisions that have long-term implications. A discretionary cost is a cost that is based on a management choice to spend a certain amount for some purpose; these costs can usually be readily changed in the short run.

D. Both the organization and the cost driver are key determinants of the cost behavior of cost items. Some illustrations are the following:

1. In manufacturing firms, production quantity, direct-labor hours, and machine hours are typical cost drivers. Examples of variable costs are direct materials, direct labor, indirect materials, and indirect labor. Examples of fixed costs are depreciation on plant and equipment, property taxes on plant facilities, and the foreman's salary. Examples of semivariable costs or curvilinear costs are utilities and plant-equipment maintenance. Supervisory salaries are usually step-fixed costs. Fixed costs are becoming more prevalent in many manufacturing firms; this is due to increased automation and stable work forces negotiated by labor unions. In the advanced manufacturing environment many costs that were once essentially variable have become committed fixed costs; a large part of the manufacturing process is now computerized, and much of the labor force consists of highly skilled computer experts and operators of sophisticated production equipment.
2. In merchandising organizations, the cost driver is usually sales revenue. The cost of merchandise sold is a variable cost. Examples of fixed costs are depreciation on building and furnishings, and property taxes. Labor costs are usually fixed or step-fixed.

E. Four methods of estimating costs are as follows:

1. The account-classification method is based on an examination of an organization's ledger accounts. Each cost item in the ledger is classified as variable, fixed, or semivariable.
2. The visual-fit method consists of plotting the observations of cost and their associated cost-driver levels on a graph. This plot is called a scatter diagram. The analyst then visually fits a line to the plotted data points. This method helps the analyst to locate outliers—data points that are way off from the other plotted points. This method is easy to use, but it is very subjective.
3. The high-low method estimates semivariable costs by passing a line through exactly two data points—one corresponding to the low level of activity and the other corresponding to the high level of activity. For this method the unit variable cost (or slope of the line) is computed as:

$$\text{Variable cost per unit} = \frac{\text{Difference in cost levels}}{\text{Difference in activity levels}}$$

   The fixed-cost portion is determined by subtracting from one cost level (either the high or the low) the product of the variable cost per unit and the corresponding activity level. This method has a major shortcoming in that it ignores all data points except the high and low points.
4. The least-squares regression method is based on positioning the cost line so as to minimize the sum of the squared deviations between the cost line and the data points. This method is very useful for statistical analysis. The cost driver is referred to as the independent variable, and the cost is the dependent variable. This method is objective and makes use of all the data points that are available. The cost estimation line determined by this method can be evaluated by various criteria, such as:

a. Economic plausibility—the extent to which the line makes reasonable economic sense.
b. Goodness of fit—this is a quantitative measure of how well the line fits the data points.

The application of least-squares regression to a situation where there is more than one independent variable is called multiple regression; this technique may be more appropriate when the analyst believes that using only one cost driver is insufficient in cost estimation.

F. Six problems frequently encountered when collecting data for cost-estimation purposes are as follows:

1. Some data are missing due to lost documents or lack of recorded information.
2. Outliers may represent errors or highly unusual circumstances; such outliers should be omitted from the data set.
3. The units of time for which the dependent and independent variables are measured may not match.
4. There may be a conflict in objectives when choosing the time period for the data set. Many data points are desired, which implies a short time period, but accurately associating costs with time periods often requires longer time periods.
5. Some allocated and discretionary costs appear as variable even though they are fixed.
6. Historical data may not reflect the future behavior of cost because of inflation.

G. The engineering method of cost estimation consists of a detailed study of the production technology, materials, and labor that are employed in the manufacturing process. This approach is time-consuming and expensive, but it often provides highly accurate estimates of cost behavior.

H. Production efficiency often increases with experience in manufacturing. In these instances the average labor time needed decreases as cumulative production output increases. This situation is described graphically as a learning curve. Learning curves have been used in aircraft production, shipbuilding, and electronics to help predict costs.

I. All cost-estimation methods are based on certain simplifying assumptions. Two key assumptions are:

1. Usually only one cost driver is used. Even multiple regression employs only a few independent variables.
2. The estimated cost functions are linear; their graphs are straight lines within the relevant range.

J. Work measurement is the systematic analysis of a task for the purpose of finding the inputs needed to perform the task. The measure of work or activity is frequently called a control factor unit. Work measurement has been successfully used in a wide variety of organizations.

K. (Appendix) The method of least-squares regression consists of solving so-called normal equations to determine the regression parameters (estimates). The goodness of fit of a regression line may be measured by the coefficient of determination, denoted by R^2.

KEY TERMS

Account-classification method (or account analysis) 276
Committed cost 274
Control factor unit 287
Cost behavior 263
Cost estimation 264
Cost prediction 264
Curvilinear cost 271
Dependent variable 282
Discretionary cost 274
Engineered cost 273
Engineering method 285
Fixed cost 267
Goodness of fit 283
High-low method 279
Independent variable 282
Learning curve 285
Least-squares regression method 280
Multiple regression 283
Outlier 279
Regression line 280
Relevant range 272
Scatter diagram 277
Semivariable (or mixed) cost 270
Simple regression 283
Step-fixed costs 268
Step-variable costs 265
Variable cost 265
Visual-fit method 277
Work measurement 287

KEY TERMS: APPENDIX

SELF-EVALUATION QUESTIONS AND ANSWERS

True-False Questions

_____ 1. A fixed cost remains unchanged in total as the associated cost-driver level varies.

_____ 2. If the steps in a step-variable cost behavior pattern are large enough, this cost can be approximated by a variable cost without much loss in accuracy.

_____ 3. A semivariable cost is the same as a step-variable cost.

_____ 4. A variable cost per unit changes in direct proportion to a change in the associated cost-driver level.

_____ 5. Management is interested in cost behavior that is within the organization's relevant range.

_____ 6. Cost behavior is relevant to management functions of planning, control, and decision making.

_____ 7. Managerial accountants often use a step-variable cost-behavior pattern to approximate a curvilinear cost.

_____ 8. Fixed cost per unit does not change as the associated cost-driver level varies.

_____ 9. A marginal cost is the cost of making the next unit in a production process.

_____ 10. The slope of a total semivariable cost line is the variable cost per unit of activity.

_____ 11. Total variable cost remains constant as the associated cost-driver level changes.

_____ 12. In any cost analysis, it is preferable to work with total fixed costs rather than fixed cost per unit.

_____ 13. Cost prediction is an important part of the planning process.

_____ 14. Management can change committed costs only through relatively major decisions that have short-term implications.

_____ 15. The primary drawback of the visual-fit method is its lack of objectivity.

_____ 16. In any cost-estimation method, the estimate of a cost-behavior pattern should be restricted to the relevant range.

_____ 17. Both the nature of an organization and the cost driver are crucial determinants of the cost behavior of cost items in the organization.

_____ 18. Under the least-squares regression method, the cost line is positioned so as to minimize the sum of the deviations between the cost line and the data points.

_____ 19. All cost-estimation methods are usually based on the assumption that cost-behavior patterns are linear within the relevant range.

_____ 20. As a firm gets experience with a product, estimates of direct labor costs should be adjusted upward.

_____ 21. (Appendix) Under the least-squares regression method, the coefficient of determination is a measure of the goodness of fit.

Fill-in-the-Blank Questions

1. _______________ is a forecast of a cost at a specific level of activity.
2. Costs that are nearly variable, but increase in small steps, are called _______________ costs.
3. A(n) _______________ cost has both fixed and variable elements.
4. A(n) _______________ cost-behavior pattern has a curve for its graph.
5. The range of activity within which the management of an organization expects to operate is called the _______________.
6. A cost that bears a definite physical relationship to the activity measure used is called a(n) _______________ cost.
7. A(n) _______________ helps the analyst to visualize the relationship between cost and the level of a cost driver.

8. ________________ is the process of determining how a particular cost behaves.

9. A cost that remains fixed over a wide range of activity, but jumps to a different amount for activity levels outside that range, is called a(n) ________________ cost.

10. A(n) ________________ cost results from an organization's ownership or use of facilities and its basic organizational structure.

11. A(n) ________________ cost comes about as a result of a management decision to spend a certain amount of money for some purpose.

12. A(n) ________________ is a data point that falls away from other points in a scatter diagram and is not representative of the data.

13. In the ________________ method of cost estimation, the semivariable cost approximation is computed using exactly two data points.

14. The ________________ method of cost estimation involves a careful examination of the organization's ledger accounts to determine which costs are variable, fixed, or semivariable.

15. In regression analysis, where the regression line is given by $Y = a + bX$, X is referred to as the ________________ and Y is called the ________________.

16. Two criteria used to evaluate a particular regression line based on a given data set are ________________ and ________________.

17. ________________ is a statistical method that estimates a linear relationship between one dependent variable and two or more independent variables.

18. The ________________ method of cost estimation is a detailed study of the production technology, materials, and labor used in the manufacturing process.

19. A graphical expression of the situation where the average labor time needed per unit decreases as cumulative production output increases is called a(n) ________________.

20. ________________ is the systematic analysis of a task for the purpose of determining the inputs needed to perform that task.

21. The measure of work or activity in work measurement is often called a(n) ________________.

Multiple-Choice Questions

_____ **1.** Consider the following two statements:
I. Direct materials and direct labor are usually considered variable costs.
II. Fixed manufacturing costs are generally the costs of creating production capacity.
Which is (are) true?
(a) Only I
(b) Only II
(c) Both I and II
(d) Neither I nor II

_____ **2.** Which of the following is a disadvantage of the visual-fit method of cost estimation?
(a) The method lacks objectivity.
(b) The method is difficult to use.
(c) The method does not give a useful view of the overall cost-behavior pattern.
(d) The method does not provide a means of detecting outliers.

_____ **3.** The following data are available:

Activity level	Cost
300 hr	$ 900
500	1,900
400	1,500
200	1,000

Under the high-low method of cost estimation, the variable cost per hour of activity is
(a) $5. **(b)** $3. **(c)** $4. **(d)** $2.

_____ **4.** Fixed costs are becoming more prevalent in many industries due to which of the following reasons?

I. Labor unions have been increasingly successful in negotiating agreements that result in a relatively stable work force.

II. Labor is replacing automation to an increasing extent.

Which is (are) true?

(a) Only I
(b) Only II
(c) Both I and II
(d) Neither I nor II

_____ **5.** Which of the following is true?

(a) Supervisory salaries are usually step-variable costs.
(b) Depreciation on plant and production equipment is a variable cost.
(c) In merchandising firms, the cost driver is usually sales revenue.
(d) In merchandising firms, the cost of merchandise sold is a fixed cost.

_____ **6.** A disadvantage of the high-low method of cost estimation is that:

(a) Only two data points are used and the rest are ignored.
(b) It is less objective than the visual-fit method.
(c) The computations involved are complex.
(d) It is not appropriate for semivariable costs.

_____ **7.** Which of the following statements is *not* true about the least-squares regression method?

(a) It is an objective method of cost estimation.
(b) It makes use of all available data.
(c) It requires less computation than does the high-low method.
(d) It has desirable statistical properties for making cost predictions and inferences about the relationship between cost and activity.

_____ **8.** Which of the following are problems in data collection for cost-estimation purposes?

I. Misplaced source documents or failure to record a transaction can result in missing data.

II. The units of time for which the dependent and independent variables are measured may not match.

Which is (are) true?

(a) Only I
(b) Only II
(c) Both I and II
(d) Neither I nor II

Exercises

6.1 You are a management accountant for Hunter Enterprises, Inc. The president of Hunter, John Box, was recently at a conference where he heard the term "mixed cost" used by one of the speakers. The president asked you the meaning of that term, and your immediate response was "Oh! That's the same as a semivariable cost." The president's reply was, "You accountants are forever using jargon that doesn't explain much of anything; would you write me a memo explaining the meaning of this term in plain English?"

Required:

Prepare a memo to the president of Hunter that clearly and concisely explains the meaning and significance of the term "mixed or semivariable cost."

Solution Space for Exercise 6.1:

INTERNAL MEMORANDUM

To: Mr. John Box, President

From: ______________________________

Date: ______________________________

Subject: The Meaning and Significance of the Term "Mixed or Semivariable Cost"

6.2 The claims department of the Ebert Insurance Company uses labor hours as the cost driver of the department's costs. The department had the following cost data for May and June:

Month	Fixed Costs	Variable Costs	Total Costs	Labor Hours
May	$7,000	$14,400	$21,400	1,800
June	7,000	12,800	19,800	1,600

Required:

(a) Find the variable cost per labor hour.
(b) Find the fixed cost per labor hour for May and for June.
(c) Find the total cost per labor hour for May and for June.
(d) Suppose that in July the department expects to use 2,000 labor hours. What is the predicted total department cost for July?

Solution Space for Exercise 6.2:

(a) ______________________________

(b) ______________________________

____

(c) ______________________________

____

(d) ______________________________

6.3 The Delaney Company has tracked the cost of material handling for the past two months and has found the following results:

Month	Material Requisitions	Total Cost of Material Handling
February	180	$11,320
March	240	14,560

The company uses the high-low method of cost estimation.

Required:

(a) Find the variable cost per unit for material handling.
(b) Find the fixed cost per month of material handling.
(c) If 300 material requisitions are expected to be processed in April, what is the predicted total cost of material handling for April?

Solution Space for Exercise 6.3:

(a) ______________________________

(b) ______________________________

(c) ______________________________

6.4 The Honsinger Company makes and sells garden tractors and lawn mowers. A company accountant has recently completed a cost study of the Billing Department in which she used work measurement to quantify the department's activity. The control factor unit in the work measurement was number of invoices processed by the department. The following data were assembled:

Month	Control Factor Units of Activity (in hundreds of invoices processed)	Billing Department Costs (in $100 units)
July	20	57
August	23	62
September	25	64
October	21	58
November	19	59
December	15	54

Required:

(a) Find a cost-estimation equation for the Billing Department costs as a function of the control factor units (invoices processed) using the high-low method.

(b) Use the equation found in part (a) to predict the Billing Department cost for January if it is estimated that 2,200 invoices will be processed.

(c) (Appendix) Repeat parts (a) and (b) using the least-squares regression method.

Solution Space for Exercise 6.4:

(a) ______________________________

____

(b) ______________________________

(c)

x	y	$x \times x$	$x \times y$

____

____

____

____

Answers to True-False Questions

1. T
2. F The steps need to be small enough to approximate the cost by a variable cost.
3. F A semivariable cost has no steps; it is linear, with variable and fixed components.
4. F A variable cost per unit is constant as the associated cost-driver level changes.
5. T
6. T
7. F They often use a semivariable cost to approximate a curvilinear cost.
8. F Fixed cost per unit varies as the associated cost-driver level varies.
9. T
10. T
11. F Total variable cost varies directly as the associated cost-driver level changes.
12. T
13. T
14. F These committed costs can change only through relatively major decisions having long-term implications.
15. T
16. T
17. T
18. F It is positioned so as to minimize the sum of the squares of the deviations between the cost line and the data points.
19. T
20. F They should be adjusted downward to take into account the learning effect.
21. T

Answers to Fill-in-the-Blank Questions

1. Cost prediction
2. step-variable
3. semivariable
4. curvilinear
5. relevant range
6. engineered
7. scatter diagram
8. Cost estimation
9. semifixed
10. committed
11. discretionary
12. outlier
13. high-low
14. account-classification
15. independent variable, dependent variable
16. economic plausibility, goodness of fit
17. Multiple regression
18. engineering
19. learning curve
20. Work measurement
21. control factor unit

Answers to Multiple-Choice Questions

1. (c)
2. (a) The method is very subjective.
3. (b) The variable cost per hour is (1,900 – 1,000)/(500 – 200) = $3.
4. (a) Automation is replacing labor to an increasing extent.
5. (c) The other statements are false.
6. (a) The other statements are false.
7. (c) It requires much more computation than does the high-low method.
8. (c)

Solutions to Exercises

6.1 A mixed or semivariable cost is one that has both variable and fixed components. The variable component changes in direct proportion to changes in the driver of this cost while the fixed component remains constant in the short run with respect to this driver. The fact that cost is a mix of these two components helps to explain why it is sometimes referred to as a "mixed cost."

The idea of a mixed or semivariable cost is significant because this type of cost is common to many different organizations. The costs of maintenance, utilities, and energy are good examples of this type of cost. Consider maintenance cost as an illustration; the fixed component is the cost of having maintenance service available when there is no consumption of the cost driver, and the variable component is the proportional cost of maintenance that results from the usage of that maintenance service in relation to the specified cost driver.

6.2 (a) $14,400/1,800 hr. = $8.00/hr.
(b) $7,000/1,800 hr. = $3.89/hr. in May
$7,000/1,600 hr. = $4.38/hr. in June
(c) $21,400/1,800 hr. = $11.89/hr in May
$19,800/1,600 hr. = $12.38/hr in June
(d) $7,000 + $8 × 2,000 = $23,000

6.3 (a) Variable cost per unit = ($14,560 – $11,320)/(240 – 180) = $54
(b) Fixed cost per month = $11,320 – $54 × 180 = $1,600
(c) Total cost = $1,600 + $54 × 300 = $17,800

6.4 **(a)** The high point occurs in September and the low point in December.
Variable cost per unit = ($64 – $54)/(25 – 15) = $1
Fixed cost per month = 64 – 1 × 25 = 39 or $3,900

(b) For January: 39 + 1 × 22 = 61, or $6,100

(c)

x	y	$x \times x$	$x \times y$
20	57	400	1,140
23	62	529	1,426
25	64	625	1,600
21	58	441	1,218
19	59	361	1,121
15	54	225	810
123	354	2,581	7,315

$a = (354 \times 2{,}581 - 123 \times 7{,}315)/(6 \times 2{,}581 - 123 \times 123)$
$= 39.02$

$b = (6 \times 7{,}315 - 123 \times 354)/(6 \times 2{,}581 - 123 \times 123)$
$= 0.9748$

Thus,

$y = 39.02 + 0.9748 \times x$

If $x = 22$, then

$y = 39.02 + 0.9748 \times 22 = 60.46$ or $6,046

Chapter 7

Cost-Volume-Profit Analysis

CHAPTER OVERVIEW AND LEARNING OBJECTIVES

This chapter is central to many of the ideas presented in subsequent chapters. Analyzing the relationships among cost, volume, and profit is fundamental to providing information to managers to help them make decisions. After finishing this chapter, you should understand:

1. The computation of a break-even point using both the contribution-margin approach and the equation approach
2. How to compute the contribution-margin ratio and use it to find break-even sales dollars
3. The preparation of a cost-volume-profit (CVP) graph and its use
4. The use of cost-volume-profit analysis in determining the effect on profit of changes in fixed expenses, variable expenses, sales prices, and sales volume
5. The computation of a break-even point and the preparation of a profit-volume graph for a multi-product firm
6. The key assumptions of CVP analysis
7. The preparation and interpretation of a contribution income statement
8. The role of cost structure and operating leverage in CVP relationships
9. The effects of advanced technology on CVP relationships
10. The implications of activity-based costing for CVP analysis

AN OUTLINE FOR CHAPTER STUDY

A. Cost-volume-profit (CVP) analysis is a technique for examining the effects of changes in an organization's volume of activity on its costs, revenue, and profits. It is used by nonprofit organizations as well as profit-seeking enterprises. Analyzing an organization's cost behavior (as discussed in Chapter 6) is an essential first step in any CVP analysis.

B. Unit contribution margin is defined as unit sales price minus unit variable cost. It represents the contribution made by one unit of product toward covering fixed costs and profit. The unit contribution margin divided by the unit sales price is called the contribution-margin ratio; when this ratio is expressed as a percentage, it is called the contribution-margin percentage. The contribution-margin ratio represents the portion of a sales dollar that is contributed to the coverage of fixed costs and profit.

C. The break-even point is the volume of activity at which the organization's revenues and expenses are equal. It is the point at which there is no profit or loss.

1. The break-even point in units equals fixed expenses/unit contribution margin.
2. The break-even point in dollars equals fixed expenses/contribution-margin ratio.

D. An alternative method (called the equation approach) for calculating the break-even point in dollars is to use the profit equation:

Sales revenue − Variable expenses − Fixed expenses = Profit

and then solve for the sales revenue where profit equals zero. The equation approach to finding the break-even point in units is to use the profit equation:

$$\begin{pmatrix}\text{Unit}\\ \text{sales}\\ \text{price}\end{pmatrix} \times \begin{pmatrix}\text{Sales}\\ \text{volume}\\ \text{in units}\end{pmatrix} - \begin{pmatrix}\text{Unit}\\ \text{variable}\\ \text{expense}\end{pmatrix} \times \begin{pmatrix}\text{Sales}\\ \text{volume}\\ \text{in units}\end{pmatrix} - \begin{pmatrix}\text{Fixed}\\ \text{expenses}\end{pmatrix} = \text{Profits}$$

and then solve for sales volume in units where profit equals zero.

E. A CVP graph is often used to show how profit changes as activity changes. This graph has sales units on the horizontal axis and dollars on the vertical axis. The graph can be drawn according to the following steps:

1. Draw the axes of the graph.
2. Draw the fixed-expense line.
3. Compute total expense at any convenient volume.
4. Draw the variable-expense line above the fixed-expense line.
5. Compute total sales revenue at any convenient volume.
6. Draw the total revenue line.
7. Label the graph properly.

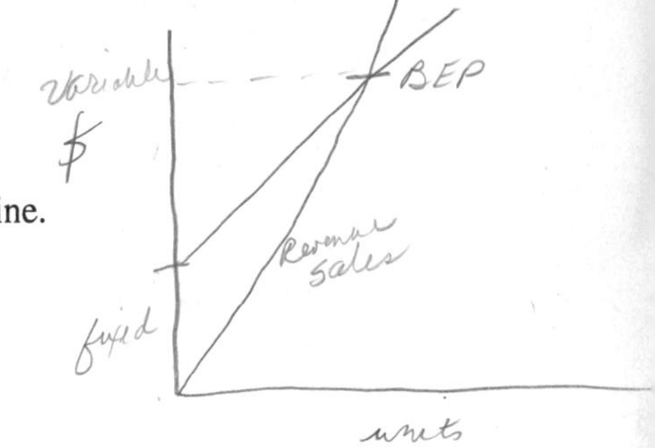

The following observations can be made about the CVP graph:

1. The break-even point is where the total-revenue line and the total-expense line intersect.
2. A manager can see the effects on profit of changes in volume.
3. The position of the break-even point within the organization's relevant range of activity gives management important information.

An alternative format to the graphical procedure just indicated is to graph fixed expenses above variable expenses; note that in the preceding graphical procedure fixed expenses were below variable expenses.

Finally, one other way to graph CVP relationships is to graph sales units on the horizontal axis and profit on the vertical axis; this format is called a profit-volume graph. This graph crosses the horizontal axis at the break-even point.

F. Target net profit is the level of profit management would like to aim at. The level of sales units needed to achieve a given target net profit is given by the formula

(Fixed expenses + Target net profit)/Unit contribution margin

Also, the level of sales dollars needed to achieve a target net profit is given by the formula

(Fixed expenses + Target net profit)/Contribution-margin ratio

The equation approach discussed in Section D can also be used to compute the sales units or sales dollars required to reach a given target net profit; it is used exactly as in the calculation of a break-even point, except that profit in the profit equation is replaced with the target net profit. Observe that break-even is the same as a target net profit of zero.

G. The safety margin of an organization is the difference between budgeted sales revenue and the break-even sales revenue. It gives management a feeling of how close projected operations are to the organization's break-even point.

H. CVP analysis can provide valuable information for management by looking at various possible changes in the elements of the profit equation to study the effects on break-even point computations. The following observations should be made, assuming that other conditions stay the same.

1. Increasing fixed expenses increases the break-even point, and decreasing fixed expenses decreases the break-even point.
2. Increasing the unit variable expense increases the break-even point, and decreasing the unit variable expenses decreases the break-even point.
3. Increasing the unit sales price decreases the break-even point, and decreasing the unit sales price increases the break-even point.

It should be noted that sometimes a change in one key element in the profit equation will cause a change in another key element of the profit equation. Varying the elements in the profit equation to study their effects on the break-even point or on profit is sometimes called "sensitivity analysis." Electronic spreadsheets are very useful for sensitivity analysis.

I. The total contribution margin is the difference between total sales revenue and total variable expenses. This is the total amount left to cover fixed expenses and profit after total variable expenses have been covered.

J. For an organization that sells multiple products (at least two), the relative proportion of each type of product sold is called the sales mix. This sales mix is used to calculate the weighted-average unit contribution margin. This is the average of the several products' unit contribution margins, weighted by the relative sales units' proportion of each product. Using this concept, the multiproduct organization's break-even point is given by the formula

Fixed expenses/Weighted-average unit contribution margin

It should be observed that this break-even point in units is valid only for the given sales mix; the break-even point will change when the sales mix changes. (Notice the similarity between the break-even formula here and the one for the single product case given in Section C.1.) With multiproduct CVP analysis the managerial accountant can investigate the impact on profit of changes in sales volume, prices, variable costs, fixed costs, or the sales mix itself.

K. The following assumptions underlie CVP analysis:

1. The behavior of total revenue is linear. This means that the unit sales price remains stable over the relevant range.
2. The behavior of total expenses is linear. This means the following:
   a. Total fixed expenses and unit variable expenses remain constant over the relevant range.
   b. The efficiency and productivity of the production process and workers remains constant.
   c. In multiproduct firms, the sales mix is stable over the relevant range.
   d. In manufacturing firms, beginning and ending inventory levels are the same.

L. The traditional income statement consists of reporting the cost of goods sold, which includes both variable and fixed manufacturing expenses and does not usually report fixed and variable expenses separately. The contribution income statement does highlight the distinction between fixed and variable expenses. In the contribution income statement, total variable expenses are subtracted from total sales revenue to obtain the total contribution margin. Then, total fixed expenses are subtracted from total contribution margin to get net income. The contribution income statement is significant because it dovetails exactly with CVP analysis, whereas the traditional income statement does not. The following points should be observed in relation to the contribution income statement when sales volume increases:

1. Net income increases by the same amount that the total contribution margin increases.
2. The total contribution margin changes in direct proportion to the change in sales volume.
3. Increase in sales revenue times contribution margin percentage equals increase in net income.

M. The cost structure of an organization is the relative proportion of its fixed and variable costs. The greater the proportion of fixed costs in a firm's cost structure, the greater will be the impact of a change in sales revenue on profit. The extent to which a firm uses fixed costs in its cost structure is called "operating leverage." In other words, operating leverage refers to the firm's ability to generate an increase in net income when sales revenue increases. The following points should be noted:

1. The operating leverage factor is contribution margin/net income. This factor depends on a given sales volume.
2. The operating leverage factor for a given sales volume is a measure of the percentage impact on net income that a given percentage changes in sales revenue will have.
3. A firm with proportionately high fixed costs will have a relatively high operating leverage.
4. A firm with a high operating leverage will have a relatively high break-even point.
5. Management must weigh the benefits of a high operating leverage against the large committed fixed costs and the correspondingly high break-even point.
6. A movement toward an advanced manufacturing environment will often cause higher fixed costs than the traditional labor-intensive production system. This will result in a higher break-even point, higher operating leverage, and lower safety margin; it will also have greater throughput, allowing a greater potential for profit, but the risk of achieving this profit will be greater due to the higher fixed costs.

N. Traditional CVP analysis focuses on units sold as the sole cost and revenue driver; this can be misleading. An activity-based costing system can provide a more complete picture of CVP relationships and thus better information for management. Costs which are fixed with respect to units sold are not fixed with respect to cost drivers such as number of setups and hours of material handling; activity-based costing CVP analysis recognizes this issue. Thus, activity-based costing provides a richer and more informative description of a firm's cost behavior.

O. (Appendix) A profit-oriented firm's after-tax net income is its before-tax income less income tax expense. The following relationships are important:

1. Sales – Variable expense – Fixed expenses = Before-tax income

2. $$\text{After tax net income} = \text{Before-tax income} \times (1 - t)$$

   where t is the tax rate.

3. $$\text{Target after-tax net income} = \text{Target before-tax income} \times (1 - t)$$

   where t is the tax rate.

4. $$\text{Sales units needed for target after-tax net income} = \frac{\text{Fixed expenses} + \dfrac{(\text{Target after-tax net income})}{(1 - t)}}{\text{Unit contribution margin}}$$

   where t is the tax rate.

KEY TERMS

Break-even point 319
Contribution income statement 337
Contribution-margin ratio 320
Contribution-margin, total 319
Cost structure 338
Cost-volume-profit (CVP) analysis 317
Cost-volume-profit graph 322
Operating leverage 339
Operating leverage factor 339
Profit-volume graph 325
Safety margin 327
Sales mix 333
Sensitivity analysis 335
Target net profit (or income) 326
Total contribution margin 319
Unit contribution margin 320
Weighted-average unit contribution margin 333

KEY TERMS: APPENDIX

After-tax net income 348 Before-tax income 348

SELF-EVALUATION QUESTIONS AND ANSWERS

True-False Questions

____ 1. Cost-volume-profit analysis is not used by nonprofit organizations.

____ 2. Analyzing an organization's cost behavior is a necessary first step in any cost-volume-profit analysis.

____ 3. In a profit-volume graph, the break-even point is where the graph crosses the vertical axis.

____ 4. If the unit contribution margin is $12 and period fixed expenses are $57,960, then the period break-even units are 4,380.

____ 5. Total contribution margin for a single product changes in direct proportion to sales revenue from that product.

____ 6. If a firm sells 2,800 units a month, the unit selling price is $15, the unit variable cost is $5, and monthly fixed costs are $18,000, then monthly profit is $12,000.

____ 7. Sales revenue equals variable expenses plus fixed expenses plus profit.

____ 8. The position of the break-even point within an organization's relevant range of activity provides important information to management.

____ 9. In a cost-volume-profit graph, the break-even point is determined by the intersection of the total-revenue line and the total-variable-expense line.

____ 10. If the unit selling price is $20 and the unit variable cost is $12, then the contribution margin percent is 60 percent.

____ 11. Decreasing fixed expenses decreases the break-even point, assuming that the unit contribution margin stays constant.

____ 12. Sometimes a change in one key variable in the profit formula will cause a change in another key variable.

____ 13. The break-even point in units in a multiproduct firm is the same for every possible sales mix.

____ 14. In a traditional income statement, the cost of goods sold includes both fixed and variable manufacturing costs.

____ 15. Increasing the unit variable expense decreases the break-even point, assuming that the fixed expenses and the unit selling price remain unchanged.

____ 16. Assume that fixed costs remain unchanged. If contribution margin increases by a given amount, then net income will increase by exactly the same amount.

____ 17. The greater the proportion of fixed costs in a firm's cost structure, the less will be the impact on profit from a given percentage change in sales revenue.

____ 18. Decreasing the unit sales price will decrease the break-even point, assuming that the fixed expenses and unit variable expense stay constant.

____ 19. In a contribution income statement, all fixed costs are subtracted from the contribution margin to obtain net income.

____ 20. If contribution margin is $40,000 and net income is $10,000, then the operating leverage factor is 0.25.

____ 21. The operating leverage factor is independent of the level of sales.

____ 22. A movement toward an advanced manufacturing system usually results in a higher operating leverage.

____ 23. (Appendix) If the target after-tax net income is $42,000 and the tax rate is 30 percent, then the target before-tax income is $60,000.

Fill-in-the-Blank Questions

1. ________________ is a technique that summarizes the effects of changes in an organization's volume of activity on its cost, revenue, and profit.
2. The ________________ is the volume of activity where an organization's profit is zero.
3. The difference between the unit sales prices and the unit variable cost is called the ________________.
4. Fixed expenses divided by the contribution-margin ratio equals the ________________.

5. A(n) ______________ graph shows the relationship between profit and volume of activity and crosses the horizontal axis at the break-even point.

6. The difference between the budgeted sales revenue and the break-even sales revenue is called the ______________.

7. Increasing fixed expenses causes the break-even point to ______________, assuming that the unit contribution margin remains unchanged.

8. ______________ is the difference between total sales revenue and total variable expenses.

9. For a multiproduct firm, the relative proportion of each type of product sold is called the ______________.

10. In performing a CVP analysis, the use of different estimates for prices, unit variable expenses, and fixed expenses to study the impact on profit is called ______________.

11. The contribution income statement highlights the distinction between ______________ and ______________ expenses.

12. Decreasing the unit variable expenses will ______________ the break-even point, assuming that the fixed expenses and the unit selling price stay constant.

13. The increase in sales revenue times ______________ equals the increase in net income.

14. The ______________ of a firm is the relative proportion of its fixed and variable costs.

15. Increasing the unit sales price will ______________ the break-even point, assuming that the fixed expenses and unit variable expense do not change.

16. The extent to which an organization uses fixed costs in its cost structure is called ______________.

17. A firm with proportionately high fixed costs has relatively ______________ operating leverage.

18. A firm with high operating leverage has a relatively ______________ break-even point.

19. (Appendix) If the factor 1 minus the tax rate is multiplied by the before-tax income, the result is ______________.

Multiple-Choice Questions

_____ 1. A firm makes and sells a single product. The selling price is $32 and the unit variable cost is $24. Monthly fixed costs are $28,800. Which of the following statements is true?
   (a) The contribution margin ratio is 0.25.
   (b) The unit contribution margin is $6.
   (c) The monthly break-even point in units is 4,800.
   (d) The monthly break-even sales dollars are $38,400.

_____ 2. An organization makes and sells only one product. If the target net profit for the month is $26,000, monthly fixed expenses are $39,000, and the unit contribution margin is $13, then the number of sales units needed to earn the monthly target net profit is
   (a) 2,000. (b) 3,000. (c) 4,000. (d) 5,000.

_____ 3. Consider the following two statements:
   I. In CVP analysis, the behavior of total revenue is assumed to be linear.
   II. In CVP analysis, the behavior of total expenses is assumed to be linear.
   Which is (are) true?
   (a) Only I
   (b) Only II
   (c) Both I and II
   (d) Neither I nor II

_____ 4. A firm makes and sells a single product. If monthly fixed expenses are $19,500, monthly unit sales are 3,000, and the unit contribution margin is $20, then monthly net profit is
   (a) $45,000. (b) $40,500. (c) $21,000. (d) $35,000.

a 5. Suppose that a firm makes two products, *A* and *B*. The sales mix in units for the period is 70 percent for *A* and 30 percent for *B*. If the unit contribution margin for *A* is $8 and the unit contribution margin for *B* is $5, then the weighted-average unit contribution margin is
(a) $7.10. **(b)** $5.90. **(c)** $6.20. **(d)** $4.80.

b 6. Consider the following two statements:
I. In CVP analysis, it is assumed that in multiproduct firms the sales mix ~~varies~~ is constant over the relevant range.
II. In CVP analysis, it is assumed that in manufacturing firms beginning and ending inventory levels are the same.
Which is (are) true?
(a) Only I
(b) Only II
(c) Both I and II
(d) Neither I nor II

____ 7. (Appendix) A firm makes and sells a single product. Monthly fixed expenses are $18,000, the unit contribution margin is $10, and the target after-tax monthly net income is $28,000. If the tax rate is 30 percent, the number of sales units needed in one month to achieve the target after-tax monthly net income is
(a) 11,133. **(b)** 4,600. **(c)** 5,800. **(d)** 8,250.

Exercises

7.1 The Robbins Company makes and sells only one product. This product has a unit sales price of $40 and a unit variable cost of $24. Fixed expenses are $32,000 per month.

Required:

(a) Find each of the following:
  (1) Unit contribution margin
  (2) Contribution-margin ratio
  (3) Monthly break-even point in units
  (4) Monthly break-even point in dollars
  (5) The monthly sales units needed to achieve a monthly before-tax income of $28,000

(b) Suppose that during July the company plans to sell 3,500 units. Compute each of the following for July based on planned sales:
  (1) Total revenue
  (2) Total contribution margin
  (3) Before-tax income
  (4) Safety margin
  (5) Operating leverage factor

(c) Draw the CVP graph for the Robbins Company. Clearly label each axis and all lines drawn. Also, indicate the monthly break-even point in units on the graph.

Solution Space for Exercise 7.1:

(a) **(1)** $40 − $24 = $16

(2) $16 / $40 = .40

(3) $32,000 / $16 = 2000

(4) $32,000 / .40 = $80,000

(5) __________

(b) **(1)** $40 X 3500 = 140,000

(2) $24 X 3500 units = 84,000   140,000 − 84,000 = $56,000

(3) 56,000 − 32,000 = 24,000

(4) (TR) 140,000 − 80,000 (BEP$) = 60,000

(5)

(c)

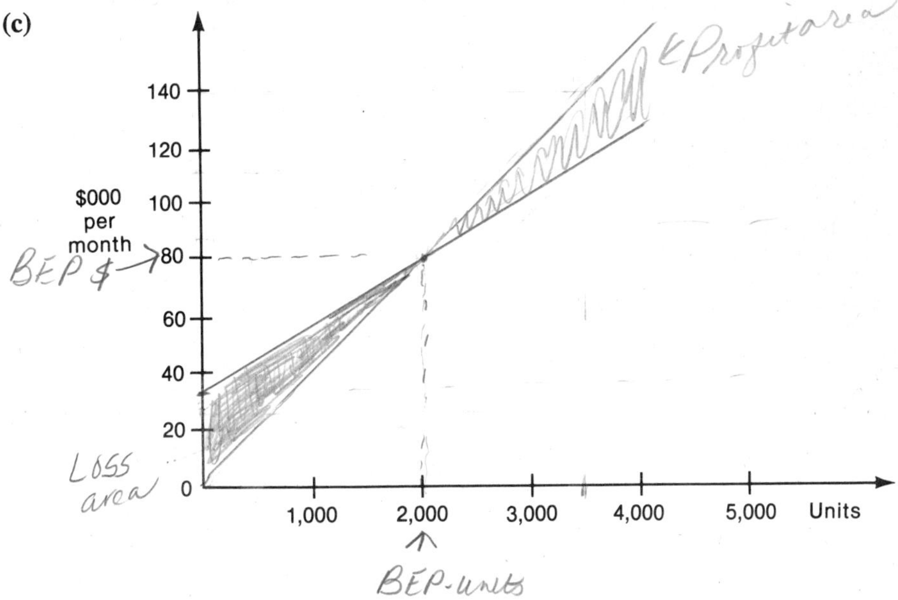

7.2 The Waldron Company produces a single product for sale. Based on current accounting records, the company's unit sales price is $20, unit variable expense is $12, and monthly fixed costs are $49,600.

Required:

(a) Compute the monthly break-even point in units.

(b) Suppose it is estimated that monthly fixed costs will increase by 10 percent. What effect will this increase have on the monthly break-even point in units? (All other factors stay the same.)

(c) Returning to the original data, suppose that variable costs decrease by 5 percent. What effect will this decrease have on the monthly break-even point in units? (All other factors remain constant.)

(d) Returning again to the original data, suppose that the unit sales price increases by 15 percent while other factors stay the same. What effect will this increase have on the monthly break-even point in units?

(e) Return to the original data. Suppose that during October the company sold 10,000 units.

- **(1)** What was the total sales revenue for October?
- **(2)** What was the before-tax income for October?
- **(3)** Use the operating leverage factor for October to compute the dollar increase in before-tax income that would result from selling 11,000 units instead of 10,000.
- **(4)** (Appendix) Suppose that the company's tax rate is 30 percent. What was October's after-tax net income?

(f) (Appendix) Return to the original data and assume that the tax rate is 30 percent. How many monthly sales units are needed to achieve a target after-tax net income of $42,000?

Solution Space for Exercise 7.2:

(a) ____________________

(b) ____________________

____

____

(c) ____________________

____

____

(d) ____________________

____

____

(e) (1) ____________________

(2) ____________________

(3) ____________________

____

____

____

(4) ____________________

(f) ____________________

____

7.3 The Kramer Company manufactures and sells two products, *X* and *Y*, in its Huntsville Division. Data concerning these products are as follows:

	Product	
	X	*Y*
Unit selling price	$200	$160
Unit variable cost	120	112

Monthly fixed costs are $480,000. Of the total units typically sold in one month, 20 percent are product *X* and 80 percent are product *Y*.

Required:

(a) Find the contribution margin per unit for each product.
(b) Find the weighted-average unit contribution margin based on the given sales mix.
(c) Find the number of units of each product that must be sold in one month in order to break even, assuming the given sales mix.

Solution Space for Exercise 7.3:

(a) ____

____

(b) ____

(c) ____

____

____

7.4 The Sanders Company makes and sells a board game called Starburst which currently has the following revenue and cost data:

Unit sales price	$30
Unit variable manufacturing cost	$16
Annual fixed selling and administrative cost	$48,000
Unit variable selling cost	$2
Annual fixed manufacturing cost (with respect to sales volume):	
Depreciation	$63,000
Setups (52 setups @ $90 each)	$4,680
Inspections (1,040 inspections @ $18 each)	$18,720
Material handling (1,248 hrs @ $10/hr.)	$12,840

Management is considering the installation of new computer-controlled equipment that will streamline the production process and generate output of higher quality than the present production system. With the new equipment there will be a reduction of direct labor costs, but fixed costs with respect to sales volume will increase; the new revenue and cost data will be as follows:

Unit sales price	$30
Unit variable manufacturing cost	$10
Annual fixed selling and administrative cost	$48,000
Unit variable selling cost	$2
Annual fixed manufacturing cost (with respect to sales volume):	
Depreciation	$195,030
Setups (365 setups @ $32 each)	$11,680
Inspections (365 inspections @ $10 each)	$3,650
Material handling (120 hrs @ $13/hr.)	$1,560

The management of Sanders would like to have a target net profit next year of $198,000.

Required:

(a) Find the break-even point in annual sales units under:
  (1) the present production system
  (2) the new production system, which uses computer-controlled equipment

(b) Find the annual sales units needed to achieve management's desired target net profit for next year under:
  (1) the present production system
  (2) the new production system, which uses computer-controlled equipment

(c) Write a paragraph that explains why the answers in Parts (a) and (b) have different break-even points and different sales units needed to achieve the same target net income.

Solution Space for Exercise 7.4:

(a) (1)

(2)

(b) (1)

(2)

(c)

Answers to True-False Questions

1. F CVP analysis is used by nonprofit organizations as well as profit-oriented firms.
2. T
3. F It is where the graph crosses the horizontal axis.
4. F The break-even point is 57,960/12 = 4,830 units.
5. T
6. F Profit equals 2,800 × ($15 − $5) − $18,000 = $10,000.
7. T
8. T
9. F It is determined by the intersection of the total-revenue line and the total-expenses line.
10. F It is 8/20 = 40 percent.
11. T
12. T
13. F It varies with the sale mix.
14. T
15. F It increases the break-even point.
16. T
17. F The impact on profit will be greater in this case.
18. F It will increase the break-even point.
19. T
20. F The operating leverage factor is $40,000/$10,000 = $4.
21. F It does depend on sales, because net income depends on sales.
22. T
23. T

Answers to Fill-in-the-Blank Questions

1. CVP analysis
2. break-even point
3. unit contribution margin
4. break-even point in sales dollars
5. profit-volume
6. safety margin
7. increase
8. Total contribution margin
9. sales mix
10. sensitivity analysis
11. fixed, variable
12. decrease
13. contribution-margin percentage
14. cost structure
15. decrease
16. operating leverage
17. high
18. high
19. after-tax net income

Answers to Multiple-Choice Questions

1. (a) The contribution-margin ratio is 8/32 = .25. The unit contribution margin is 8. Monthly break-even units are $28,800/$8 = 3,600. Monthly break-even sales dollars are $28,800/.25 = $115,200.
2. (d) ($39,000 + $26,000)/$13 = 5,000 units.
3. (c)
4. (b) 3,000 × $20 − $19,500 = $40,500.
5. (a) .7 × $8 + .3 × $5 = $7.10.
6. (b) It is assumed that the sales mix is constant over the relevant range.
7. (c) ($18,000 + $28,000/.7)/$10 = 5,800 units.

Solutions to Exercises

7.1 **(a)** (1) \$40 – \$24 = \$16
(2) 16/40 = 0.4
(3) \$32,000/\$16 = 2,000 units
(4) \$32,000/.4 = \$80,000
(5) (\$32,000 + \$28,000)/\$16 = 3,750 units

(b) (1) 3,500 × \$40 = \$140,000
(2) 3,500 × \$16 = \$56,000
(3) \$56,000 – \$32,000 = \$24,000
(4) \$140,000 – \$80,000 = \$60,000
(5) \$56,000/\$24,000 = 2.33

(c)

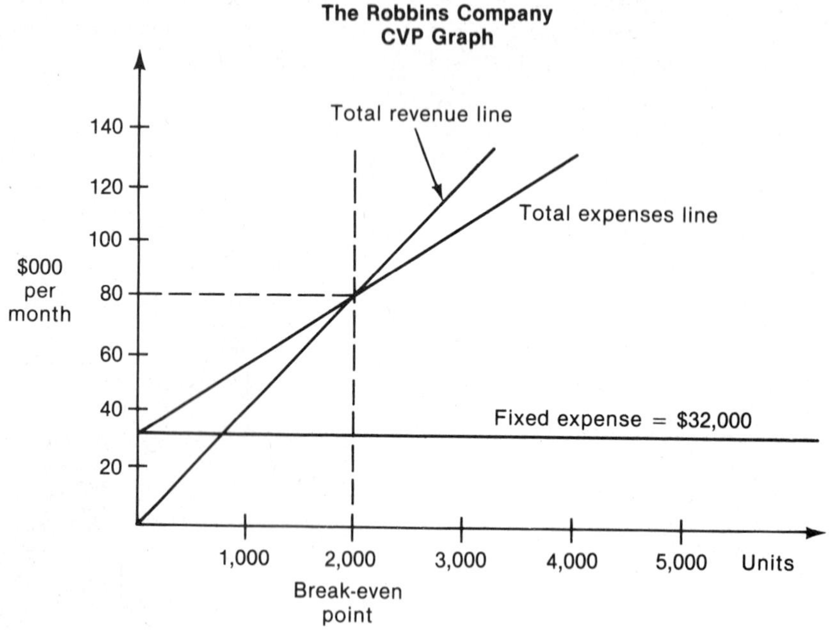

7.2 **(a)** \$49,600/\$(20 – 12) = 6,200 units

(b) \$49,600 × 1.1 = \$54,560
\$54,560/\$8 = 6,820
The break-even point went up by 10 percent.

(c) \$12 × .95 = \$11.40
\$49,600/\$(20 – 11.40) = 5,768 units
The break-even point decreased.

(d) \$20 × 1.15 = \$23
\$49,600/\$(23 – 12) = 4,510 units
The break-even point decreased.

(e) (1) 10,000 × \$20 = \$200,000
(2) 10,000 × \$8 – \$49,600 = \$30,400
(3) Operating leverage factor = \$80,000/\$30,400 = 2.632. 11,000 = 1.1 × 10,000.
If sales units (and hence sales revenue) increase by 10 percent, then before-tax income will increase by .1 × 2.632, or 26.32 percent. Thus, .2632 × \$30,400 = \$8,001.
(4) \$30,400 – .3 × \$30,400 = \$21,280

(f) (\$49,600 + \$42,000/.7)/\$8 = 13,700 units

7.3 **(a)** For *X:* \$200 – \$120 = \$80
For *Y:* \$160 – \$112 = \$48

(b) .2 × \$80 + .8 × \$48 = \$54.40

(c) Total break-even units = \$480,000/\$54.40 = 8,824
Units of *X* needed to break even = .2 × 8,824 = 1,765
Units of *Y* needed to break even = .8 × 8,824 = 7,059

7.4 **(a)** **(1)** Annual fixed costs = $147,240

Contribution margin per unit = $12

Break-even sales units = $147,240/$12 = 12,270

(2) Annual fixed costs = $259,920

Contribution margin per unit = $18

Break-even sales units = $259,920/$18 = 14,440

(b) **(1)** Units needed = ($147,240 + $198,000)/$12 = 28,770

(2) Units needed = ($259,920 + $198,000)/$18 = 25,440

(c) The cost structure of the new production system with the computer-controlled equipment has a lower proportion of variable cost than the present system because of the reduction in direct labor. Also, the new system has a larger proportion of fixed costs (with respect to sales volume) than the present system, primarily because of the increased depreciation expense on the computer-controlled equipment. This shift in cost structure usually results in different break-even points and different levels of sales units needed to achieve a given target net profit, as is the case in this situation.

Chapter **8**

Budgeting: Profit Planning and Control Systems

CHAPTER OVERVIEW AND LEARNING OBJECTIVES

This chapter covers the overall master budget that is used by most organizations. You should carefully follow the logical procedures that are used in building this budget. Each part of this budget depends on the previous parts that have been constructed. After finishing this chapter, you should understand:

1. The five purposes of budgeting systems
2. The similarities and differences in the operational budgets prepared by manufacturers, service-oriented firms, merchandising firms, and nonprofit organizations
3. How to prepare the component budgets of the master budget and the logical order in which they are prepared (Exhibit 8-1 in the text should be thoroughly understood)
4. A typical organization's process of budget administration
5. The role of assumptions and predictions in budgeting
6. The process of identifying and eliminating non-value-added activities
7. The behavioral implications of budgetary slack and participative budgeting
8. The importance of budgeting life-cycle costs
9. The differences between the economic-order-quantity and just-in-time approaches to inventory management.

AN OUTLINE FOR CHAPTER STUDY

A. A budget is a detailed plan, expressed quantitatively, that shows how resources will be acquired and used during a given period of time. Budgeting is a critical step in planning any economic activity. The prime purposes of budgeting are as follows:

   1. To quantify a plan of action
   2. To facilitate communication and coordination throughout the organization
   3. To allocate limited resources among competing uses
   4. To serve as a benchmark with which to compare actual results
   5. To serve as a basis for evaluating performance and providing incentives to managers

B. There are several different kinds of budgets. They include:

   1. A capital budget, which is a plan for the acquisition of capital assets
   2. A financial budget, which is a plan that shows how an organization will acquire its financial resources

3. A short-range budget, which is a budget covering a period of one year at most
4. A long-range budget, which is a budget covering a period of more than one year
5. A rolling budget, which is a budget that is continually being updated by adding an incremental time period and dropping the period just finished

C. A master budget is a comprehensive set of budgets covering all phases of an organization's operations for a given period of time. The components of a master budget for a manufacturing firm are:

1. A sales budget
2. Operational budgets, including a production budget, a direct-material budget, a direct-labor budget, an overhead budget, a selling and administrative expense budget, and a cash budget
3. Budgeted financial statements, including a budgeted income statement, a budgeted balance sheet, and a budgeted statement of cash flows (*Note:* You should study Exhibit 8-1 in the text until you understand the logical connections between these various component budgets.)

D. The sales budget depends on the forecast of sales for the budget period. Major factors that are considered when forecasting sales are:

1. Past sales levels and trends of the organization
2. General economic trends
3. Economic trends in the organization's industry
4. Other external factors expected to affect sales in the industry (for example, weather)
5. Political and legal events
6. The intended pricing policy of the organization
7. Planned advertising and promotion
8. Anticipated actions of competitors
9. New products or services that might affect products presently sold
10. Market research studies

E. The operational budgets are built upon information contained in the sales budget. These operational budgets specify how operations will be carried out to meet the sales demand. In a merchandising firm, a purchases budget is developed from information on sales demand and planned inventory levels. In a service-oriented firm, a set of budgets for services is established to show how the demand for services will be met.

F. The operational budgets for a manufacturing firm are constructed according to the following steps:

1. From the sales budget and information about planned beginning and ending period inventory levels, a production budget of units is developed. The number of units to be produced over the given budget period is given by the formula:

Planned unit sales	+	Desired ending inventory in units	−	Beginning inventory in units	=	Units to be produced

2. The production units needed for the budget period as determined from the production budget is the basis for preparing the direct-material budget. The following formula is used in preparing the budget for direct-material purchases for the budget period:

Direct materials needed for production	+	Desired ending inventory of direct materials	−	Beginning inventory of direct materials	=	Direct materials to be purchased

3. Based on the production budget, a direct-labor budget and a manufacturing overhead budget will be prepared. The two budgets will set forth all the conversion costs needed during the period to satisfy the requirements of the production budget.
4. The selling and administrative budget is then prepared to reflect all the period expenses needed for marketing the products and administering the firm.
5. The last operational budget to be prepared is the cash budget. This budget is made up of three parts:

a. The cash receipts budget presents all the cash that is to be received, together with the source of that cash, over the budget period.
b. The cash disbursements budget displays a schedule of cash payments, and what the payments are for, over the budget period
c. The summary cash budget presents the planned change in the cash balance over the budget period

Information from the cash receipts budget and the cash disbursements budget is used in the summary cash budget according to the following formula:

$$\text{Period cash receipts} - \text{Period cash disbursements} + \text{Beginning period cash balance} = \text{Ending period cash balance}$$

G. For a manufacturing firm the information from the sales budget, direct-material budget, direct-labor budget, overhead budget, and selling and administrative expense budget is used to prepare a budgeted income statement. The budgeted income statement and the cash budget are used to prepare the budgeted balance sheet. Finally, information from the budgeted balance sheet is used to prepare the budgeted statement of cash flows.

H. Nonprofit organizations begin their budgeting process with budgets that indicate the level of services to be provided. These organizations also prepare budgets showing their anticipated funding.

I. Large organizations usually employ a budget director, who oversees budget data collection and the preparation of the master budget. Often this director develops and disseminates a budget manual indicating the details and procedures of budget preparation. Some large organizations have a budget committee made up of key executives who advise the budget director. The authority for final approval of the master budget usually resides with the board of directors or board of trustees of the organization.

J. A financial planning model is a set of mathematical relationships that expresses the interaction among the operational, financial, and environmental events that determine the outcomes of an organization's activities.

K. Zero-based budgeting assumes that the budget for virtually every activity in the organization is initially set at zero. In order to obtain funding for an activity during the budgeting process, that activity must be justified as to its continued usefulness. This approach to budgeting forces management to rethink each phase of an organization's operations before resources are allocated. A modified version of this approach is to use base budgeting, which sets the initial budget of an activity in accordance with a base package; any increases from the initial base must be justified according to costs and benefits.

L. The base-budgeting concept is compatible with the philosophy of a cost management system, which seeks to identify and eliminate non-value-added costs and activities. Non-value-added costs result from activities that are either unnecessary and dispensable or necessary but inefficient. The following steps give a strategy for reducing or eliminating non-value-added costs.

1. Identify the activities in the firm.
2. Separate out the non-value-added activities.
3. Understand activity linkages and cost drivers.
4. Establish meaningful performance measures.
5. Report the non-value-added costs.

After the non-value-added costs have been uncovered, these costs can be reduced by reducing or eliminating the activities that generate these costs. Sharing activities with related products or using alternative activities where possible can also help reduce the cost of activities.

M. When a product is being considered for introduction into the marketplace, it is important to plan for all of the costs that will be incurred throughout the product's life cycle. This is especially important for products with short product life cycles. Product life-cycle costs that need to be budgeted relate to the five phases in a product's life cycle, namely:

1. Product planning and concept design
2. Preliminary design
3. Detailed design and testing
4. Production
5. Distribution and customer service

N. The budgeting process can have a significant impact on people's behavior. An example of the behavioral effects of budgets is padding the budget; this means overestimating costs and underestimating revenues. The difference between the budgeted amount a person provides and a realistic estimate of that amount is called budgetary slack. Reasons why people pad budgets are as follows:

1. They perceive that their performance will look better if they can "beat the budget."
2. It is a way to cope with uncertainty.
3. Often cost projections are cut in the resource-allocation process.

Padding the budget for one's personal gain is an ethical violation.

O. Participative budgeting is an approach to budgeting that seeks to involve employees throughout an organization in the budgeting process. This approach gives employees a sense that "this is our budget," and it can be very effective in motivating employees to be more concerned about budgetary matters. A disadvantage of this approach is that excessive participation can cause vacillation and delay in the budget process. Management by objectives is an approach where a firm's goal is subdivided into specific objectives; a budget is then developed to meet each objective.

P. (Appendix) Inventory decisions involve a delicate balance between ordering costs, holding costs, and shortage costs. A mathematical tool that has traditionally been used to minimize the cost of ordering and holding inventory is the economical-order-quantity (EOQ) model. The basic formula of the EOQ model is

$$\text{Economic order quantity} = \left[\frac{2 \times \text{Annual requirement} \times \text{Cost per order}}{\text{Annual holding cost per unit}}\right]^{1/2}$$

Another important inventory management problem is when to place an order; this depends on the lead time, which is the time needed for the material to be received after an order has been placed.

The basic philosophies of just-in-time (JIT) inventory management and the EOQ approach are different. The EOQ method says that some inventory is necessary and the cost of ordering should be balanced against the cost of holding inventory. The JIT philosophy strives for minimum or zero inventory levels and seeks to reduce the non-value-added costs, which include holding and ordering costs.

KEY TERMS

Base budgeting 397
Base budget package 397
Budget 374
Budget administration 394
Budgetary slack 401
Budget committee 395
Budget director (or chief budget officer) 395
Budgeted balance sheet 391
Budgeted financial (or pro forma) statements 375
Budgeted income statement 391
Budgeting system 374
Budget manual 395
Capital budget 375
Cash disbursements budget 387
Cash receipts budget 386
Direct-material budget 381
Direct-professional-labor budget 383
Financial budget 375
Financial planning model 396
Incremental budget package 397
Indirect professional labor budget 384
Management by objectives (MBO) 403
Master budget (or profit plan) 374
Operational budgets 376
Overhead budget 385
Padding the budget 401
Participative budgeting 402
Production budget 380
Professional services and sales budget 379
Profit plan (or master budget) 374
Rolling budgets (or revolving or continuous) 375
Sales forecasting 375
Selling and administrative expense budget 386
Summary cash budget 390
Zero-base budgeting 397

KEY TERMS: APPENDIX

Economic order quantity (EOQ) 406 | Lead time 409 | Safety stock 410

SELF-EVALUATION QUESTIONS AND ANSWERS

True-False Questions

_____ 1. Pro forma financial statements show the financial condition and performance for a period of time that has occurred in the past.

_____ 2. A long-range budget covers a period from 6 months to 1 year.

_____ 3. Developing a budget is a critical step in any economic activity.

_____ 4. The starting point for any master budget is a sales revenue budget.

_____ 5. The selling and administrative expense budget is an example of a budgeted financial statement.

_____ 6. The direct-material budget is developed from the production budget.

_____ 7. Sales forecasting is a useful, but not a critical, step in the budgeting process.

_____ 8. Every business should prepare a cash budget.

_____ 9. Nonprofit organizations begin their budgeting process with a budget that shows the level of services to be provided.

_____ 10. The summary cash budget is the same as the cash disbursements budget.

_____ 11. The cash budget is an example of an operational budget.

_____ 12. A merchandising firm develops a budget for merchandise purchases instead of a production budget.

_____ 13. Based on the direct-material budget, a direct-labor budget and an overhead budget are prepared.

_____ 14. The cash balance on May 1 is $15,000, cash receipts for May are $92,000, and cash disbursements for May are $105,000. The cash balance on May 31 is $28,000.

_____ 15. Budget activity is a major activity in every large organization.

_____ 16. The participative budgeting approach is sometimes used so as not to go to the extreme of zero-based budgeting.

_____ 17. Nonprofit organizations do not prepare budgets showing their anticipated funding, because this information is not useful for planning purposes.

_____ 18. Human reactions to the budgeting process have negligible influence on an organization's overall effectiveness.

_____ 19. Budget padding means underestimating cost and overstating revenues.

_____ 20. Planning life-cycle costs is a crucial step in making a decision about the introduction of a new product.

_____ 21. (Appendix) Inventory decisions involve a delicate balance among ordering costs, holding costs, and shortage costs.

Fill-in-the-Blank Questions

1. A(n) _______________ is a detailed plan in quantitative terms that specifies how resources will be acquired and used in a specific period of time.
2. A(n) _______________ budget is a comprehensive set of budgets covering all phases of an organization's operations for a specified period of time.
3. A(n) _______________ budget is a plan for the acquisition of capital assets.
4. A(n) _______________ budget shows the number of product units to be manufactured.
5. The _______________ budget shows expected cash receipts and planned cash disbursements.
6. Budgeted _______________ show the overall financial results of the organization's planned operations for the budget period.
7. A(n) _______________ budget is continually updated by periodically adding a new incremental time period and dropping the period just covered.
8. The _______________ budget shows the dollar amount of materials that need to be purchased during the budget period.

9. In large organizations, the ________________ is usually the person who specifies the process by which budget data will be gathered, collects the information, and prepares the master budget.

10. The ________________ is the document which says who is responsible for providing various types of information, when the information is required, and what form the information is to take.

11. Often a(n) ________________ is appointed to advise the budget director during the preparation of the budget.

12. Under ________________ budgeting, the budget for virtually every activity of an organization is initially set to zero.

13. A(n) ________________ is a set of mathematical relationships that expresses the interactions among various operational, financial, and environmental events that determine the overall results of an organization's activities.

14. The difference between the revenue or cost projection that a person provides and a realistic estimate of the revenue or cost is called ________________.

15. The idea of ________________ budgeting is to involve employees throughout an organization in the budgetary process.

16. (Appendix) The ________________ is the length of time it takes for material to be received after an order is placed.

Multiple-Choice Questions

____ **1.** Which of the following are major factors when forecasting sales?

I. Past sales levels and trends
II. Economic trends in the company's industry
III. Political and legal events

(a) Only I and II
(b) Only II and III
(c) Only I and III
(d) I, II, and III

____ **2.** Which of the following is *not* a primary purpose of budgeting?

(a) Facilitating communication and coordination throughout the organization
(b) Providing basic information in determining tax obligations for a previous period's operations
(c) Controlling profits and operations
(d) Quantifying a plan of action

____ **3.** The March 1 inventory of finished units at the J Company is 3,000. During March the company plans to sell 35,000 units and desires a March 31 inventory of 5,000 units. The number of units that the company should plan on producing in March is:

(a) 53,000.
(b) 37,000.
(c) 42,000.
(d) 33,000.

____ **4.** The Jason Company plans to produce 24,000 units during January. Each unit of finished product requires 1.5 direct-labor hours, and each direct-labor hour costs $12. The amount that should be budgeted for direct labor to meet the planned production in January is:

(a) $288,000.
(b) $36,000.
(c) $432,000.
(d) $360,000.

____ **5.** The Graham Company plans to sell 20,000 units in April, 30,000 in May, and 25,000 in June. Each unit sells for $25, and sales in any month consist of 80 percent credit sales and 20 percent cash sales. All credit sales are paid for in the month following the month of sale. The cash receipts in May from all planned sales amount to:

(a) $60,000.
(b) $550,000.
(c) $150,000.
(d) $500,000.

_____ **6.** The Finley Company plans to produce 25,000 units during July. Each unit of finished product requires 2 pounds of direct material *X*. This direct material costs $4 per pound. The July 1 inventory of *X* is 2,000 pounds, and the desired July 31 inventory of *X* is 1,000 pounds. The cost of material *X* purchases in July is planned to be:
(a) $204,000.
(b) $196,000.
(c) $200,000.
(d) $180,000.

_____ **7.** The Hanover Company sells only one product and plans to sell 80,000 units in November and 120,000 units in December. The unit sales price is $4.80. The sales each month consist of 30 percent cash sales and the rest on credit; however, credit sales are always paid for in the month following the month of sale. The planned accounts receivable balance on November 30 is:
(a) $268,800.
(b) $56,000.
(c) $384,000.
(d) $403,200.

_____ **8.** Which of the following would *not* be done to help achieve the goal of eliminating all non-value-added costs?
(a) Identify all significant activities of the firm.
(b) Identify the non-value-added activities.
(c) Understand activity linkages and cost drivers.
(d) Eliminate performance measures.

_____ **9.** (Appendix) The Munson Company needs 12,000 units of material *Y* annually. This material is ordered periodically from a regular supplier. The cost of placing one order is $60, and the annual holding cost per unit is $.16. For material *Y* the economic order quantity is:
(a) 2,000 units.
(b) 3,000 units.
(c) 4,000 units.
(d) 3,280 units.

Exercises

8.1 The Sharkey Company makes and sells a single product. Forecasted sales of this product for October are 30,000 units; for November, 50,000 units; for December, 45,000 units; and for January, 35,000 units. This product is made from a liquid *Z*, and one unit of finished product requires 2 gallons of *Z*. The price of liquid *Z* is $8 per gallon. Because of the nature of liquid *Z*, the company wants no ending inventories of *Z* at all, and they do not have any work-in-process inventories. The company does desire to have an ending inventory of finished product equal to 5 percent of next month's sales in units. On September 30 the inventory of finished product amounted to 1,700 units.

Required:

(a) Prepare a production budget for October, November, and December.
(b) Prepare a direct-material budget for October, November, and December.

Solution Space for Exercise 8.1:

(a)

SHARKEY COMPANY
Production Budget
For the Fourth Quarter

	October	November	December

(b)

SHARKEY COMPANY
Direct-Material Budget
For the Fourth Quarter

	October	November	December

8.2 General Eye Care, Inc., is a large, all-around eye-care practice which expects 50,400 office visits next year; these visits are spread evenly over the year. Seventy percent of these visits will be for 20-minute appointments, and the rest will be for 40-minute appointments. On average, a 20-minute appointment will generate $80 in revenue and a 40-minute appointment $140 in revenue. Forty percent of the revenue goes for professional labor. Eighty percent of the revenue in one month is paid for during the month, and the remainder is paid for in the month following the appointment. There are no bad debts.

Required:

(a) Prepare a professional-labor budget for February.
(b) Determine the cash collections during February for professional eye care.

Solution Space for Exercise 8.2:

(a)

GENERAL EYE CARE, INC.
Direct-Professional-Labor Budget
For the Month of February

(b)

GENERAL EYE CARE, INC.
Schedule of Cash Collections
For the Month of February

8.3 Harwit Nurseries sells a variety of plants, shrubs, and lawn products. It is now February 28. The following data are available:

1. Sales are budgeted at $280,000 for March and $340,000 for April. February sales were $250,000.
2. Collections from the sale of nursery items will be 75 percent in the month of sale and the rest in the month following sale. There are no bad debts.
3. The cost of sales is expected to be 70 percent of sales revenue.
4. Sixty percent of the nursery products are purchased in the month prior to sale, and 40 percent are bought in the month of sale. Payment for nursery items bought from suppliers is always in the month following the purchase.
5. The annual depreciation amounts to $240,000.
6. Other monthly expenses amount to $38,000 and are paid for in cash.
7. The income tax rate is 30 percent; taxes are paid in cash. The balance sheet on February 28 was as follows:

HARWIT NURSERIES
Balance Sheet
February 28

Assets

Cash	$ 20,000
Accounts receivable	62,500
Inventory (nursery products)	117,600
Property, plant, and equipment (net of $540,000 accum. depr.)	660,000
Total assets	$860,100

Liabilities and Equities

Accounts payable (nursery products)	$187,600
Common stock	600,000
Retained earnings	72,500
Total liabilities and equity	$860,100

Required:

(a) Prepare a cash receipts budget for March.
(b) Prepare a budgeted income statement for March.
(c) Prepare a cash disbursements budget for March.
(d) Prepare a budgeted balance sheet as of March 31.

Solution Space for Exercise 8.3:

(a)

HARWIT NURSERIES
Cash Receipts Budget
For March

(b)

HARWIT NURSERIES
Budgeted Income Statement
For March

(c)

HARWIT NURSERIES
Cash Disbursements Budget
For March

(d)

HARWIT NURSERIES
Budgeted Balance Sheet
As of March 31

Computations:

8.4 The headmaster of Loudonville Academy told the budget committee, "In preparing next year's budget we would be wise to underestimate our revenues and overstate our expenses." You are a member of this budget committee and are asked by the chairman of the committee to give your views on the statement made by the headmaster.

Required:

Prepare a paragraph that explains the meaning of the headmaster's statement and the reasons why managers often follow this philosophy.

Solution Space for Exercise 8.4:

Answers to True-False Questions

1. F They show the projected financial condition and performance for a future time period.
2. F It covers a period of more than 1 year.
3. T
4. T
5. F It is an example of an operational budget.
6. T
7. F It is a critical step in the budgeting process.
8. T
9. T
10. F The summary cash budget shows the change that is expected to occur over the budget period.
11. T
12. T
13. F The direct-labor and overhead budgets are based on the production budget.
14. F The ending balance is \$15,000 + \$92,000 – \$105,000 = \$2,000.
15. T
16. F Base budgeting is sometimes used so as to not go to the extreme of zero-based budgeting.
17. F These organizations do prepare budgets showing their anticipated funding.
18. F It has a significant influence on overall effectiveness.
19. F It means underestimating revenues and overstating expenses.
20. T
21. T

Answers to Fill-in-the-Blank Questions

1. budget
2. master
3. capital
4. production
5. cash
6. financial statements
7. rolling
8. direct-material
9. budget director
10. budget manual
11. budget committee
12. zero-based
13. financial planning model
14. budgetary slack
15. participative
16. lead time

Answers to Multiple-Choice Questions

1. (d)
2. (b) Budgeting pertains to future events, not information on a previous period's tax obligations.
3. (b) 35,000 + 5,000 – 3,000 = 37,000 units.
4. (c) \$12 × 1.5 × 24,000 = \$432,000.
5. (b) 30,000 × 25 × .2 + 20,000 × 25 × .8 = \$550,000.
6. (b) (25,000 × 2 + 1,000 – 2,000) × 4 = \$196,000.
7. (a) 80,000 × \$4.80 × .7 = \$268,800.
8. (d) Performance measures should be established.
9. (b) $(2 \times 12{,}000 \times \$60/\$.16)^{1/2}$ = 3,000 units.

Solutions to Exercises

8.1 (a)

SHARKEY COMPANY
Production Budget
For the Fourth Quarter

	Month		
	October	**November**	**December**
Sales in units	30,000	50,000	45,000
Add: desired ending inventory	2,500	2,250	1,750
Total units needed	32,500	52,250	46,750
Less: beginning inventory	1,700	2,500	2,250
Units to be produced	30,800	49,750	44,500

(b)

SHARKEY COMPANY
Direct-Material Budget
For the Fourth Quarter

	Month		
	October	**November**	**December**
Units to be produced	30,800	49,750	44,500
Direct material needed per unit (gal)	× 2	× 2	× 2
Direct material needed for production and to be purchased*	61,600	99,500	89,000
Price per gallon	× $8	× $8	× $8
Cost of direct material purchases	$492,800	$796,000	$712,000

*No beginning or ending inventories of material *Z* are desired.

8.2 (a)

GENERAL EYE CARE, INC.
Direct-Professional-Labor Budget
For the Month of February

20-minute appointments:	
(50,400/12) × 0.7 = 2,940 appointments	
Revenue from appointments = 2,940 × $80 = $235,200	
Direct professional labor needed = $235,200 × 0.4 =	$ 94,080
40-minute appointments:	
(50,400/12) × 0.3 = 1,260 appointments	
Revenue from appointments = 1,260 × $140 = $176,400	
Direct professional labor needed = $176,400 × 0.4 =	$ 70,560
Total direct professional labor needed	$164,640

(b)

GENERAL EYE CARE, INC.
Schedule of Cash Collections
For the Month of February

Collections from January services:		
January revenue	$411,600	
February collections	$411,600 × .2 =	$ 82,320
Collections from February services:		
February revenue	$411,600	
February collections	$411,600 × .8 =	329,280
Total cash collections in February		$411,600

($235,200 + 176,400 = $411,600)

8.3 (a)

HARWIT NURSERIES
Cash Receipts Budget
For March

Cash collections from February sales:	.25 × $250,000 =	$ 62,500
Cash collections from March sales:	.75 × $280,000 =	210,000
Total cash receipts		$272,500

(b)

HARWIT NURSERIES
Budgeted Income Statement
For March

Sales revenue	$280,000
Cost of goods sold (70% of sales)	196,000
Gross margin	$ 84,000
Operating expenses (besides depreciation)	38,000
Depreciation	20,000
Income before taxes	$ 26,000
Income taxes	7,800
Net income after taxes	$ 18,200

(c)

HARWIT NURSERIES
Cash Disbursements Budget
For March

Cash payments for February purchases	$187,600
Cash payments for other March expenses	38,000
Cash payment for March income taxes	7,800
Total cash disbursements	$233,400

(d)

HARWIT NURSERIES
Budgeted Balance Sheet
As of March 31

Assets

Cash (1)	$ 59,100
Accounts receivable (2)	70,000
Inventory (3)	142,800
Property, plant, and equipment (net) (4)	640,000
Total assets	$911,900

Liabilities and Equity

Accounts payable (5)	$221,200
Common stock	600,000
Retained earnings (6)	90,700
Total liabilities and equity	$911,900

Computations:

(1) $20,000 + $272,500 – $233,400
(2) 0.25 × $280,000
(3) $117,600 + 0.4 × 0.7 × $280,000 + 0.6 × 0.7 × $340,000 – 0.7 × $280,000
(4) $660,000 – $240,000/12
(5) 0.4 × 0.7 × $280,000 + 0.6 × 0.7 × $340,000
(6) $72,500 + $18,200

8.4 The statement made by the headmaster is commonly referred to as "budgetary slack" or "padding the budget." It occurs when those preparing the budget intentionally understate anticipated revenues and overstate anticipated expenses. Some reasons for doing this are:

(1) It increases the chances of obtaining favorable budget variances, and this makes performance look better.
(2) It is a way to help cope with budget uncertainties.
(3) It is a way of dealing with budget cuts made in resource-allocation decisions.

Chapter **9**

Standard-Costing and Performance Measures for the New Manufacturing Environment

CHAPTER OVERVIEW AND LEARNING OBJECTIVES

In this chapter you begin your study of standard costing. In Chapter 3 you learned about the use of predetermined overhead rates based on budgeted data. This idea is now extended to material and labor in standard-costing systems as well. After finishing this chapter, you should understand:

1. How standard costing is used to help control costs
2. Two ways of setting standards
3. The difference between perfection and practical standards
4. How to compute and interpret the direct-material price and quantity variances and the direct-labor rate and efficiency variances
5. Several methods for determining the significance of cost variances
6. Some behavioral effects of standard costing
7. How standard costs are used in product costing
8. How to journalize the recording and closing out of cost variances
9. Some advantages of standard costing
10. The changing role of standard-costing systems in the new manufacturing environment
11. How to describe the operational performance measures appropriate for the new manufacturing environment

AN OUTLINE FOR CHAPTER STUDY

A. At the end of a budget period, managers use the budget as a benchmark against which the results of actual operations are compared. Thus, the budget serves as a control device as well as a planning tool. This budgetary-control system operates according to these steps:

 1. Determine the budget for the production of one unit of product or service. This budget is called a standard cost.
 2. Measure the actual cost incurred in the production process during the period.
 3. Compare the actual cost with the standard cost for the period. The difference between the actual cost and the standard cost is called a cost variance. If actual cost less standard cost is negative, the cost variance is favorable; if actual cost exceeds standard cost, the cost variance is unfavorable.

 The process of following up only on significant cost variances is called management by exception.

B. Two methods used by managerial accountants for setting standards are as follows:

1. Analysis of historical data to determine cost behavior and to make cost predictions, as was done in Chapter 6.
2. Analysis of the process of making a product to determine what is should cost. This is called task analysis and is often done by the managerial accountant in conjunction with engineers.

Often both of these approaches are used together. Sometimes people involved in the production process participate in setting standards.

C. There are two key types of standards.

1. Perfection standards are standards that can be attained only under nearly perfect operating conditions. Some managers favor these standards on the grounds that they will motivate employees to try hard to approach these ideal standards.
2. Practical standards are standards that are as tight as practical but can still be attained. These standards allow for such things as machine breakdowns and normal material waste.

These standards can be applied to service-oriented firms, nonprofit organizations, and governmental units as well as manufacturing firms.

D. The standard quantity of material allowed in a manufacturing process is the total amount of material normally required to produce a finished product, including allowances for normal waste or inefficiency. The standard price of material is the total delivered cost less any related purchase discounts. The standard quantity of direct labor is the number of labor hours normally needed to make one unit of product. The standard labor rate is the total hourly cost of compensation, including fringe benefits. The standard costs for direct-material and direct-labor inputs that are allowed are based on the actual output achieved. These standard costs are benchmarks against which actual costs are compared.

E. The direct-material price variance is the difference between actual material cost and the actual quantity purchased times the standard price. In symbols, this variance is

$$PQ \times AP - PQ \times SP = PQ \times (AP - SP)$$

where PQ = quantity purchased
AP = actual price
SP = standard price

Notice that this variance exists because the actual price differs from the standard price. Also, notice that it depends on the quantity purchased, not the quantity used.

F. The direct-material quantity variance is the difference between actual quantity used times the standard price and the standard quantity allowed for the output achieved times the standard price. In symbols, this variance is

$$AQ \times SP - SQ \times SP = SP \times (AQ - SQ)$$

where AQ = actual quantity used
SP = standard price
SQ = standard quantity allowed for the output achieved

Observe that this variance exists because the actual quantity used differs from the standard quantity allowed.

G. The direct-labor rate variance is the difference between actual labor cost and the actual hours used times the standard rate. In symbols, this variance is

$$AH \times AR - AH \times SR = AH \times (AR - SR)$$

where AH = actual hours
AR = actual rate per hour
SR = standard rate per hour

Notice that this variance exists because the actual rate differs from the standard rate.

H. The direct-labor efficiency is the difference between actual hours used times the standard rate and the standard hours allowed for the output achieved times the standard rate. In symbols, this variance is

$$AH \times SR - SH \times SR = SR \times (AH - SH)$$

where AH = actual hours
SH = standard hours allowed for the output achieved
SR = standard rate per hour

Observe that this variance exists because actual hours used differ from the standard hours allowed for the output achieved.

I. Managers use several guidelines in deciding whether cost variances are significant enough to be investigated. These guidelines include the following:

1. The size of the variances in question; often managerial accountants will report the relative magnitude of variances in order to put the variance measures on a comparable footing.
2. The extent to which variances recur; if a variance occurs repeatedly, management may want to investigate why.
3. Trends in variances; if a variance is following a certain pattern or trend, it may merit inquiry.
4. Ability to control; if a variance can be controlled, it may be worth investigating; if a variance is not controllable, then little is achieved by investigating it.
5. It can be just as important to investigate favorable variances as unfavorable variances.
6. Cost to investigate in relation to benefits; if the benefits from investigation don't exceed the cost to do so, the investigation may not be done.

Sometimes managerial accountants use statistical control charts to determine whether variances are worthy of investigation. In this situation, cost variances are plotted over time to see if they exceed statistically determined critical values; if the variances are outside the critical values, an investigation is likely to be made.

J. The purchasing manager is generally in the best position to influence material price variances. The production supervisor is usually the one who has the most influence over the material quantity variance. Likewise, the production manager is usually most responsible for the labor-efficiency variance. Direct-labor rate variances often result from using a difference mix of employees than was anticipated when standards were set. Interaction among variances often makes it difficult to ascertain who is responsible for a particular variance.

K. Firms that use standard costs for control also use them for product costing. In standard costing the standard costs of direct material and direct labor are entered into Work-in-Process Inventory. Examples of journal entries to record direct-material and direct-labor variances are as follows:

		Debit	Credit
1.	Raw-Materials Inventory	$$$	
	Direct-Material Price Variance	$$$	
	Accounts Payable		$$$
	To record the purchase of direct materials with an unfavorable price variance.		
2.	Work-in-Process Inventory	$$$	
	Direct-Material Quantity Variance		$$$
	Raw-Materials Inventory		$$$
	To record the direct materials used in production with a favorable quantity variance.		
3.	Work-in-Process Inventory	$$$	
	Direct-Labor Efficiency Variance	$$$	
	Direct-Labor Rate Variance		$$$
	Accounts Payable		$$$
	To record the use of direct labor in production with a favorable rate variance and an unfavorable efficiency variance.		

4. Cost of Goods Sold $$$
Direct-Material Quantity Variance $$$
Direct-Labor Rate Variance $$$
Direct-Material Price Variance $$$
Direct-Labor Efficiency Variance $$$
To record the disposition of the period cost variances where the net of the combined variances is unfavorable (positive). [If this net were favorable (negative), Cost of Goods Sold would be credited.]

An alternative method of disposing of the cost variances is to prorate the variances to Work-in-Process Inventory, Finished-Goods Inventory, and Cost of Goods Sold, instead of closing all variances to Cost of Goods Sold.

L. The traditional advantages of standard costing include the following:

1. Standard costs provide a basis for sensible cost comparisons.
2. Computation of standard-cost variances enables managers to employ the techniques of management by exception.
3. Variances give a means of evaluating performance.
4. Variances can provide motivation for employees to adhere to standards.
5. Standard costs provide more stable product costs.
6. Standard costing is generally less costly to use.

M. The new manufacturing environment is causing changes in the role of standard costing. Some drawbacks attributed to traditional standard costing in an advanced manufacturing setting are:

1. The computed variances are at too aggregate a level and come too late to be useful.
2. Variances are not tied to specific product lines, production batches, or FMS cells.
3. The focus is too much on the cost and efficiency of direct labor.
4. Production processes should be stable for standard costing to be successful.
5. For short product life cycles the standards are relevant for only a short time.
6. Costs are not defined broadly enough to capture various important aspects of performance.
7. The focus is too much on cost minimization rather than on increase in product quality or better customer service.
8. Since automated production processes tend to be fairly consistent in meeting specifications, variances from standards will be small or nonexistent.

N. Despite the drawbacks mentioned in the previous section, standard costing is being adapted to advanced manufacturing methods. Some changes in the use of standard costing in the new manufacturing environment are due to factors such as the following:

1. Reduced importance of labor standards and variances
2. More emphasis on material and overhead costs
3. Greater use of cost drivers for the activities of production
4. A shift in the cost structure with more costs being fixed
5. An emphasis on high quality and zero defects in production
6. The reduction or elimination of non-value-added costs
7. Shorter product life cycles, which are becoming more common
8. Information systems, which now operate on a real-time basis
9. Nonfinancial measures for operational control, which are now being used (a representative list of these measures is given in Exhibit 9-7 in the text)

O. The following concepts pertaining to nonfinancial performance measures should be understood:

1. The theory of constraints stresses the importance of identifying and reducing a firm's constraints. A bottleneck operation, which is one that limits the productive capacity of the entire facility, is an example of an organizational constraint.
2. Customer-acceptance measures focus on the extent to which a firm's customers perceive its product to be of high quality. Some firms prepare quality cost reports, which detail the costs incurred in ensuring product quality.
3. Delivery cycle time is the average time between the receipt of a customer order and the deliver of goods. Manufacturing cycle time is the total amount of production time per unit. Manufacturing cycle efficiency is processing time divided by the sum of processing time, inspection time, waiting time, and move time.

4. While financial performance measures summarize the results of past actions, nonfinancial performance measures concentrate on current activities which will be the drivers of future financial performance.

P. (Appendix) The direct-labor rate variance can be further decomposed into a pure rate variance and a joint rate-efficiency variance. Using the symbols discussed above in this outline, we have the following relationships:

1. Pure rate variance = SH × (AR −SR)
2. Joint rate-efficiency variance = (AH − SH) × (AR − SR)

Note that these two variances add up to AH × (AR − SR), which is the direct-labor rate variance.

KEY TERMS

Aggregate (or total) productivity 471
Controllability 457
Cost variance 446
Critical value 458
Customer-acceptance measures 470
Delivery cycle time 471
Direct-labor efficiency variance 453
Direct-labor rate variance 453
Direct-material price variance (or purchase price variance) 451
Direct-material quantity variance 451
In-process quality controls 470
Management by exception 446
Manufacturing cycle efficiency (MCE) 471
Manufacturing cycle time 471
Partial (or component) productivity 471
Perfection (or ideal) standard 448
Practical (or attainable) standard 448
Standard cost 446
Standard-costing system 462
Standard direct-labor quantity 450
Standard labor rate 450
Standard material price 450
Standard material quantity 450
Statistical control chart 458
Task analysis 447
Velocity 471

KEY TERMS: APPENDIX

Joint rate-efficiency variance 478
Pure rate variance 478

SELF-EVALUATION QUESTIONS AND ANSWERS

True-False Questions

_____ **1.** People will generally be less committed to meeting standards if they are allowed to participate in the process of setting them.

_____ **2.** Perfection standards allow for such occurrences as occasional machine breakdowns.

_____ **3.** Managers use the budget as a benchmark against which to compare the results of actual operations.

_____ **4.** The standard quantity of direct materials allowed for a given budget period depends on the actual production output for that period.

_____ **5.** Standard costs are used by manufacturing firms, but not by nonprofit organizations.

_____ **6.** The direct-material price variance is unfavorable if actual purchase price exceeds the standard price.

_____ **7.** The direct-labor rate variance is unfavorable when the actual labor rate exceeds the standard rate.

_____ **8.** The direct-material quantity variance is unfavorable if the actual quantity of direct material used is less than the standard quantity allowed for the output achieved.

_____ **9.** Standard costs and variance analysis are useful in diagnosing organizational performance.

_____ **10.** The standard hours allowed for a given budget period depend on the actual hours used during that period.

_____ **11.** The production manager is generally in the best position to influence material price variances.

_____ **12.** The direct-labor efficiency variance is favorable when the actual hours used exceed the standard hours allowed for the output achieved.

_____ 13. The production manager is usually in the best position to influence material quantity variances.

_____ 14. Firms use standard costs for control, but never for product costing.

_____ 15. The journal entry to record the purchase of raw materials with an unfavorable material price variance in a standard-costing system would include a credit to the Direct-Material Price Variance account.

_____ 16. The production supervisor is usually most responsible for the efficient use of employee time.

_____ 17. The journal entry to record the usage of direct labor with a favorable labor efficiency variance in a standard-costing system would include a debit to the Direct-Labor Efficiency Variance account.

_____ 18. A consequence of unfavorable cost variances is that they decrease net income.

_____ 19. In the new manufacturing environment there is a reduced emphasis on labor standards and variances.

_____ 20. The emergence of the JIT philosophy has diminished the role of standard costs in product costing.

_____ 21. Traditional standard costing focuses too much on increasing product quality rather than cost minimization.

_____ 22. (Appendix) The pure rate variance and the joint rate-efficiency variance add up to the direct-labor rate variance.

Fill-in-the-Blank Questions

1. A(n) _______________ is a budget for the production of one unit of product or service.
2. The difference between actual cost and standard cost is called a(n) _______________.
3. A(n) _______________ standard is one that can be attained only under nearly perfect operating conditions.
4. The _______________ is the total amount of material normally required to produce a finished product, including allowances for normal waste or inefficiency.
5. The _______________ variance is the difference between the actual material quantity used times the standard price and the standard material quantity allowed for the output achieved times the standard price.
6. The _______________ is the number of labor hours normally needed to manufacture one unit of product.
7. The process of following up only on significant cost variances is called _______________.
8. The _______________ variance is the difference between actual material cost and the actual quantity purchased times the standard price.
9. The _______________ of material is the total delivered cost, after subtracting any purchase discounts.
10. _______________ standards are standards that are as tight as practical, but still are expected to be attainable.
11. The _______________ is the typical total hourly cost of compensation, including fringe benefits.
12. The _______________ variance is the difference between actual labor cost and the actual hours used times the standard rate.
13. A(n) _______________ plots cost variances over time and compares them with statistically determined critical values.
14. In a(n) _______________ costing system the standard costs of direct material and direct labor are entered into Work-in-Process Inventory.
15. The _______________ variance is the difference between the actual hours used times the standard rate and the standard hours allowed for the output achieved times the standard rate.
16. _______________ is a method of disposing cost variances that apportions them to Work-in-Process Inventory, Finished-Goods Inventory, and Cost of Goods Sold.
17. The _______________ stresses the importance of identifying and easing the constraints on a firm's operations.
18. Processing time divided by the sum of process time, inspection time, waiting time, and move time is called _______________.
19. _______________ is a productivity measure defined as total output divided by total input.

Multiple-Choice Questions

____ **1.** Consider the following statements about a control system:
I. It has a standard performance level.
II. It has a measure of actual performance
III. It compares standard and actual performance.
Which is (are) true?
(a) Only I and II
(b) Only I
(c) Only II
(d) I, II, and III

____ **2.** The direct-material standards for making one unit of output are 4 pounds at $7 per pound. During December, 3,000 units of output were made and 11,500 pounds of direct material were used. The December direct-material quantity variance is
(a) $500 favorable.
(b) $500 unfavorable.
(c) $3,500 favorable.
(d) $3,500 unfavorable.

____ **3.** The direct-labor standards for making one chair are 2.5 hours at $14 per hour. During April, 1,800 chairs were made and the actual hours used were 4,800. The April direct-labor efficiency variance is
(a) $4,200 favorable.
(b) $4,200 unfavorable.
(c) $4,500 favorable.
(d) $4,500 unfavorable.

____ **4.** Which of the following are methods used by managerial accountants for setting cost standards?
I. Analysis of historical data
II. Task analysis
(a) Only I
(b) Only II
(c) Both I and II
(d) Neither I nor II

____ **5.** The direct-material standards for making one bottle of Wif are 10 ounces at $3 per ounce. During February, 8,000 ounces of direct material were purchased for $26,000. The February direct-material price variance is
(a) $2,000 unfavorable.
(b) $2,000 favorable.
(c) $4,000 unfavorable.
(d) $4,000 favorable.

____ **6.** Which of the following is *not* a guideline factor in determining when a variance should be investigated?
(a) Size of variance
(b) Whether or not the variance occurs repeatedly
(c) The cost-flow assumption used in product costing
(d) A trend in the variance

____ **7.** The direct-labor standards for making one unit of finished product are 3 hours at $12 per hour. During May the company used 9,000 actual direct-labor hours at a cost of $101,070. The May direct-labor rate variance is
(a) $6,930 unfavorable.
(b) $6,930 favorable.
(c) $7,240 unfavorable.
(d) $7,240 favorable.

_____ 8. Which of the following is *not* an advantage of a standard-costing system?
   (a) It enables managers to employ management by exception.
   (b) It provides a means of performance evaluation.
   (c) It eliminates the need to maintain work-in-process inventories.
   (d) It is usually less expensive than actual costing.

Exercises

9.1 The Nelson Company makes Product 823 and uses standard costing. Standards for making one unit of this product include the following:

Three quarts of material *Q* at $2.30 per quart
One-half hour of direct labor at $9.50 per hour

Required:

Find each of the following:

(a) The standard cost of material *Q* for one unit of Product 823
(b) The standard cost of direct labor for one unit of Product 823
(c) The number of quarts of material *Q* that should be used if 2,500 units of Product 823 are made
(d) The number of direct-labor hours that should be used if 2,500 units of Product 823 are made
(e) The number of units of Product 823 that should have been produced if 7,440 quarts of material *Q* are used

Solution Space for Exercise 9.1:

(a) ____________________

(b) ____________________

(c) ____________________

(d) ____________________

(e) ____________________

9.2 The Schell Company makes nails in batches of 8,000. The standard cost for one batch includes the following:

Direct material: 300 pounds at $.25 per pound
Direct labor: 5 hours at $12.50 per hour

During June the following events occurred:

1. Two hundred and twenty batches were produced.
2. Direct material purchased and used was 62,000 pounds at an actual cost of $17,360.
3. Direct labor used was 1,350 hours at an actual cost of $16,335.

Required:

(a) Find each of the following variances using the formula approach:
   (1) Direct-material price variance
   (2) Direct-material quantity variance
   (3) Direct-labor rate variance
   (4) Direct-labor efficiency variance
   (*Note:* Indicate whether the variances are favorable or unfavorable.)
(b) Repeat part (a) using the diagram approach as in Exhibits 9-2 and 9-3 in the text.

Solution Space for Exercise 9.2:

(a) (1) ______________________

(2) ______________________

(3) ______________________

(4) ______________________

(b) Direct-material variances:

Actual costs	Actual qty. at std. price	Std. qty. at std. price
________	________	________

Direct-labor variances:

Actual costs	Actual hours at std. rate	Std. hours at std. rate
________	________	________

9.3 The Ramsey Company makes baseball bats in its Edaville Plant. The company uses standard costing, with standards for one baseball bat including the following:

Direct material: 3 board-feet at $.60 per board-foot
Direct labor: 0.6 hour at $11.50 per hour

During September the company had the following results at the Edaville Plant:

1. Direct material purchased and used in production amounted to 11,200 board-feet at a cost of $5,600.
2. Direct labor used in production was 1,950 hours at a cost of $23,595.
3. Three thousand bats were produced.

Required:

(a) Compute each of the following variances for September:
(1) Material price variance
(2) Material quantity variance
(3) Labor rate variance
(4) Labor efficiency variance
Indicate whether each variance is favorable or unfavorable.

(b) Prepare journal entries to record each of the following for September:
(1) The purchase of direct materials
(2) The use of direct materials in production
(3) The use of direct labor in production

(c) (Appendix) Compute the pure rate variance and the joint rate-efficiency variance for September.

Solution Space for Exercise 9.3:

(a) (1) ______________________

(2) ______________________

(3) ____

(4) ____

Compute these variances by the diagram method:

(b)

(1)

(2)

(3)

(c)

9.4 The Gates Company makes a certain type of crate and uses standard costing. The following data are available for November:

1. Material price variance: $1,200, favorable
2. Material quantity variance: $640, unfavorable
3. Seven thousand crates were finished.
4. Direct materials purchased: 60,000 lb.
5. Standard direct-material pounds per crate: 8 lb.
6. Standard direct-material cost per pound: $0.32
7. Actual direct-labor hours used: 1,600
8. Standard direct-labor hours per crate: 0.2
9. Standard direct-labor cost per crate: $2.40
10. Labor rate variance: $800, favorable
11. There were no inventories of any kind on Nov. 1, and there was no work-in-process inventory on Nov. 30.

Required:

Find each of the following for November:

(a) Actual cost of direct materials purchased
(b) Actual quantity of direct materials used
(c) Standard direct-labor cost per hour
(d) Labor efficiency variance
(e) Actual cost of direct labor

Solution Space for Exercise 9.4:

Answers to True-False Questions

1. F They will be more committed.
2. F Perfection standards are standards that can be achieved only under nearly perfect operating conditions. Practical standards allow for occasional machine breakdowns.
3. T
4. T
5. F They are also used by nonprofit organizations.
6. T
7. T
8. F This variance is unfavorable when actual quantity used exceeds the standard quantity allowed.
9. T
10. F The standard hours allowed depend on the actual output achieved.
11. F The purchasing manager is generally in the best position to influence this variance.
12. F It is favorable when actual hours used are less than standard hours allowed.
13. T
14. F They also use standard costs for product costing.
15. F It would include a debit to the Direct-Material Price Variance account.
16. T
17. F It would include a credit to the Direct-Labor Efficiency Variance account.
18. T
19. T
20. F The role of standard costs has not diminished under the JIT philosophy.
21. F Traditional standard costing does focus on cost minimization and not on increasing product quality.
22. T

Answers to Fill-in-the-Blank Questions

1. standard
2. cost variance
3. perfection (ideal)
4. standard quantity of materials
5. direct-material quantity
6. standard quantity of direct labor
7. management by exception
8. direct-material price
9. standard price
10. Practical
11. standard labor rate
12. direct-labor rate
13. statistical control chart
14. standard-
15. direct-labor efficiency
16. Variance proration
17. theory of constraints
18. manufacturing-cycle efficiency
19. Aggregate productivity

Answers to Multiple-Choice Questions

1. **(d)**
2. **(c)** (11,500 – 3,000 × 4) × \$7 = (\$3,500)
3. **(b)** (4,800 – 1,800 × 2.5) × \$14 = \$4,200
4. **(c)**
5. **(a)** \$26,000 – 8,000 × \$3 = \$2,000
6. **(c)** The cost-flow assumption used in product costing has no bearing on variance investigation.
7. **(b)** \$101,070 – 9,000 × \$12 = (\$6,930)
8. **(c)** Work-in-process inventories are still needed in standard-costing systems.

Solutions to Exercises

9.1 **(a)** 3 qt × \$2.30/qt = \$6.90
(b) 0.5 hr × \$9.50/hr. = \$4.75
(c) 2,500 × 3 qt. = 7,500 qt.
(d) 2,500 × 0.5 hr. = 1,250 hr.
(e) 7,440/3 = 2,480 units

9.2 Actual purchase price = \$17,360/62,000 = \$0.28
Actual labor rate = \$16,335/1,350 = \$12.10

(a) **(1)** Material price variance = PQ × (AP – SP) = 62,000 × (.28 – .25) = \$1,860 unfavorable
(2) Material quantity variance = SP × (AQ – SQ) = \$.25 × (62,000 – 220 × 300) = \$1,000 favorable
(3) Labor rate variance = AH × (AR – SR) = 1,350 × (12.10 – 12.50) = \$540 favorable
(4) Labor efficiency variance = SR × (AH – SH) = \$12.50 × (1,350 – 220 × 5) = \$3,125 unfavorable

(b) Direct-material variances:

Actual costs	Actual qty. at std. price	Std. qty. at std. price
\$17,360	62,000 × \$.25 = \$15,500	220 × 300 × \$.25 = \$16,500

\$1,860 unfavorable	\$1,000 favorable
Material price variance	Material quantity variance

Direct-labor variances:

Actual costs	Actual hours at std. rate	Std. hours at std. rate
\$16,335	1,350 × \$12.50 = \$16,875	220 × 5 × \$12.50 = \$13,750

\$540 favorable	\$3,125 unfavorable
Labor rate variance	Labor efficiency variance

9.3 Actual purchase price = \$5,600/11,200 = \$.50
Actual labor rate = \$23,595/1,950 = \$12.10

(a) (1) Material price variance = PQ × (AP – SP) = 11,200 × (.5 – .6) = \$1,120 favorable
(2) Material quantity variance = SP × (AQ – SQ) = .6 × (11,200 – 3,000 × 3) = \$1,320 unfavorable
(3) Labor rate variance = AH × (AR – SR) = 1,950 × (12.10 – 11.50) = \$1,170 unfavorable
(4) Labor efficiency variance = SR × (AH – SH) = 11.50 × (1,950 – 3,000 × 0.6) = \$1,725 unfavorable

Computation of variances by the diagram method:

Direct-material variances:

Actual costs	Actual qty. at std. price	Std. qty. at std. price
\$5,600	11,200 × \$.60 = \$6,720	3,000 × 3 × \$.60 = \$5,400

\$1,120 favorable	\$1,320 unfavorable
Material price variance	Material quantity variance

Direct-labor variances:

Actual costs	Actual hours at std. rate	Std. hours at std. rate
\$23,595	1,950 × \$11.50 = \$22,425	3,000 × .6 × \$11.50 = \$20,700

\$1,170 unfavorable	\$1,725 unfavorable
Labor rate variance	Labor efficiency variance

Note that the diagram approach to computing variances makes it convenient for preparing journal entries, because the journal-entry amounts have already been computed in the diagram.

(b)

		Debit	Credit
1.	Raw-Materials Inventory	6,720	
	Direct-Materials Price Variance		1,120
	Accounts Payable		5,600
2.	Work-in-Process Inventory	5,400	
	Material Quantity Variance	1,320	
	Raw-Materials Inventory		6,720
3.	Work-in-Process Inventory	20,700	
	Labor Rate Variance	1,170	
	Labor Efficiency Variance	1,725	
	Wages Payable		23,595

(c) (Appendix)
Pure rate variance = SH × (AR – SR) =
3,000 × .6 × (\$12.10 – \$11.50) = \$1,080 unfavorable
Joint rate-efficiency variance = (AH – SH) × (AR – SR) =
(1,950 – 3,000 × .6) × (\$12.10 – \$11.50) = \$90 unfavorable
Note that \$1,080 unfavorable + \$90 unfavorable =
\$1,170 unfavorable = labor rate variance

9.4 The required items can be computed in the following sequence:

(b) Standard quantity of direct material at standard price = 7,000 × 8 × 0.32 = \$17,920
Actual quantity of direct material used at standard price = 17,920 + 640 = \$18,560
Actual quantity of direct material used = 18,560/0.32 = 58,000 lb.

(a) Actual quantity of direct material at standard price = 60,000 × 0.32 = \$19,200
Actual cost of direct material = 19,200 − 1,200 = 18,000

(c) Standard direct labor cost/hr. = \$2.40/0.2 = \$12/hr.

(d) Labor efficiency variance = 1,600 × 12 − 7,000 × 2.40 = \$2,400, unfavorable

(e) Actual cost of direct labor = 1,600 × 12 − 800 = \$18,400

Chapter 10

Flexible Budgets and Control of Overhead Costs

CHAPTER OVERVIEW AND LEARNING OBJECTIVES

This chapter continues the study of standard costing. In Chapter 9 standard-costing ideas were applied to direct material and direct labor; in this chapter the focus is on standard costing for overhead. After completing this chapter, you should understand:

1. The difference between a static budget and a flexible budget
2. The advantages of a flexible overhead budget
3. How to prepare a flexible budget in two formats
4. How overhead is applied to work in process under standard costing
5. Some important issues in selecting an activity measure for overhead budgeting and the application of overhead
6. How to measure and interpret the variable-overhead spending and efficiency variances and the fixed-overhead budget and volume variances
7. How to prepare an overhead cost performance report
8. How to prepare journal entries to record and close out overhead cost variances
9. How an activity-based flexible budget differs from a conventional flexible budget
10. How to prepare a quality cost report
11. How to compute and interpret sales-price and sales-volume variances (if you study the appendix)

AN OUTLINE FOR CHAPTER STUDY

A. A flexible budget is a detailed plan for controlling budgeted items and is based on various levels of activity within the firm's relevant range of activity. It differs from a static budget in that a static budget (like those studied in Chapter 8) is based on only one level of activity. A flexible overhead budget is a flexible budget for controlling overhead costs. The following points about flexible budgets should be noted.

   1. The flexible budget provides the proper basis for comparing actual and budgeted costs, given the actual activity level.
   2. The flexible overhead budget should be based on input activity levels rather than output levels. In a firm having several outputs, there is no common denominator for measuring budget items using output, whereas there is one when using an input measure. Moreover, managers can control outputs only by first controlling inputs.

3. Flexible overhead budgets are divided into fixed and variable costs. In fact, it is the variable cost that puts the "flex" into the flexible overhead budget.
4. Flexible budgets are used by nonmanufacturing organizations as well as manufacturing firms.

B. There are two ways to prepare flexible budgets. The columnar flexible budget consists of a schedule of budget items listed in a column for a few specific levels of activity. The formula flexible budget is given in terms of a formula which expresses the relationship between activity and the budget items. For example, the total budgeted overhead cost can be expressed by the formula

$$\text{Total budgeted period overhead cost} = \text{Budgeted variable cost per activity unit} \times \text{Level of activity in units} + \text{Budgeted period fixed overhead cost}$$

The budgeted variable cost per activity unit is also called the budgeted variable-overhead rate; it can be found by dividing total budgeted variable cost for a specific activity level by that level of activity. Note that the formula flexible budget is more general than the columnar flexible budget because it can give budgeted amounts at any level of activity.

C. Overhead application refers to the addition of overhead cost to work in process. In a standard-costing system, overhead application is based on standard hours allowed, given actual output. In normal costing, overhead application is based on actual hours used. In standard costing the predetermined overhead rate is also called the standard overhead rate. This standard overhead rate is usually the combination of a variable-overhead rate and a fixed-overhead rate.

D. Choosing the appropriate activity measure for the flexible overhead budget is crucial, because the flexible budget is the main tool for controlling overhead costs. This activity measure should be such that variable-overhead cost changes roughly in proportion to changes in the activity measure. The new manufacturing environment has had a profound impact on the choice of activity measures; firms are switching to measures such as machine hours or process time instead of direct-labor hours. These activity measures are also called cost drivers. It should be observed that dollar measures should be avoided as activity measures; they are subject to price-level changes and tend to fluctuate more than physical measures.

E. At the end of each accounting period, the flexible overhead budget is used to determine the level of budgeted overhead cost that should have been incurred, given the actual level of output achieved. This budgeted overhead cost is compared with the actual overhead cost incurred to determine the combined budget overhead variance for the period. This variance is the actual overhead cost less the budgeted cost for overhead and is divided into three components which are useful for controlling overhead costs. These component variances are presented in the next three sections of this outline. In discussing these three component variances, it will be assumed that machine hours is the cost driver or activity measure.

F. The variable-overhead spending variance is actual variable overhead cost less the product of actual machine hours and the standard variable-overhead rate. (Machine hours is the assumed cost driver.) In symbols, this variance is:

$$AH \times AVR - AH \times SVR = AH \times (AVR - SVR)$$

where
AH = actual machine hours
AVR = actual variable-overhead rate
SVR = standard variable-overhead rate

AVR is computed by dividing total actual variable-overhead cost for the period by the actual machine hours used during the period. An unfavorable spending variance means that the actual cost of variable overhead is greater than expected, after adjusting for the actual level of machine hours used. This variance is the real control variance for variable overhead.

G. The variable-overhead efficiency variance is defined as the difference between actual machine hours times the standard variable-overhead rate and the standard machine hours allowed for the actual output achieved times the standard variable-overhead rate. In symbols, this variance is:

$$AH \times SVR - SH \times SVR = SVR \times (AH - SH)$$

where AH = actual machine hours
SH = standard machine hours for the output achieved
SVR = standard variable-overhead rate

This variance will be unfavorable if the actual machine hours used exceed what is allowed for the output achieved during the period. This variance is a dollar measure of the fact that actual machine hours differ from what should have been used; it does not directly measure inefficiencies in the use of overhead items such as electricity and indirect materials.

H. The fixed-overhead budget variance is the difference between actual fixed overhead and budgeted fixed overhead. This variance is the real control variance for fixed overhead; it is unfavorable if the actual fixed overhead exceeds the budgeted fixed overhead. Note that no activity level need be specified to determine budgeted fixed overhead.

I. The fixed-overhead volume variance is defined as the difference between budgeted fixed overhead and applied fixed overhead. The standard fixed-overhead rate (SFR) is defined as budgeted fixed overhead divided by budgeted machine hours (BH). Budgeted machine hours is a static amount determined at the beginning of the planning period. In symbols, the fixed-overhead volume variance is:

$$SFR \times BH - SFR \times SH = SFR \times (BH - SH)$$

where SFR = standard fixed overhead rate
BH = budgeted machine hours (determined at the beginning of the period)
SH = standard machine hours (determined at the end of the period and based on the actual output achieved)

This volume variance provides a means of reconciling the two purposes of a cost-accounting system—control and product costing. This variance, by itself, does not serve any control purpose, nor does it provide a real measure of the utilization of productive capacity.

J. Instead of breaking down the total manufacturing overhead variance into four component variances as indicated in the previous four sections, managerial accountants sometimes add the variable-overhead spending variance to the fixed-overhead budget variance to get a combined spending variance; this gives a three-component decomposition of the total manufacturing-overhead variance—a combined spending variance, a variable-overhead efficiency variance, and a fixed-overhead volume variance. Instead of this, the combined spending variance can be added to the variable-overhead efficiency variance to obtain a combined budget variance; this results in a two-component decomposition of the total manufacturing-overhead variance—the combined budget variance and the fixed-overhead volume variance. Finally, note that the difference between the total actual manufacturing overhead and the total applied manufacturing overhead is the under- (or over-) applied overhead. If the combined budget variance is presented along with the actual and budgeted costs for each overhead item, the resulting document is called an overhead cost performance report.

K. In a standard-costing system the entries to handle the manufacturing overhead include:

1.	Manufacturing Overhead	$$$	
	Various Accounts		$$$
	To record the incurrence of manufacturing overhead at actual costs.		
2.	Work-in-Process Inventory	$$$	
	Manufacturing Overhead		$$$
	To record the application of overhead to production at standard cost.		
3.	Cost of Goods Sold	$$$	
	Manufacturing Overhead		$$$
	To record the disposition of underapplied overhead at the end of the period. (If this were overapplied overhead, Cost of Goods Sold would be credited.)		

An alternative method, instead of journal entry 3, for disposing of under- or overapplied overhead is to prorate this under- or overapplied overhead to Work-in-Process Inventory, Finished-Goods Inventory, and Cost of Goods Sold.

L. The activity-based costing (ABC) approach can also be used as the basis of a flexible budget for planning and control purposes. The key difference between this type of flexible budget and the traditional flexible budget is that costs classified as fixed in the traditional flexible budget may be variable in the ABC flexible budget because of the use of several cost drivers for the budget. For example, while the traditional budget treats inspection, setup, engineering, and material-handling costs as fixed, the ABC budget assumes they are variable with respect to the appropriate cost driver.

M. Product quality is now a key factor in determining a firm's success in the global marketplace. A product's quality of design refers to how well it was designed for its intended use. Quality of conformance refers to the extent to which a product meets the specifications of its design. There are basically four types of quality costs:

1. Prevention costs: the cost of preventing defects
2. Appraisal costs: the costs of ascertaining whether defects exist
3. Internal failure costs: the costs of repairing defects found before a product is sold
4. External failure costs: the costs incurred after defective products have been sold

Exhibit 10-13 in the text provides some good examples of these types of costs.

N. (Appendix) The sales-price variance is defined as actual sales volumes times the difference between the actual sales price and the expected sales price. The sales-volume variance is defined as the budgeted unit contribution margin times the difference between actual sales volume and budgeted sales volume. It should be observed that these are revenue variances, not cost variances. This means that if the difference between an actual amount and a budgeted amount is negative, the revenue variance is unfavorable; if the difference is positive, the revenue variance is favorable.

KEY TERMS

Activity-based flexible budget 520
Appraisal costs 522
External failure costs 522
Fixed-overhead budget variance 513
Fixed-overhead volume variance 514
Flexible budget 502
Internal failure costs 522
Overhead cost performance report 517
Prevention costs 522
Quality of conformance 522
Quality of design 522
Static budget 502
Variable-overhead efficiency variance 510
Variable-overhead spending variance 510

KEY TERMS: APPENDIX

Sales-price variance 528
Sales-volume variance 528
Total contribution margin 527
Unit contribution margin 527

SELF-EVALUATION QUESTIONS AND ANSWERS

True-False Questions

_____ **1.** A flexible budget is based on only one level of activity.

_____ **2.** Units of output is usually not a meaningful measure in a multiproduct firm.

_____ **3.** The overhead costs in a flexible overhead budget are divided into fixed and variable costs.

_____ **4.** The static budget provides the correct basis for comparison between actual and expected costs, given the actual level of activity.

_____ **5.** Total budgeted variable-overhead cost does not change with increasing levels of activity.

_____ **6.** A flexible overhead budget should be based on input activity measures instead of output measures.

_____ **7.** Manufacturing overhead costs are not traceable to individual products.

_____ **8.** If total budgeted fixed overhead is $150,000 at 7,500 machine hours, then the budgeted variable-overhead rate is $20 per machine hour.

_____ 9. Flexible budgeted overhead cost can be used at the end of an accounting period as a benchmark against which actual overhead costs for the period can be compared.

_____ 10. Total budgeted fixed overhead changes with increasing levels of activity.

_____ 11. Both normal- and standard-costing systems use a predetermined overhead rate.

_____ 12. The flexible overhead budget is the chief tool for controlling overhead costs.

_____ 13. As automation increases, more and more firms are switching to labor hours as an activity measure for flexible overhead budgets.

_____ 14. Dollar measures are better than physical measures as cost drivers for flexible overhead budgets.

_____ 15. If actual machine hours exceed standard machine hours allowed for output achieved, then the variable overhead efficiency variance based on machine hours is unfavorable.

_____ 16. Suppose that the activity measure is machine hours. Then the variable-overhead efficiency variance gives a dollar measure of the inefficiencies associated with overhead items such as electricity and indirect materials.

_____ 17. The volume variance is the real control variance for fixed overhead.

_____ 18. The fixed-overhead volume variance does not depend on any actual operating inputs.

_____ 19. If the budgeted activity level at the beginning of the accounting period equals the standard activity level for the output achieved in the period, then the fixed-overhead volume variance is zero.

_____ 20. Nonmanufacturing organizations do not use flexible budgets to control overhead.

_____ 21. An activity-based flexible budget treats inspection and setup costs as fixed costs.

_____ 22. (Appendix) If the actual sales price exceeds the expected sales price, then the sales-price variance is favorable.

Fill-in-the-Blank Questions

1. A(n) _______________ budget is a detailed plan for controlling overhead costs that is valid in the firm's relevant range of activity.
2. A(n) _______________ budget is based on a particular single planned level of activity.
3. In a(n) _______________, each budgeted overhead cost item is listed in a column under a particular activity level.
4. Dividing total budgeted variable overhead cost by the associated activity level yields a(n) _______________ rate.
5. The activity measure chosen as a basis for the flexible overhead budget should be such that variable overhead cost and the activity measure move _______________ as overall productive activity changes.
6. The difference between total actual overhead cost and total applied overhead cost is called _______________.
7. Assume that machine hours is used as the activity measure. The variable-overhead spending variance is unfavorable when actual variable overhead cost _______________ the expected amount, after adjusting that expectation for the actual number of machine hours used.
8. The _______________ variance is the real control variance for variable overhead.
9. We do not need to specify an activity level to determine budgeted _______________ overhead.
10. Actual fixed overhead less budgeted fixed overhead equals the _______________ variance.
11. The _______________ variance is defined as budgeted fixed overhead minus applied fixed overhead.
12. The _______________ variance provides a means of reconciling two difference purposes of a cost-accounting system—a control purpose and a product-costing purpose.
13. The _______________ variance equals the sum of the variable-overhead spending variance and the fixed-overhead budget variance.
14. When the itemized variances of the combined budget variance are presented along with actual and budgeted costs for each item, the result is a(n) _______________ report.
15. The _______________ refers to the extent to which a product meets the specifications of its design.

Multiple-Choice Questions

_____ **1.** If the budgeted fixed overhead per month is $18,000 and the budgeted variable-overhead rate is $15.20 per machine hour, then the total budgeted monthly overhead cost corresponding to 1,300 machine hours is

(a) $37,760.
(b) $37,500.
(c) $19,760.
(d) $18,000.

_____ **2.** Suppose that the standard variable-overhead rate is $12 per machine hour, actual machine hours used in February were 1,800, and the February actual variable-overhead cost was $23,900. The February variable-overhead spending variance is

(a) $2,300 favorable.
(b) $2,300 unfavorable.
(c) $3,600 favorable.
(d) $3,600 unfavorable.

_____ **3.** The standard variable-overhead rate is $25 per hour of process time. During May, 840 units of output were produced and 670 hours of process time were actually used. If the standard process time to make one unit is 0.75 hour, the May variable-overhead efficiency variance is

(a) $4,250 favorable.
(b) $4,250 unfavorable.
(c) $1,000 favorable.
(d) $1,000 unfavorable.

_____ **4.** If actual fixed overhead for June equals $154,000 and the May budgeted fixed-overhead is $163,000, then the fixed-overhead budget variance is

(a) $19,000 favorable.
(b) $19,000 unfavorable.
(c) $9,000 favorable.
(d) $9,000 unfavorable.

_____ **5.** The Olmstead Company uses process time as the activity measure for its flexible overhead budget. For July the company budgeted fixed overhead at $45,000 and budgeted 20,000 hours of process time. During July, 43,000 units of finished product were made. The standard process time for one unit of product is 0.5 hour. The fixed-overhead volume variance for July is

(a) $3,375 unfavorable.
(b) $3,375 favorable.
(c) $2,000 unfavorable.
(d) $2,000 favorable.

_____ **6.** The journal entry to record overhead costs applied to production includes a

(a) debit to Manufacturing Overhead.
(b) credit to Work-in-Process Inventory.
(c) credit to Manufacturing Overhead.
(d) credit to Accounts Payable.

_____ **7.** Consider the following two statements:

I. Appraisal costs are quality costs.
II. Advertising costs are quality costs.

Which is (are) true?

(a) Only I
(b) Only II
(c) Both I and II
(d) Neither I nor II

_____ **8.** (Appendix) If the budgeted unit contribution margin is $8, the expected sales price is $23, the budgeted sales-volume is 4,000 units, and the actual sales volume is 4,500 units, then the sales-volume variance is

(a) $4,000 unfavorable.
(b) $4,000 favorable.
(c) $11,500 unfavorable.
(d) $11,500 favorable.

Exercises

10.1 The Valley View Health Care Center uses a flexible budget to plan and control costs. The accountant at Valley View has assembled the following budget data for one month:

Patient days	6,000
Variable costs	
Utilities	$ 4,200
Maintenance	2,400
Medical supplies	7,200
Laundry	1,200
Housekeeping	3,000
Fixed costs	
Health care salaries	24,000
Administrative salaries	10,000
Depreciation	7,000

Required:

(a) Prepare a columnar flexible budget indicating each of the given cost categories for 7,000, 7,500, and 8,000 patient days. Be sure to label your flexible budget properly.

(b) Find a flexible budget formula for Valley View.

Solution Space for Exercise 10.1:

(a)

VALLEY VIEW HEALTH CARE CENTER
Flexible Budget for One Month

(b) ____

____

____

____

10.2 The Pitman Company uses standard costing for the product it makes in its Hadley Plant. The standards for one unit of this product include:

Variable overhead, 1.5 machine hours at $4 per machine hour
Fixed overhead, 1.5 machine hours at $12 per machine hour

During January, 27,000 machine hours were budgeted. The following actual results occurred in January:

1. Sixteen thousand units of product were made.
2. Variable overhead incurred was $102,000.
3. Fixed overhead incurred was $295,000.
4. Actual machine hours used were 26,000.

Required:

(a) For January, find each of the following using the formula approach:
(1) Variable-overhead spending variance
(2) Variable-overhead efficiency variance
(3) Fixed-overhead budget variance
(4) Fixed-overhead volume variance
Indicate whether each variance is favorable or unfavorable.

(b) Repeat part (a) using the diagram approach similar to Exhibits 10-6 and 10-8 in the text.

Solution Space for Exercise 10.2:

(a) **(1)** ____

(2) ____

(3) ____

(4) ____

(b)	Actual cost	Flex. budget at actual hours	Flex. budget at std. hours	Applied costs
Variable	________	________	________	________
Fixed	________	________	________	________

10.3 The Wagner Company makes wibbits in its Bushland Division and uses standard costing. Flexible overhead budget data for one month are as follows:

Budgeted fixed overhead	$80,000
Budgeted process time	3,200 hours
Process time per wibbit	0.8 hours
Standard variable-overhead rate	$4.20 per hour of process time

The actual operating results for March were as follows:

Actual variable overhead	$17,500
Actual wibbits produced	4,200
Actual fixed overhead	$76,800
Actual process time used	3,900 hours

Required:

(a) Find each of the following variances for March using the diagram approach similar to Exhibits 10-6 and 10-8 in the text:
(1) Variable-overhead spending variance
(2) Variable-overhead efficiency variance
(3) Fixed-overhead budget variance
(4) Fixed-overhead volume variance
(5) Combined spending variance
(6) Combined budget variance
(7) Under- or overapplied overhead
Indicate whether each variance is favorable or unfavorable.

(b) Prepare journal entries to record the following events for March:
(1) The incurrence of actual overhead costs
(2) The application of overhead to production
(3) The disposition of under- or overapplied overhead to Cost of Goods Sold

Solution Space for Exercise 10.3:

(a)

(b)

(1)

(2)

(3)

10.4 Classify each of the following costs as:

P: Prevention costs
I: Internal failure costs
A: Appraisal costs
E: External failure costs

(a) Reliability engineering
(b) Product liability
(c) Supplies inspection
(d) Rework
(e) Customer complaints
(f) Scrap
(g) Quality training
(h) Reliability testing
(i) Warranty costs
(j) Out-of-warranty repairs

Solution Space for Exercise 10.4:

(a) ______________

(b) ______________

(c) ______________

(d) ______________

(e) ______________

(f) ______________

(g) ______________

(h) ______________

(i) ______________

(j) ______________

Answers to True-False Questions

1. F It is based on any given level of activity.
2. T
3. T
4. F The static budget does not provide the correct basis. It is the flexible budget that provides the correct basis.
5. F It does change with increasing levels of activity.
6. T
7. T
8. F The $20 is the budgeted fixed-overhead rate.
9. T
10. F It remains fixed as the level of activity increases.
11. T
12. T
13. F They are moving away from labor hours to other measures of activity as automation increases.
14. F Dollar measures are to be avoided as cost drivers if possible, since they tend to fluctuate more than physical measures.
15. T
16. F This overhead efficiency variance based on machine hours does not reflect the direct inefficiencies associated with items such as electricity and indirect materials.
17. F The volume variance is not a measure of control. The real control variance for fixed overhead is the fixed-overhead budget variance.
18. T
19. T
20. F They do use flexible budgets to control overhead.
21. F It treats them as variable costs.
22. T

Answers to Fill-in-the-Blank Questions

1. flexible overhead
2. static
3. columnar flexible budget
4. budgeted variable-overhead
5. together
6. under- or overapplied overhead
7. exceeds
8. variable-overhead spending
9. fixed
10. fixed-overhead budget
11. volume
12. volume
13. combined spending
14. overhead cost performance
15. quality of conformance

Answers to Multiple-Choice Questions

1. (a) $18,000 + $15.2 × 1,300 = $37,760.
2. (b) $23,900 − $12 × 1,800 = $2,300.
3. (d) $25 × (670 − 840 × .75) = $1,000.
4. (c) $154,000 − $163,000 = ($9,000).
5. (b) ($45,000/20,000) × (20,000 − .5 × 43,000) = ($3,375).
6. (c)
7. (a) Advertising costs are marketing costs, not quality costs.
8. (b) $8 × (4,500 − 4,000) = $4,000. This is a favorable revenue variance.

Solutions to Exercises

10.1 (a)

VALLEY VIEW HEALTH CARE CENTER
Flexible Budget For One Month

	Cost per Patient Day	Patient Days 7,000	7,500	8,000
Variable costs				
Utilities	$ .70	$ 4,900	$ 5,250	$ 5,600
Maintenance	.40	2,800	3,000	3,200
Medical supplies	1.20	8,400	9,000	9,600
Laundry	.20	1,400	1,500	1,600
Housekeeping	.50	3,500	3,750	4,000
Fixed costs				
Health care salaries	—	24,000	24,000	24,000
Administrative services	—	10,000	10,000	10,000
Depreciation	—	7,000	7,000	7,000
Total		$62,000	$63,500	$65,000

(b) Total cost = $41,000 + $3 × (Number of patient days)

10.2 **(a)** **(1)** Variable spending variance = $102,000 – (26,000 × $4) = $2,000 favorable
(2) Variable efficiency variance = $4 × (26,000 – 16,000 × 1.5) = $8,000 unfavorable
(3) Fixed budget variance = $295,000 – (27,000 × $12) = $29,000 favorable
(4) Fixed volume variance = $12 × (27,000 – 16,000 × 1.5) = $36,000 unfavorable

(b) Budgeted fixed overhead = 27,000 × $12 = $324,000

	Actual cost	Flex. budget at actual hours	Flex. budget at std. hours	Applied costs
Variable	$102,000	26,000 × $4 = $104,000	16,000 × 1.5 × $4 = $96,000	$96,000
	$2,000 favorable Var. spending variance		$8,000 unfavorable Var. efficiency variance	
Fixed	$295,000	$324,000	$324,000	16,000 × 1.5 × $12 = $288,000
	$29,000 favorable Fixed budget variance			$36,000 unfavorable Fixed volume variance

10.3 **(a)** Standard fixed-overhead rate = $80,000/3,200 = $25/hr

	Actual cost	Flex. budget at actual hours	Flex. budget at std. hours	Applied costs
Variable	$17,500	3,900 × $4.20 = $16,380	4,200 × .8 × $4.20 = $14,112	$14,112
	$1,120 unfavorable **(1)** Var. spending variance		$2,268 unfavorable **(2)** Var. efficiency variance	
Fixed	$76,800	$80,000	$80,000	4,200 × .8 × 25 = $84,000
	$3,200 favorable **(3)** Fixed budget variance			$4,000 favorable **(4)** Fixed volume variance
Totals	$94,300	$96,380	$94,112	$98,112

(5) Combined spending variance = $1,120 unfavorable + $3,200 favorable = $2,080 favorable
(6) Combined budget variance = $2,080 favorable + $2,268 unfavorable = $188 unfavorable
(7) Overapplied overhead = $188 unfavorable + $4,000 favorable = $3,812 favorable

Check: Overapplied overhead = $94,300 – $98,112 = $3,812 favorable

(b)

	Account	Debit	Credit
(1)	Manufacturing Overhead	94,300	
	Various Accounts		94,300
(2)	Work-in-Process Inventory	98,112	
	Manufacturing Overhead		98,112
(3)	Manufacturing Overhead	3,812	
	Cost of Goods Sold		3,812

10.4 **(a)** P
(b) E
(c) A
(d) I
(e) E
(f) I
(g) P
(h) A
(i) E
(j) E

Chapter **11**

Responsibility Accounting and Income Reporting

CHAPTER OVERVIEW AND LEARNING OBJECTIVES

This chapter covers the topics that relate to reporting income and evaluating performance in segments of an organization. After completing this chapter, you should understand:

1. Several benefits and costs of decentralization
2. The role of responsibility accounting in fostering goal congruence
3. The meaning of a cost center, a revenue center, a profit center, and an investment center
4. How to prepare a performance report and the relationships among the performance reports for various responsibility centers
5. How to use a cost allocation base to allocate costs
6. How to prepare a segmented income statement
7. How to prepare an income statement under either absorption or variable costing
8. The reconciliation of income under absorption and variable costing

AN OUTLINE FOR CHAPTER STUDY

A. When large organizations are divided into segments (divisions, subunits, or departments), goal congruence results when the managers of these segments strive to achieve the goals set by top management. Responsibility accounting is the set of accounting concepts and tools used by managerial accountants to measure the performance of managers responsible for segments in order to foster goal congruence.

B. A responsibility center is a segment of an organization in which the manager of that segment is held accountable for the financial results of the segment's activities. The types of responsibility centers are as follows:

   1. A cost center is a segment in which the manager is held accountable for the costs incurred in that segment.
   2. A revenue center is a segment in which the manager is held accountable for the revenues earned by that segment.
   3. A profit center is a segment in which the manager is held accountable for the profit of that segment.
   4. An investment center is a segment in which the manager is held accountable for the segment's profit in relation to the capital invested in that segment. Divisions of large corporations are usually investment centers.

C. A performance report shows the budgeted and actual amounts and the corresponding variances of key financial results appropriate to the type of responsibility center involved. The data in this report help managers use management by exception for control purposes. Some organizations use performance reports that distinguish between controllable and uncontrollable costs and revenues.

D. A collection of costs to be assigned is called a cost pool. The products, services, or responsibility centers to which costs are to be assigned are called cost objects. The process of assigning costs in the cost pool to the cost objects is called cost allocation.

E. A cost allocation base is a measure of activity or some characteristic associated with the responsibility centers; these centers are the cost objects in the allocation process. This cost allocation base is also called a cost driver. Allocation procedures should be such that the behavior of one responsibility center does not affect the costs allocated to the other responsibility centers; very often this is best accomplished by using budget data instead of actual data.

F. The following points concerning a responsibility accounting system should be noted.

1. In activity-based responsibility accounting, management's attention is directed not only to the cost incurred in an activity, but also to the activity itself.
2. The focus of the system is on information and should not emphasize blame; when this is the case, managers react constructively and strive for improved performance.
3. The system is often used to motivate the actions considered desirable by upper-level management.
4. A function of the system is to assign all the organization's costs to the segments that caused those costs to be incurred.

G. Segment reporting refers to the preparation of accounting reports by segment and for the organization as a whole. Segmented income statements show the income for major segments and the whole organization. Common costs, which are costs incurred to benefit more than one segment, are often left unallocated on segmented income statements, because any basis for allocating common costs is arbitrary. It should be noted that some costs that are traceable to a segment may be beyond the influence of the segment manager. Some key features of segmented income statements are as follows:

1. They are in contribution format.
2. They highlight costs that can be controlled by the segment manager.
3. They report income for each major segment and the organization as a whole.

H. In absorption costing (or full costing), all manufacturing-overhead costs are applied to production, both fixed and variable. That is, product costs (or inventoried costs) under absorption costing include fixed manufacturing costs. Under variable costing (or direct costing), fixed manufacturing overhead is not inventoried, but rather is treated as a period cost; that is, it is expensed in the period in which it is incurred. Absorption costing is inconsistent with CVP analysis, while variable costing dovetails exactly with CVP analysis.

I. Absorption-costing income statements present expenses according to management function. Cost of goods sold includes all costs of production; selling and administrative expenses are shown below gross margin. On the other hand, variable-costing income statements use the contribution format, which separates all fixed and variable costs. In this case, fixed manufacturing overhead is shown as a period expense along with other fixed expenses. The reconciliation of the income shown under each of these two statements for a single-product firm can be accounted for by the formula:

$$\text{Difference in reported net income} = \text{Change in inventory level in units} \times \text{Predetermined fixed-overhead rate per unit}$$

If beginning period inventory exceeds ending inventory, then absorption-costing net income is less than variable-costing net income. If beginning inventory is less than ending inventory, net income under absorption costing is greater than under variable costing. If beginning inventory equals ending inventory, net income under the two costing methods is the same. It should be noted that in a JIT environment, income differences under absorption and variable costing will generally be insignificant.

J. Many managers prefer to use absorption-cost data in cost-based pricing decisions on the ground that variable costing data understate the cost of a product. There are those who argue in favor of absorption costing because products are inventoried (valued as assets) at their full cost of production; on the other hand, others argue in favor of variable costing on the ground that the fixed-cost component of a product's cost under absorption costing has no future service potential; that is, attaching fixed overhead to a product in one period does not prevent that fixed cost from occurring in the next period. By contrast, a variable cost that is incurred in a period and attached to a product will not be incurred again, simply because it is a variable cost. It should be observed that generally accepted accounting principles require that income reporting be based on absorption costing. Likewise, federal tax laws require the use of absorption costing in computing net income for tax purposes.

K. (Appendix) In standard absorption costing, the fixed-overhead volume variance is treated as an adjustment to the gross margin. If this variance is favorable, it is added to gross margin; if this variance is unfavorable, it is subtracted from gross margin.

KEY TERMS

Absorption (or full) costing 567
Activity-based responsibility accounting 562
Allocation base 560
Common costs 564
Cost allocation (or distribution) 560
Cost center 554
Cost objects 560
Cost pool 560
Goal congruence 554
Investment center 554
Performance report 556
Profit center 554
Responsibility accounting 554
Responsibility center 554
Revenue center 554
Segmented income statement 564
Variable (or direct) costing 567

SELF-EVALUATION QUESTIONS AND ANSWERS

True-False Questions

____ **1.** Most large organizations are centralized.

____ **2.** The data in a performance report do not provide any help for the use of management by exception to control an organization's operations effectively.

____ **3.** The topics of budgeting, variance analysis, and responsibility accounting are closely interrelated.

____ **4.** A division of a large corporation is typically designated as a profit center.

____ **5.** Goal congruence results when the managers of segments throughout an organization strive to achieve the goals set by top management.

____ **6.** A responsibility center is a subunit in an organization, the manager of which is held accountable for specified financial results of the subunit's activities.

____ **7.** The proper focus of a responsibility-accounting system is information.

____ **8.** All costs which are controllable over a long time frame are also controllable within a short time period.

____ **9.** Some organizations use performance reports that distinguish between controllable and uncontrollable costs or revenues.

____ **10.** A cost driver is not the same thing as a cost allocation base.

____ **11.** One function of a responsibility-accounting system is to assign all of an organization's costs to the segments that cause those costs to be incurred.

____ **12.** Managerial accountants often use the responsibility-accounting system to motivate actions considered desirable by upper-level management.

____ **13.** An important use of a responsibility-accounting system is to emphasize the blame for wrong actions on the part of segment managers.

_____ 14. The managerial accountant should design an allocation procedure so that the behavior of one responsibility center does not affect the costs allocated to other responsibility centers.

_____ 15. If sales revenue is to be used as an allocation base, it is better to use actual sales revenue than budgeted sales revenue.

_____ 16. Common costs can be allocated to segments only on some arbitrarily chosen cost allocation base.

_____ 17. Costs that are traceable to segments at one level in an organization will never be common costs at a lower level in the organization.

_____ 18. Absorption costing is consistent with CVP analysis.

_____ 19. In a JIT environment, the income differences under absorption and variable costing will be insignificant.

_____ 20. (Appendix) In standard absorption costing, a fixed volume variance that is favorable is subtracted from gross margin in the income statement.

Fill-in-the-Blank Questions

1. _______________ accounting consists of the various concepts and tools used by managerial accountants to measure the performance of people and departments so as to foster goal congruence.
2. A(n) _______________ center is a segment of an organization in which the manager is held responsible for the revenue attributed to the segment.
3. A(n) _______________ center is a segment of an organization in which the manager is held accountable for the profit of the segment.
4. A(n) _______________ shows the budgeted and actual amounts of key financial results appropriate to the type of responsibility center involved.
5. A collection of costs to be assigned is called a(n) _______________.
6. A(n) _______________ is a measure of activity or some physical or economic characteristic associated with the responsibility centers, which are the cost objectives of allocation.
7. _______________ refers to the preparation of accounting reports by segment and for the organization as a whole.
8. A(n) _______________ center is a segment of an organization in which the manager is held accountable for the profit of the segment in relation to the capital invested in that segment.
9. The process of assigning costs in a cost pool to cost objects is called _______________.
10. Costs of an organization that are incurred to benefit more than one segment are called _______________.
11. A(n) _______________ center is a segment of an organization in which the manager is held accountable for the costs incurred by the segment.
12. The responsibility centers, products or services to which costs are to be assigned, are called _______________.
13. In a(n) _______________-costing system, fixed manufacturing overhead is inventoried.
14. In a(n) _______________-costing system, fixed manufacturing overhead is treated as a period expense.
15. Generally accepted accounting principles require that income reporting be based on _______________ costing.

Multiple-Choice Questions

_____ **1.** Consider the following two statements about decentralized organizations:
I. Managers of the organization's subunits have specialized skills that enable them to manage their departments most effectively.
II. Managers with some decision-making authority usually exhibit less motivation than those who merely execute the decisions of others.
Which is (are) benefits of decentralization?
(a) Only I
(b) Only II
(c) Both I and II
(d) Neither I nor II

_____ **2.** Consider the following two statements:
I. Proponents of absorption costing argue that to include fixed cost in the inventoried cost of a product will overstate the cost of the product.
II. Defenders of variable costing argue that the fixed-cost component of a product's absorption-costing value has no future service potential.
Which is (are) true?
(a) Only I
(b) Only II
(c) Both I and II
(d) Neither I nor II

_____ **3.** The Harkness Company makes and sells a single product. The March 1 inventory was 3,000 units, and the March 31 inventory was 5,000 units. If the predetermined fixed-overhead rate is $12 per unit, then the reported income for March under absorption costing in relation to variable costing is
(a) $24,000 less.
(b) $24,000 more.
(c) $60,000 less.
(d) $60,000 more.

_____ **4.** Which of the following is *not* a key feature of segment reporting?
(a) Income statements are in the contribution format.
(b) Income statements highlight costs that can be controlled by segment managers.
(c) Income statements show income for the company as a whole and for its major segments.
(d) Costs are reported by management function with fixed and variable costs not segregated.

Exercises

11.1 The Phillips Photocopy Service had the following data for May:

	Flexible budget	Actual results
Paper products bought and used	$3,200	$3,492
Revenue from copying government reports	2,800	2,614
Variable overhead	400	238
Fixed overhead	1,200	1,288
Revenue from other copying services	2,300	2,593

Required:

Prepare a performance report for May similar to the lower portion of Exhibit 11-4 in the text. Use three columns in your report.

Solution Space for Exercise 11.1:

PHILLIPS PHOTOCOPY SERVICE
Performance Report for May

11.2 Hill-Top Hospital has two divisions—Health Care and Pharmacy. The hospital accountant has decided to allocate the costs of power and heat to the divisions on the basis of square footage and the cost of business administration to the divisions on the basis of payroll dollars. The following information is available for the month of September:

Division	Budgeted Payroll	Square Footage
Health care	$81,000	15,000
Pharmacy	9,000	1,000

Department	Direct Costs
Power and heat	$ 5,300
Business administration	12,000

Required:

Allocate the costs of power and heat and of business administration to the divisions using the cost allocation bases chosen by the hospital accountant.

Solution Space for Exercise 11.2:

11.3 The Kretser Company sells three products: *X, Y,* and *Z.* Data for the last quarter of the year are as follows:

	Products		
	X	*Y*	*Z*
Sales revenue	$150,000	$220,000	$180,000
Contribution margin (%)	45%	55%	40%
Controllable fixed expenses	$ 29,000	$ 54,000	$ 32,000
Fixed expenses controllable by others	$ 16,000	$ 12,000	$ 18,000

Besides the expenses given above, Kretser had $42,000 of common fixed costs. The tax rate is 30 percent.

Required:

Prepare a segmented income statement for Kretser for the last quarter of the year. Use the contribution format.

Solution Space for Exercise 11.3:

KRETSER COMPANY
Segmented Income Statement
For the Last Quarter of the Year

11.4 The Stearns Company makes and sells a single product and had the following data for February:

Units sold	6,500
Variable manufacturing overhead	$23,750
Finished-goods inventory, Feb. 1	none
Variable selling and administrative expenses	$ 3,900
Direct materials used	$37,500
Planned production (in units)	12,500
Fixed selling and administrative expenses	$27,100
Fixed manufacturing overhead	$28,750
Units produced	12,500
Direct labor incurred	$20,000

There were no work-in-process inventories on February 1 or February 28.

Required:

(a) Compute the finished-goods inventory cost under
- **(1)** Absorption costing
- **(2)** Variable costing

(b) Determine which costing method, variable costing or absorption costing, will show the higher income for February. By what amount?

Solution Space for Exercise 11.4:

(a)

(1)

(2)

(b)

11.5 Harold Jameson is the controller of the Southern Division of Arctic Products, Inc. The Southern Division had the following divisional income statement data (in $1,000) for 19x5:

	Actual	Budgeted
Sales	320	284
Variable expenses	180	159
Variable selling and administrative expenses	26	23
Contribution margin	206	102
Fixed overhead expenses	120	49
Fixed selling and administrative expenses	58	23
Net income	28	30

Arctic provides a bonus to each division manager (including the controller) if the division's actual annual net income is at least as large as the budgeted annual income. Before finalizing the actual income statement for 19x5 and sending it to corporate headquarters, Jameson is contemplating deferring those fixed expenses that haven't been paid until the first quarter of 19x6. By doing this, the actual annual net income will exceed the budgeted net income for 19x5.

Required:

Write a paragraph commenting on the unethical behavior that Jameson is contemplating. State explicitly why such behavior would be in violation of the Standards of Ethical Conduct for Management Accountants.

Solution Space for Exercise 11.5:

Answers to True-False Questions

1. F Large organizations are usually decentralized.
2. F The performance report provides very helpful information for the use of management by exception.
3. T
4. F It is typically designated as an investment center.
5. T
6. T
7. T
8. F Some costs, such as a two-year contract to buy merchandise, can be controlled in the long run but not in the short run.
9. T
10. F It is the same thing.
11. T
12. T
13. F Blame should not be emphasized in a responsibility-accounting system. The approach should be constructive, not destructive.
14. T
15. F It is better to use budgeted sales revenue.
16. T
17. F These costs could be common costs at a lower level in the organization.
18. F It is inconsistent with CVP analysis; variable costing is consistent with CVP analysis.
19. T
20. F It is added to gross margin.

Answers to Fill-in-the-Blank Questions

1. Responsibility
2. revenue
3. profit
4. performance report
5. cost pool
6. allocation base
7. Segment reporting
8. investment
9. cost allocation (cost distribution)
10. common costs
11. cost
12. cost objects
13. absorption
14. variable
15. absorption

Answers to Multiple-Choice Questions

1. **(a)** Managers who have decision-making authority are usually more motivated than those who merely execute the decisions of others.
2. **(b)** Statement I is not true at all.
3. **(b)** $12 × (5,000 – 3,000) = $24,000.
4. **(d)** This choice is not true.

Solutions to Exercises

11.1

PHILLIPS PHOTOCOPY SERVICE
Performance Report
For May

	Flexible Budget	Actual Results	Variance
Revenue			
Copying government reports	$2,800	$2,614	$186 U
Other copy services	2,300	2,593	293 F
Total revenue	$5,100	$5,207	$107 F
Expenses			
Paper products	3,200	3,492	292 U
Variable overhead	400	238	162 F
Fixed overhead	1,200	1,288	88 U
Total expenses	$4,800	$5,018	218 U
Profit	$ 300	$ 189	$111 U

11.2

Department	Division	Allocation Base	Percent of Total	Cost Allocated
Power and heat	Health care	15,000 $ft.^2$	93.75%	$ 4,968.75
	Pharmacy	1,000 $ft.^2$	6.25%	331.25
		16,000 $ft.^2$	100 %	$ 5,300.00
Business adm.	Health care	$81,000	90 %	$10,800.00
	Pharmacy	9,000	10 %	1,200.00
		$90,000	100 %	$12,000.00

11.3

KRETSER COMPANY
Segmented Income Statement
For the Last Quarter of the Year

		Product Line		
	Total	*X*	*Y*	*Z*
Sales revenue	$550,000	$150,000	$220,000	$180,000
Variable expenses	289,500	82,500	99,000	108,000
Contribution margin	$260,500	$ 67,500	$121,000	$ 72,000
Less: Controllable fixed expenses	115,000	29,000	54,000	32,000
Controllable segment margin	$145,500	$ 38,500	$ 67,000	$ 40,000
Less: Fixed expenses controllable by others	46,000	16,000	12,000	18,000
Segment margin	$ 99,500	$ 22,500	$ 55,000	$ 22,000
Less: Common fixed costs	42,000			
Income before taxes	$ 57,500			
Less: Income tax expense	17,250			
Net income after taxes	$ 40,250			

11.4 **(a)** Manufacturing costs for February:

Direct materials	$ 37,500
Direct labor	20,000
Variable manufacturing overhead	23,750
Total variable product cost	$ 81,250
Fixed manufacturing overhead	28,750
Total product cost	$110,000

(1) Unit product cost under absorption costing: $110,000/12,500 = $8.80
Finished-goods inventory, February 28, under absorption costing is valued at $8.80 × 6,000 = $52,800
(*Note:* Finished-goods inventory, February 28, in units = 0 + 12,500 − 6,500 = 6,000)

(2) Unit product cost under variable costing: $81,250/12,500 = $6.50
Finished-goods inventory, February 28, under variable costing is valued at $6.50 × 6,000 = $39,000

(b) The higher income will be obtained under absorption costing because ending inventory of finished goods is valued higher by $13,800 under absorption costing than under variable costing. Note that 6,000 × $2.30 = $13,800, where $2.30 is the fixed-overhead rate.

11.5 If Jameson carries out his contemplated behavior, he is unethical in several respects. First, he is not performing his professional duties in accord with relevant technical standards. The fixed expenses were incurred in 19x5 and therefore should be reported on the 19x5 Income Statement. Secondly, he is failing to communicate information fairly and objectively. Finally, he is allowing his own interests to influence the financial reporting and hence is compromising his professional integrity.

Chapter 12

Investment Centers and Transfer Pricing

CHAPTER OVERVIEW AND LEARNING OBJECTIVES

In this chapter you will study the various methods employed by managerial accountants to evaluate investment centers and the performance of their managers. Also, you will study the important issues involved in transfer pricing in decentralized organizations. When you have finished this chapter, you should understand:

1. The role of managerial accounting in achieving goal congruence
2. How to compute an investment center's return on investment and residual income
3. How a manager can improve the return on investment by increasing either the sales margin or capital turnover
4. Some advantages and disadvantages of both return on investment and residual income when used as divisional performance measures
5. How to measure a division's income and invested capital
6. The use of the general economic rule for setting optimal transfer prices
7. How to base transfer prices on market prices, costs, or negotiations

AN OUTLINE FOR CHAPTER STUDY

A. In decentralized organizations the biggest challenge is to obtain goal congruence among autonomous divisional managers so that the organization will function effectively. Goal congruence is realized when the managers of the divisions strive to achieve the goals set by top management. In all of this the managerial accountant's objective is to design and have in place a responsibility-accounting system that will direct the efforts of managers toward the goals of the organization. This system is used to evaluate the performance of managers in achieving the organization's goals. If the managers participate in setting these goals, the approach is called management by objectives. As organizations grow and become more decentralized, the responsibility-accounting system should adapt and will most likely become more complex.

B. Two primary goals of a profit-oriented firm are maximizing its profits and utilizing its invested capital effectively. To evaluate the performance of managers in achieving these goals, managerial accountants use two measures—return on investment (ROI) and residual income. These two measures will be summarized in the next two sections.

C. Return on investment (ROI) is defined as follows:

$$ROI = \frac{\text{Income}}{\text{Invested capital}}$$

This formula measures the income of a division in relation to capital invested in that division. The formula can be expanded as follows:

$$ROI = \left(\frac{\text{Income}}{\text{Sales}}\right) \times \left(\frac{\text{Sales}}{\text{Invested capital}}\right)$$

where (Income/Sales) is called sales margin and (Sales/Invested capital) is called capital turnover.

This formula shows that ROI can be improved by either increasing sales margin or increasing capital turnover. Sales margin can be increased by increasing profit without increasing sales revenue; this might be done by either decreasing expenses or selling a smaller quantity at a higher per-unit price. Capital turnover can be increased by either increasing sales revenue or reducing invested capital. ROI is the most popular performance measure in an investment center; it is simple and is in the form of a ratio or percentage. The ROI measure has a shortcoming in that it ignores the firm's cost of raising invested capital; thus it might undermine goal congruence.

D. Residual income is defined for an investment center as:

$$\text{Income} - (\text{Invested capital} \times \text{Imputed interest rate})$$

The imputed interest rate is simply the firm's minimum required rate of return on invested capital; it is sometimes called the cost of capital. Thus, residual income is what is left from division income after deducting a charge for invested capital to reflect a minimum required rate of return on this invested capital. The formula for residual income requires three pieces of data—division income, invested capital, and imputed interest rate. Residual income can also be expressed in the form

$$\text{Residual income} = \text{Invested capital} \times (\text{ROI} - \text{Imputed interest rate})$$

This form tells us that residual income will be positive only if the ROI exceeds the imputed interest rate. One drawback of the residual-income measure is that is should not be used to compare the performance of different-size investment centers.

E. There are various methods used by managerial accountants to measure invested capital. Generally, average asset balances are used to compute ROI and residual income. They include the following:

1. Total assets are used if the division manager has considerable authority in making decisions about all of these assets.
2. Only productive assets are used in those situations where division managers are directed by top management to keep nonproductive assets, such as vacant land or construction in progress.
3. In cases where division managers are allowed to secure short-term credit, invested capital is often measured as average total assets less average current liabilities.

F. An issue to be addressed in measuring invested capital is whether to use the gross or the net book value of long-term assets. Net book value has these advantages:

1. It maintains consistency with the balance sheet prepared for external reporting purposes.
2. It is also more consistent with the definition of income, which is used in the ROI and residual-income computations.

On the other hand, gross book value has these advantages:

1. The methods of computing depreciation are arbitrary and thus should not influence the ROI and residual income.
2. Over time, net book value declines, whereas gross book value does not; this could give a misleading increase in the ROI and residual income over time.

Another issue in measuring invested capital is that older assets will often show higher ROI figures than newer assets, because newer assets usually cost more; this might discourage managers from investing in new equipment, which could make the division uncompetitive. Sometimes assets used by a division, such as cash, are centrally controlled; in such cases some allocation basis is used to portion these assets to divisions for the purpose of measuring invested capital.

G. The key issue in measuring a division's income is controllability. The choice of measure will relate to the extent to which uncontrollable items are allowed to influence the income measure. Only those revenues and costs that a manager can control should influence the profit measure. Income measures often used are numbered in the following schedule for a division income statement:

	Sales revenue	\$\$\$
	Less: Variable costs	\$\$\$
	Contribution margin	\$\$\$
	Less: Fixed costs controllable by manager	\$\$\$
1.	Profit margin controllable by manager	\$\$\$
	Less: Traceable fixed costs not controllable by manager	\$\$\$
2.	Traceable profit margin	\$\$\$
	Less: Costs allocated from headquarters	\$\$\$
3.	Net income before interest and taxes	\$\$\$
	Less: Interest cost from headquarters	\$\$\$
4.	Income before taxes	\$\$\$
	Less: Income taxes	\$\$\$
5.	Net income	\$\$\$

Measure 1 best addresses the controllability issue.

H. During inflationary periods, historical-cost asset values do not reflect the cost of replacing those assets. However, most managers believe that measures based on historical-cost accounting are adequate when used together with budgets and performance targets. Moreover, historical-cost accounting is required for external reporting and so is readily available for performance-measure computations.

I. Other issues involved in divisional performance evaluation are as follows:

1. ROI and residual income put the focus on the short run, even though investment centers have long-term lives and investments are made at various times in those centers. To avoid this short-term focus, some firms use divisional profit, flexible budgets, and variances to analyze divisional performance. Investments are evaluated through a postaudit of investment decisions.
2. Nonfinancial measures are also important in evaluating divisional performance. Examples include rates of defective products produced, aircraft delays, and hotel occupancy rates.

J. The amount charged when one division sells goods or services to another division is called a transfer price. The goal in setting transfer prices is to establish incentives for autonomous division managers to make choices that support the overall goals of the organization. A general rule for transfer prices that will ensure goal congruence is given according to the formula:

$$\text{Transfer price} = \text{Outlay cost per unit for transfer} + \text{Opportunity cost per unit due to transfer}$$

An outlay cost is a cost incurred in producing the goods or services being transferred. An opportunity cost represents the profit forgone by the organization as a whole because the transfer takes place.

K. Two cases need to be considered when applying the general transfer-pricing rule:

1. When there is no excess capacity, a division is selling to the outside market all it can produce. This means that for a transfer to a sister division to take place, the selling division will have to give up some of its outside sales. This results in profit forgone, and this forgone profit should be included in the opportunity-cost component of the general transfer-pricing formula.

2. When there is excess capacity in a selling division, no profit is forgone when transferring goods or services to a buying division. This means that the opportunity cost is zero in the general transfer-pricing formula.

L. The amount determined by the general transfer-pricing formula should be viewed as a lower bound on the transfer price, since it represents zero profit (when considering opportunity cost as well as outlay cost) from the transfer for the selling division. Sometimes it is hard to implement the general transfer-pricing rule because it is difficult to measure the opportunity cost involved. These difficulties include:

1. External markets may not be perfectly competitive.
2. The transferred goods may be unique.
3. Special equipment may be needed to make the transferred goods.
4. Interdependencies may exist among several transferred products or services.

M. Other approaches to setting transfer prices include the following:

1. Use of the external market price, if it exists. The external market price will be the same as that given by the general transfer-pricing formula only when the selling division has no excess capacity and perfect competition prevails. Distress market prices should not be used to set transfer prices.
2. Use of negotiated transfer prices. In this case divisional managers negotiate the price at which transfers will be made. Any cost saving resulting from a transfer may be split between the two divisions. Sometimes negotiations can lead to divisiveness among divisional managers, which might have a negative impact on the organization as a whole.
3. Use of cost-based transfer prices. Some organizations will set the transfer price at the standard variable cost plus a markup. Other organizations may use fill cost as a basis for the transfer price. Full-cost-based transfer prices can be dysfunctional in that they lead the buying division to view fixed costs for the company as a whole as variable costs to the buying division; this can cause faulty decision making. Although the practice is common, transfer prices should not be based on full cost.

N. Other considerations pertaining to transfer prices include the following:

1. Transfer prices should be based on standard or budgeted costs rather than actual costs.
2. Top-level managers are generally reluctant to intervene in disputes among divisional managers over transfer prices, even if this leads to an occasional dysfunctional decision from the view of the organization as a whole.
3. International companies often need to consider domestic and foreign income tax rates and the imposition of import duties or tariffs when setting transfer prices.

O. The design of a managerial performance and reward system involves a trade-off between two factors:

1. Providing incentives for the manager to act in the organization's interest
2. Imposing risks on a manager who is a risk averter, because financial performance measures are only partially controllable by the manager

P. An internal control system is an integral part of an organization's effort to achieve its goals. This is a set of procedures designed to ensure that the organization's employees act in a legal, ethical, and responsible manner; these procedures are designed to prevent major lapses in responsible behavior.

KEY TERMS

Capital turnover 607
Distress market price 624
Full (or absorption) cost 625
Goal congruence 619
Imperfect competition 622
Internal control system 628
Investment centers 603
Management by objectives (MBO) 604
Perfect competition 622
Residual income 609
Return on investment (ROI) 606
Sales margin 607
Transfer price 604

SELF-EVALUATION QUESTIONS AND ANSWERS

True-False Questions

_____ 1. The greatest challenge in making a decentralized organization function effectively is to obtain goal congruence among the organization's autonomous managers.

_____ 2. As an organization grows, it is crucial that decision making become more centralized.

_____ 3. Return on investment = invested capital divided by income.

_____ 4. Most large organizations are centralized.

_____ 5. ROI can be improved by increasing sales margin and holding capital turnover constant.

_____ 6. A primary goal of a profit-making enterprise is to use its invested capital as effectively as possible.

_____ 7. It is impossible to increase profit without increasing total sales revenue.

_____ 8. The key factor in deciding how well a responsibility-accounting system works is the extent to which it directs managers' efforts toward organizational goals.

_____ 9. The ROI measure ignores the firm's cost of raising investment capital.

_____ 10. Sales margin can never be greater than 100 percent.

_____ 11. Capital turnover can never be greater than 100 percent.

_____ 12. As an organization grows, its accounting and managerial control system usually becomes more complex.

_____ 13. Sales margin can never be greater than the contribution-margin ratio.

_____ 14. Residual income is a percentage amount.

_____ 15. Residual income is a good measure to use in comparing the performance of different-sized investment centers.

_____ 16. Both ROI and residual income are computed for a period of time.

_____ 17. During periods of inflation, historical-cost asset values soon cease to reflect the cost of replacing those assets.

_____ 18. ROI and residual income are long-run performance measures.

_____ 19. In performance evaluation, nonfinancial measures are not important.

_____ 20. Transfer prices affect the profit measurement of the buying division, the selling division, and the organization as a whole.

_____ 21. Application of the general transfer-pricing formula results in goal-congruent decision making.

_____ 22. If a producing division has excess capacity and the external market is imperfectly competitive, the general-formula transfer price and the external market price will be the same.

_____ 23. Basing transfer prices on full costs can cause dysfunctional decision-making behavior.

_____ 24. Transfer prices should be based on actual costs.

Fill-in-the-Blank Questions

1. The price at which products or services are transferred between two divisions in an organization is called a(n) ________________.
2. ________________ is obtained when the managers of divisions throughout an organization strive to achieve the goals set up by top management.
3. ________________ is an approach where managers participate in setting goals which they then strive to achieve.
4. ________________ is defined as the difference between income and the product of invested capital times the imputed interest rate.
5. In measuring an investment center's income, the key issue is ________________.
6. The overall objective of performance measures in decentralized organizations is to provide incentives for ________________ behavior.
7. Sales revenue divided by invested capital is called the ________________.
8. ROI can be increased by holding sales margin and sales revenue constant and decreasing ________________.
9. ________________ exists only when more goods can be produced than the producer is able to sell, due to low demand for the product.
10. Income divided by sales revenue is called the ________________.

11. When excess capacity exists, the opportunity-cost component of the transfer price in the general transfer-pricing formula is ________________.

12. The amount determined by the general transfer-pricing formula generally provides a(n) ________________ bound on the transfer price that should be realized.

13. A(n) ________________ system is the set of procedures designed to ensure that an organization's employees act in a legal, ethical, and responsible manner.

Multiple-Choice Questions

_____ **1.** A division of the Wimple Company had a return on investment of 6 percent and a capital turnover of 30 percent last year. The sales margin last year was
- **(a)** 18 percent.
- **(b)** 20 percent.
- **(c)** 25 percent.
- **(d)** 30 percent.

_____ **2.** Consider the following two statements:
I. Capital turnover can be improved by increasing invested capital and holding sales revenue constant.
II. Sales margin can be increased by decreasing expenses and holding sales revenue constant.
Which is (are) true?
- **(a)** Only I
- **(b)** Only II
- **(c)** Both I and II
- **(d)** Neither I nor II

_____ **3.** Which of the following is *not* a reason for difficulty in measuring opportunity costs for transfer-pricing purposes?
- **(a)** External markets may have perfect competition.
- **(b)** The goods being transferred may be unique.
- **(c)** Special equipment may be needed to make the transferred goods.
- **(d)** There may be interdependencies among several products being transferred.

_____ **4.** Consider the following two statements:
I. ROI can undermine goal congruence.
II. Residual income distorts comparisons between investment centers of different sizes.
Which is (are) true?
- **(a)** Only I
- **(b)** Only II
- **(c)** Both I and II
- **(d)** Neither I nor II

_____ **5.** Which of the following would *not* be a plausible measure of a division's invested capital?
- **(a)** Bonds payable
- **(b)** Total assets less current liabilities
- **(c)** Total productive assets
- **(d)** Total assets

_____ **6.** Suppose that Division A is planning to transfer 3,000 units of a product to Division B. The outlay costs of Division A due to the transfer are $8.50 per unit. The opportunity costs to the organization because of the transfer are $11,490. The transfer price per unit according to the general transfer-pricing formula is
- **(a)** $8.50.
- **(b)** $12.33.
- **(c)** $15.80.
- **(d)** $19.99.

_____ 7. Consider the following two statements:

I. Using gross book value to measure invested capital is more consistent with the definition of income than is net book value.

II. When long-lived assets are depreciated, their gross book value declines over time.

Which is (are) true?

(a) Only I
(b) Only II
(c) Both I and II
(d) Neither I nor II

Exercises

12.1 The Wheeler Company has two divisions, X and Y. The company's cost of acquiring capital is 8 percent. The following data are available:

	Division X	Division Y
Sales revenue	(a)	(e)
Income	$270,000	(f)
Average investment	$3,000,000	(g)
Sales margin	18%	(h)
Capital turnover	(b)	3
ROI	(c)	17%
Residual income	(d)	$72,000

Required:

Find items (a) through (h) in the above table.

Solution Space for Exercise 12.1:

(a) ______________________________

(b) ______________________________

(c) ______________________________

(d) ______________________________

(e) ______________________________

(f) ______________________________

(g) ______________________________

(h) ______________________________

12.2 The Corley Company has two divisions, A and B. Division A makes and sells a product having the following data, which are expected to hold for next year:

Unit selling price	$20
Variable cost per unit	$12
Annual fixed cost	$150,000

The maximum capacity at Division A is 50,000 units. This past year Division B bought 10,000 units of this same product from an outside supplier at $18 per unit. Division B is contemplating the possibility of buying 10,000 units next year from Division A; it could buy these units from the outside supplier at $18 each.

Required:

- **(a)** According to the general transfer-pricing formula, what price should Division A charge Division B under each of the following conditions?
  - **(1)** Division A can sell only 38,000 units to the outside market next year.
  - **(2)** Division A can sell 50,000 units to the outside market next year.
- **(b)** If Division A insists on the price determined in part (a) (2), will a transfer take place? Why or why not?

Solution Space for Exercise 12.2:

(a) **(1)** ____________________

(2) ____________________

(b) ____________________

12.3 Redride Products, Inc., has two divisions: North and South. The following data are available for the South Division and the single product it makes:

Unit selling price	$20
Variable cost per unit	$12
Annual fixed costs	$280,000
Investment in South	$1,500,000

Required:

(Assume that each question is independent of the others, unless otherwise stated.)

- **(a)** How many units must South sell each year to have an ROI of 16 percent?
- **(b)** If South wants an ROI of 20 percent and wishes to sell 50,000 units, what price must be charged instead of the given selling price?
- **(c)** If South wants a residual income of $45,000 and the cost of acquiring capital is 10 percent, the annual capital turnover will have to be what value?
- **(d)** Next year South has a budgeted volume of 80,000 units, of which 10,000 units are expected to be bought by North Division. However, North Division has received an offer from an outside firm to supply the 10,000 units at $18 each. If South fails to meet the $18 price, North will buy from the outside; in such a case South could save $40,000 in fixed costs if its volume dropped to 70,000 units. Assuming that South meets the $18 price, South's annual profit would be what amount?
- **(e)** Assume the same information as in part (d) except that South does not meet the $18 price. What is the effect of this on the total profit of Redride?

Solution Space for Exercise 12.3:

(a) ____________________

____

(b) ____________________

____

____

(c) ____________________

____

(d)

(e)

12.4 The Scott Company has two divisions—the Eastern Division and the Western Division. Data for these two divisions for 19x8 are as follows:

Division	Invested Capital	Income
Eastern	$940,000	$75,200
Western	188,000	20,680

Scott uses an imputed interest rate of 4 percent in computing residual income. The president of Scott believes that the best way to compare the performance of the two divisions is to measure performance by residual income because dollar amounts are both easy to understand and concrete.

Required:

Write a paragraph commenting on the president's view of comparing the performance of the two divisions. Discuss any weaknesses in his views by using the numerical data for 19x8.

Solution Space for Exercise 12.4:

Answers to True-False Questions

1. T
2. F It is crucial that decision making become more decentralized.
3. F Return on investment equals income divided by invested capital.
4. F Most large organizations are decentralized.
5. T
6. T
7. F Profit can be increased, for example, by keeping revenue constant and decreasing expenses.
8. T
9. T
10. T
11. F It is very possible that annual sales will exceed invested capital, thus making capital turnover exceed 100 percent.
12. T
13. T
14. F Residual income is a dollar amount.
15. F It is a poor measure for comparing performance of investment centers, because it is a dollar measure rather than a percentage measure.
16. T
17. T
18. F They are short-run performance measures.
19. F Nonfinancial measures are also important.
20. F They affect profit measurement in the buying and selling divisions, but not in the organization as a whole.
21. T
22. F The external market must be perfectly competitive to ensure that the general-formula transfer price and the external market price will be the same.
23. T
24. F They should be based on budgeted or standard costs.

Answers to Fill-in-the-Blank Questions

1. transfer price
2. Goal congruence
3. Management by objectives
4. Residual income
5. controllability
6. goal-congruent
7. capital turnover
8. invested capital
9. Excess capacity
10. sales margin
11. zero
12. lower
13. internal control

Answers to Multiple-Choice Questions

1. (b) .06/.3 = .2 or 20 percent.
2. (b) When sales revenue is constant and invested capital increases, capital turnover goes down.
3. (a) Difficulty in measuring opportunity costs results when external markets are imperfectly competitive.
4. (c)
5. (a) Bonds payable is a long-term debt; it is not used to measure invested capital.
6. (b) $8.50 + $11,490/3,000 = $12.33.
7. (d) Both statements are false.

Solutions to Exercises

12.1 For Division X:

(a) Sales revenue = $270,000/.18 = $1,500,000
(b) Capital turnover = $1,500,000/$3,000,000 = 0.5
(c) ROI = $270,000/$3,000,000 = 9%
(d) Residual income = $270,000 – $3,000,000 × .08 = $30,000

For Division Y:

(g) Average investment = $72,000/(.17 – .08) = $800,000
(e) Sales revenue = $800,000 × 3 = $2,400,000
(f) Income = $800,000 × .17 = $136,000
(h) Sales margin = $136,000/$2,400,000 = 5.67%

12.2 (a) (1) Transfer price = $12 + 0 = $12
(2) Transfer price = $12 + (20 – 12) = $20
(b) No: Division B can buy the 10,000 units from the outside market at $18 each.

12.3 **(a)** Income = .16 × \$1,500,000 = \$240,000
Units needed to be sold = (280,000 + 240,000)/(20 − 12) = 65,000

(b) Income = .2 × \$1,500,000 = \$300,000
Let P be the needed sales price.
Then \$300,000 = (P × 50,000) − (\$12 × 50,000) − (\$280,000), and so P = \$23.60

(c) \$45,000 = income − \$1,500,000 × .10
Income = \$195,000
ROI = \$195,000/\$1,500,000 = 13%
\$195,000 = (\$20 − \$12) × Q − 280,000
Q = 475,000/8 = 59,375
Sales revenue = \$20 × 59,375 = \$1,187,500
Capital turnover = \$1,187,500/\$1,500,000 = .792

(d)

Revenue from outside market: 70,000 × \$20 =		\$1,400,000
Revenue from North Division: 10,000 × \$18 =		180,000
Total revenue		\$1,580,000
Variable costs: 80,000 × \$12 =	\$960,000	
Fixed costs	\$280,000	
Total costs		\$1,240,000
Profit		\$ 340,000

(e) For Redride as a whole:

Cost saving: \$40,000 + (10,000 × \$12) =	\$160,000
Extra cost: 10,000 × \$18 =	180,000
Decrease in annual profit	\$ 20,000

12.4 The view of the president is misdirected. First of all, residual income which is measured in dollars, is an absolute amount; that is, it is a number that stands alone, unrelated to any base amount. For 19x8 the residual income of Eastern is

$$\$75{,}200 - \$940{,}000 \times 0.04 = \$37{,}600$$

and for Western is

$$\$20{,}680 - \$188{,}000 \times 0.04 = \$13{,}160$$

According to the president's view, Eastern had the best performance since it had the largest residual income. In order to have a plausible comparison of divisional performance, the measure should reflect income on a relative basis, and the ROI computation does just that—it compares income to the invested capital in the form of a percentage. Thus, for 19x8 Eastern's ROI is \$75,200/\$940,000 = 8%, whereas Western's ROI is \$20,680/\$188,000 = 11%. This measure says that Western's performance in 19x8 was better than Eastern's, just the opposite result from the residual income measure. The ROI measure is much better for comparing divisional performance because it puts the divisions onto a comparable footing.

Chapter **13**

Decision Making: Relevant Costs and Benefits

CHAPTER OVERVIEW AND LEARNING OBJECTIVES

Previous chapters of the text covered accounting procedures used in evaluating managerial performance. The main focus of this chapter is how to decide what information is relevant to various common decision problems faced by managers. After completing this chapter, you should understand:

1. The six steps in the decision-making process and the role of the managerial accountant in that process
2. The relationship between quantitative and qualitative analyses in decision making
3. The two criteria that must be satisfied in relevant information
4. How to identify relevant costs and benefits, giving appropriate treatment to sunk costs, opportunity costs, and unit costs
5. How to prepare correct analyses of various special decision problems
6. The analysis of manufacturing decisions involving joint products and limited resources
7. The impact of an advanced manufacturing environment and activity-based costing on the analysis of relevant costs.

AN OUTLINE FOR CHAPTER STUDY

A. The role of the managerial accountant in the decision-making process is to provide relevant information to managers who must make decisions and choices. The six steps in the decision-making process are:

   1. Clarify the decision problem.
   2. Specify the criterion upon which a decision will be made.
   3. Identify the alternative courses of action that are available.
   4. Develop a decision model that is a simplified representation of the problem.
   5. Collect the data pertinent to the decision problem.
   6. Choose an alternative to make the decision.

   The managerial accountant's responsibility in this six-step process is primarily in step 5. Managerial decision problems have both quantitative and qualitative characteristics. The first five steps pertain to quantitative analysis, whereas the sixth step relates to qualitative considerations. These qualitative characteristics are the factors in the decision problem that cannot be expressed effectively in numerical terms.

B. There are three characteristics of information that determine its usefulness. They are:

1. Relevance—Information is relevant if it pertains to the decision problem at hand.
2. Accuracy—The information must be correct; managers cannot use effectively any information that is in error or imprecise.
3. Timeliness—The information must be available to management within a time frame that meets their needs.

C. There are four key factors that must be considered in deciding whether information is relevant to a decision problem. These factors are as follows:

1. The information must be related to a future event. Costs that were incurred or benefits that were realized in the past will not change and so are irrelevant to decisions that must be made now.
2. The information relating to competing alternative courses of action must be different for each alternative. Costs and benefits that are the same across all available alternatives have no bearing on the decision.
3. Information must be predicted because it relates to a future event. However, often the predictions of costs and benefits are based on historical data.
4. Some decision problems are unique and some are repetitive. Compiling data for unique decision problems usually requires a specialized analysis. However, cost predictions relevant to repetitive decisions typically can be built up from historical data, which is usually readily available.

It is important to isolate relevant costs and benefits because it is costly to gather information and managers can effectively use only a limited amount of information. When information overload occurs, effective decision making declines.

D. Sunk costs are costs that have already been incurred; hence they are irrelevant for decision-making purposes. Examples of sunk costs are the book value of old equipment and the book value of obsolete inventory. Other costs that are irrelevant for decision making are those that make no difference when one is evaluating competing alternatives. If the same cost is incurred under all possible alternative courses of action, then it is not relevant. When two alternatives are available, one way to identify costs that make a difference is to compute the difference of the like costs under the two alternatives. The computation of these differential costs is a convenient way of summarizing the relative advantage of one alternative over another.

E. An opportunity cost is the potential benefit given up when the choice of one action precludes a different action. An opportunity cost is a relevant cost of decision making and is just as important as any out-of-pocket expenditure. Often, people overlook or underweight opportunity costs.

F. Variable costs may or may not be relevant costs; it depends on whether or not they make a difference when compared across the competing alternative courses of action in the decision problem. The same can be said about fixed costs; if fixed costs make a difference when compared across the alternative choices, then they are relevant. Fixed costs are often irrelevant because they cannot be avoided, regardless of which alternative is chosen; however, if a fixed cost is avoidable under one course of action but not under another, then it is relevant because it makes a difference.

G. The problem of accepting or rejecting a special order is an important class of nonroutine managerial decision problems. It is a common problem in both service-oriented and manufacturing firms. This decision problem usually involves accepting or rejecting an offer to buy a product or service at less than full price. The correct way of analyzing this type of problem is to focus on only the relevant costs and benefits. When excess capacity exists, there is usually no opportunity cost involved; when there is no excess capacity, the opportunity cost of using the firm's resources to produce the special order is a relevant cost. The economic decision criterion is which action (to accept or reject a special order) gives the largest incremental net income.

H. Another important relevant costing decision problem is "Should a given product (or service) be bought or made?" This problem consists of weighing the relevant costs of making the product against the relevant costs of buying the product on the outside market. The action which gives the smallest relevant cost (and hence the largest incremental net income) is the one that is economically preferable.

I. Whether to add or drop a product line constitutes another important class of relevant costing problems. The economic advantage of adding a product line is obtained by weighing the incremental costs of adding this product against the incremental revenues obtained from this product. If the difference between the incremental revenue and the incremental costs is positive, then net income will be increased by adding the product line. Similarly, to determine whether an existing product line should be dropped, it is necessary to compare the cost savings (those costs that can be avoided by dropping the product line) from doing so with the incremental net income from keeping that product line. If this cost saving exceeds the incremental net income, then the product line should be dropped on economic grounds.

J. A joint production process consists of producing at least two products from common raw materials, where these products become identifiable only at some point beyond the start of the production process; this point is called the split-off point. An important class of relevant costing problems emerges from this production process. The relevant costing decision problem is "Should joint products, which can be sold at split-off, actually be sold, or should they be processed further?" The best economic choice in this type of problem is determined by weighing the incremental revenue from processing a product beyond split-off with the cost of further processing beyond split-off. If this incremental revenue exceeds the further processing costs beyond split-off, then processing that product beyond split-off is economically preferable. It should be noted that the production cost up to the split-off point (commonly called the joint cost of production) is irrelevant in this problem; this is because at the split-off point (where the decision problem occurs), the joint cost is a sunk cost. The production costs incurred beyond split-off are often called separable processing costs.

K. Often an organization must decide how much of each product (or service) should be made in the face of limited or scarce resources. In this situation the crucial issue is not, "Which products generate the most profit per unit of product?" but rather, "What product generates the most profit per unit of scarce resource?" Problems of this type are generally dealt with by the methods of linear programming (discussed in the appendix to this chapter).

L. Relevant costing concepts also apply to an advanced manufacturing setting and where activity-based costing is used. With ABC the decision maker can associate costs of activities with cost drivers more accurately than in traditional product costing. As a result, with ABC the decision maker is in a much better position to identify costs that are avoidable in a decision situation. Many of the costs thought to be unavoidable fixed costs in traditional relevant costing may well be avoidable when analyzed in the light of appropriate cost drivers.

M. The following additional points concerning the types of decision problems discussed above should be noted:

1. The decisions made about each of these problem situations cover a given period of time. This time period might be less than one year (a short-run decision) or more than a year (a long-run decision). In long-run decision problems, the time value of money should be considered. (This is covered in Chapters 15 and 16).
2. The criteria discussed in the previous sections for making choices in the decision problems were economic and quantitative in nature. It is also very important to consider all the relevant qualitative issues that bear on these decision problems before any final decision is made.
3. Most often the decision problems cited above involve the element of uncertainty. Two approaches that are sometimes used in this connection are:

    a. Sensitivity analysis. This approach consists of determining what would happen in a decision analysis if a key prediction or assumption proves to be wrong.
    b. Use of expected values. This approach involves computing expected profits or expected losses. These expected values are based on the probabilities that each possible value of profit or loss will occur.

4. Managers typically make decisions that maximize their perceived performance evaluations and rewards. If it is desired that managers make optimal decisions, they must be given incentives to do so.

N. (Appendix) Linear programming is a mathematical tool for maximizing profit or minimizing cost subject to linear constraints. It is often applied to product-mix decision problems—how much of each product should be made, in the face of scarce resources, so as to maximize the total contribution margin. The three steps in constructing a linear programming problem are:

1. Identify the decision variables.
2. Formulate the objective function.
3. Formulate the problem constraints.

The set of possible combinations of levels of the decision variables that satisfy the constraints is called the set of feasible solutions (or the feasible region). The combination that optimizes the objective function is called the optimal feasible solution. The method that is generally used to solve these problems is called the simplex algorithm. The managerial accountant often supplies key information needed to solve linear programming problems.

KEY TERMS

Accurate information 654
Avoidable expenses 666
Differential cost 658
Expected value 672
Information overload 656
Joint cost 668
Joint production process 668
Opportunity cost 659
Qualitative characteristics 653
Relative-sales-value method 668
Relevant information 654
Sensitivity analysis 672
Separable processing cost 669
Split-off point 668
Timely information 654
Unavoidable expenses 666

KEY TERMS: APPENDIX

Constraints 682
Decision variables 682
Feasible region 683
Objective function 682

SELF-EVALUATION QUESTIONS AND ANSWERS

True-False Questions

_____ **1.** Defining a managerial decision problem is a straightforward matter requiring little or no managerial skill.

_____ **2.** Relevant and accurate data are of value in decision making regardless of when these data are made available.

_____ **3.** A decision problem involves selecting from among more than two alternatives.

_____ **4.** The managerial accountant's role in the decision-making process is to provide relevant information to the managers who make the decisions.

_____ **5.** The managerial accountant's role in the decision-making process is primarily to be responsible for the collection of data.

_____ **6.** Decision problems involving accounting data are typically specified in qualitative terms.

_____ **7.** A decision model is a simplified representation of the issues involved in making choices in a decision problem.

_____ **8.** To be relevant to a decision, cost or benefit information must involve a future event.

_____ **9.** Information relevant to unique decisions is easier to generate than information relevant to repetitive decisions.

_____ **10.** The book value of old equipment is a sunk cost.

_____ **11.** In relevant costing problems it is more important to consider out-of-pocket expenditures than it is to consider opportunity costs.

_____ **12.** Fixed costs are irrelevant costs.

_____ **13.** Costs or benefits that are the same across all alternatives in a decision problem have a definite bearing on the choice of action to be made.

_____ **14.** The book value of obsolete inventory is a sunk cost.

_____ **15.** In the decision-making process, people seldom overlook or underweight opportunity costs.

_____ **16.** Variable costs are sometimes irrelevant costs.

_____ **17.** In a joint production process, the joint cost of production is not relevant to the decision problem of selling products at split-off or processing those products further.

_____ **18.** In the decision problem of which products to make when resources are scarce or limited, the important question to ask is "Which products have the largest contribution margin per unit of product?"

_____ **19.** Managers typically make decisions that maximize their perceived performance evaluations and rewards.

_____ **20.** ABC is superior to traditional product costing in identifying avoidable costs.

Fill-in-the-Blank Questions

1. ________________ are the factors in a decision problem that cannot be expressed effectively in numerical terms.

2. Information is ________________ if it is pertinent to a decision problem.

3. Relevant information in decision making must involve costs or benefits that ________________ among the possible alternative choices of action.

4. ________________ are decisions that arise essentially only once.

5. Costs that have occurred in the past are ________________ to a decision problem that is at hand.

6. Relevant information must involve costs and benefits to be realized in the ________________; however, the accountant's predictions of those costs and benefits are often based on data from the ________________.

7. ________________ are decisions that are made over and over again, at regular or irregular intervals.

8. ________________ refers to the precision of data.

9. ________________ consists of receiving more information than can effectively be used in the decision-making process.

10. ________________ are costs that have already been incurred.

11. The computation of ________________ costs is a convenient way of summarizing the relative advantage of one alternative over another in a decision problem.

12. A(n) ________________ cost is the potential benefit given up when the choice of one action precludes a different action.

13. When there is ________________ capacity, the opportunity cost of using a firm's facilities for a special-order decision problem is relevant to the decision.

14. For purposes of decision making, ________________ fixed costs can be misleading.

15. Expenses that a manager can escape incurring by taking a certain course of action are called ________________ expenses.

16. The point in a production process at which joint products become identifiable is called a(n) ________________ point.

17. ________________ is a technique for determining what would happen in a decision analysis if a key prediction or assumption proves to be wrong.

18. An important factor that should be considered in long-run decision problems, and which is not considered in short-run decision problems, is the ________________.

19. (Appendix) ________________ is a mathematical tool to solve the problem of optimizing a linear function subject to linear constraints.

Multiple-Choice Questions

_____ **1.** Which of the following is *not* a key characteristic of information in determining its usefulness for decision making?
- **(a)** Accuracy
- **(b)** Scope
- **(c)** Relevance
- **(d)** Timeliness

_____ **2.** The Gleason Company bought a small computer two years ago; its book value is now $2,000, and it has one more year of useful life. The company could buy a new computer now with a useful life of one year (because in one year it will be obsolete) for $1,500. The new computer would result in a cost saving over the next year of $1,800. The change in company net income for next year resulting from buying the new computer would be:
(a) $200 decrease.
(b) $500 increase.
(c) $300 increase.
(d) $400 decrease.

_____ **3.** Consider the following two statements about relevant costing problems:
I. Future costs or benefits that are identical across all decision alternatives are relevant.
II. Opportunity costs are relevant costs.
Which is (are) true?
(a) Only I
(b) Only II
(c) Both I and II
(d) Neither I nor II

_____ **4.** The Thomas Company now has a $12,000 obsolete inventory in stock. This inventory could be sold for $5,000 or modified for $6,000 and sold for $15,000. The change in company net income resulting from modifying the inventory and then selling it as opposed to selling it as is would be:
(a) $3,000 decrease.
(b) $4,000 increase.
(c) $7,000 increase.
(d) $9,000 increase.

_____ **5.** Of the following steps in the decision-making process, the one that is primarily the responsibility of the managerial accountant is
(a) Collecting the data.
(b) Specifying the criterion.
(c) Developing the decision model.
(d) Clarifying the decision problem.

_____ **6.** One of the products made and sold by the Sandler Company is a warble. The contribution margin per warble is $7.80. It takes 0.5 machine hour to make one warble. The contribution margin per machine hour in making warbles is:
(a) $3.90.
(b) $8.30.
(c) $15.60.
(d) $10.40.

_____ **7.** The Rowe Company makes products *X* and *Y* in a joint production process. The joint cost of production is $7,000. Product *X* can be sold for $12 per unit at split-off and for $18 per unit after further processing. The separable cost of producing *X* is $11 per unit. The change in company net income as a result of selling 1,200 units of *X* at split-off instead of processing these units further is:
(a) $6,000 increase.
(b) $3,400 decrease.
(c) $14,400 increase.
(d) $7,200 decrease.

Exercises

13.1 When Hazel Cooper, president of Ripton Enterprises, Inc., saw the annual income statement showing a loss for Product Line X-50, she quickly asserted, "This is first-class evidence that we should discontinue making Product X-50." As controller of Ripton, you believe it would be helpful for Hazel to know some of the issues and factors that should be considered when contemplating dropping a product line that shows a loss on the income statement.

Required:

Prepare a memo to Hazel Cooper that discusses the issues and factors that should be considered when pondering the discontinuance of a product line that shows a loss on the income statement.

Solution Space for Exercise 13.1:

RIPTON ENTERPRISES, INC.
MEMORANDUM

To: Ms. Hazel Cooper

From: ______________________________

Date: ______________________________

13.2 The Monroe Company owns a machine that produces a component for the products the company makes and sells. Presently, the company uses 18,000 units of this component in production each year. The costs of making one unit of this component are

Direct material	$ 7
Variable conversion	10
Fixed conversion	5

The fixed conversion costs are unavoidable, and the unit cost is based on the present annual usage of 18,000 units of the component. An outside supplier has offered to sell Monroe this component for $20 per unit and can supply all the units it needs.

Required:

(a) Find the change in net income per year that would result if Monroe buys the component from the outside supplier instead of making the component.

(b) Repeat part (a) if the machine could be rented to another organization for $62,000 per year.

Solution Space for Exercise 13.2:

(a) ______________________________

____

____

____

(b) ______________________________

____

____

____

____

____

____

13.3 The Hinkell Company makes and sells 32,000 pairs of bowling shoes each year. The cost of making one pair of these shoes is

Direct material	$7
Variable conversion	5
Fixed conversion	6

The fixed conversion costs are unavoidable, and the unit fixed conversion cost is based on the annual capacity of 42,000 pairs of bowling shoes that Hinkell can make. The company has recently received an offer from a company other than its regular customers that has offered to buy 6,000 pairs of shoes at $16 per pair. Regular customers buy shoes from Hinkell at $22 per pair.

Required:

(a) Find the change in annual net income that would result if this special order is accepted.

(b) Repeat part (a) if the special order is for 12,000 pairs of shoes instead of 6,000 pairs. All other conditions stay the same.

Solution Space for Exercise 13.3:

(a) ______________________________

____

____

____

(b)

13.4 The Fisher Company makes and sells two products, *H* and *K*. The income statement for last year was as follows:

	Product *H*	Product *K*
Sales	$160,000	$240,000
Variable cost of goods sold	60,000	100,000
Manufacturing contribution margin	$100,000	$140,000
Expenses:		
Fixed production	50,000	75,000
Variable selling and administration	18,000	50,000
Fixed selling and administration	14,000	21,000
Net income	$ 18,000	$ (6,000)

At Fisher, fixed costs are unavoidable and are allocated to products on the basis of sales revenue. When the president of Fisher saw this income statement, he immediately concluded that product *K* should be dropped. If *K* is dropped, sales of product *H* are expected to increase by 10 percent next year; the company's cost structure will remain the same.

Required:

Find the change in annual net income if product *K* is discontinued and only product *H* is sold.

Solution Space for Exercise 13.4:

13.5 (Appendix) The Hornick Company makes and sells two products, X and Y, in its Jacksonville plant. Product X requires 2 hours in the machining department and 0.25 hour in the packing department. Product Y requires 4 hours in the machining department and 0.2 hour in the packing department. In any one week there are available at most 16,000 hours in the machining department and at most 1,250 hours in the packing department. The contribution margin from selling one unit of X is \$18 and that of Y is \$15. The decision problem at Hornick is how many units of each product should be made each week in order to maximize the total weekly contribution margin.

Required:

(a) Formulate the given decision problem as a linear programming problem. Let x be the number of units of X made and sold each week, and let y be the number of units of Y made and sold each week.
(b) On a coordinate axis, draw the graph of the feasible region.
(c) Use the graph from part (b) to find the optimal solution to the linear programming problem in part (a).

Solution Space for Exercise 13.5:

(a) ______________________________

____

____

____

(b)

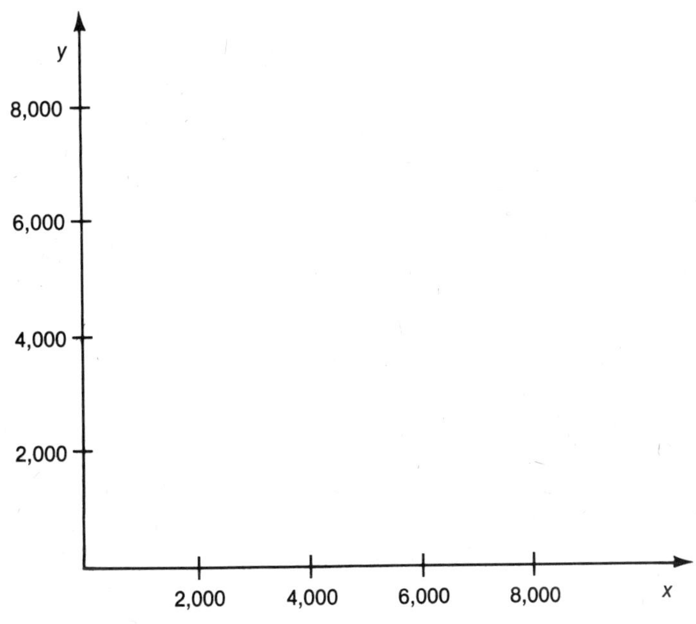

(c) ______________________________

____

____

____

Answers to True-False Questions

1. F Defining a managerial decision problem requires considerable managerial skill.
2. F These data must also be available in a timely manner.
3. F There can also be only two alternatives in a decision problem.
4. T
5. T
6. F These problems are specified in quantitative terms.
7. T
8. T
9. F It is harder to generate.
10. T
11. F Opportunity costs are just as important to consider as out-of-pocket costs.
12. F Fixed costs may be relevant; it depends on whether they make a difference when considering alternative possible actions in a decision problem.
13. F They have no bearing on the choice of action to be made.
14. T
15. F They often overlook or underweight opportunity costs.
16. T
17. T
18. F The question should be: "Which product gives the greatest contribution margin per unit of scarce resource?"
19. T
20. T

Answers to Fill-in-the-Blank Questions

1. Qualitative characteristics
2. relevant
3. differ
4. Unique decisions
5. irrelevant
6. future, past
7. Repetitive decisions
8. Accuracy
9. Information overload
10. Sunk costs
11. differential
12. opportunity
13. no excess
14. unitized
15. avoidable
16. split-off
17. Sensitivity analysis
18. time value of money
19. Linear programming

Answers to Multiple-Choice Questions

1. (b) The scope of information in not a key characteristic in determining its usefulness for decision making.
2. (c) \$1,800 – \$1,500 = \$300; the \$2,000 book value of the old computer is irrelevant.
3. (b) Future costs or benefits that are identical across all decision alternatives are irrelevant.
4. (b) (\$15,000 – \$6,000) – \$5,000 = \$4,000 increase. The \$12,000 book value of obsolete inventory is irrelevant.
5. (a)
6. (c) \$7.80/.5 = \$15.60.
7. (a) [\$12 – (\$18 – \$11)] × 1,200 = \$6,000 increase.

Solutions to Exercises

13.1 The decision to drop Product Line X-50 will ultimately relate to the impact it will have on profitability, but only the costs that are relevant to this decision should be considered in evaluating this impact. By dropping Product X-50, it may be possible to avoid some fixed costs. For sake of discussion, suppose X-50 is dropped; if the fixed costs avoided exceed the loss in contribution margin from X-50, dropping the product line is the right decision. Alternatively, if the loss in contribution margin from X-50 is greater than the avoidable fixed costs associated with X-50, dropping the product line is the wrong decision. Thus, it is important to look beyond the bottom line of the income statement and make a careful analysis of the costs that relate to this decision.

13.2

(a)	Annual cost saving from not making component: 18,000 × \$17 =		\$306,000
	Annual cost of buying component on the outside: 18,000 × \$20 =		360,000
	Annual decrease in net income due to buying component outside		\$ (54,000)
(b)	Annual cost saving from not making component: 18,000 × \$17 =	\$306,000	
	Annual rent from machine	62,000	\$368,000
	Annual cost of buying component on the outside: 18,000 × \$20 =		360,000
	Annual increase in net income due to buying component outside		\$ 8,000

13.3 **(a)** Revenue from special order: 6,000 × $16 = $ 96,000

Revenue from special order: 6,000 × $16 =		$ 96,000
Incremental cost to fill special order: 6,000 × ($7 + $5) =		72,000
Increase in net income from accepting special order		$ 24,000

(b)

Revenue from special order: 12,000 ×$16 =		$192,000
Incremental cost to fill special order: 12,000 × ($7 + $5) =	$144,000	
Opportunity loss from not selling 2,000 pairs to regular customers: 2,000 × ($22 – 12) =	20,000	164,000
Increase in net income from accepting special offer		$ 28,000

13.4 Product *H:*

Last year's contribution margin: $160,000 – $60,000 – $18,000 = $82,000

Last year's contribution-margin ratio: $82,000/$160,000 = 51.25%

Product *K:*

Last year's contribution margin: $240,000 – $100,000 – $50,000 = $90,000

Last year's contribution-margin ratio: $90,000/$240,000 = 37.5%

Incremental contribution margin from *H* if *K* is dropped: $160,000 × 0.1 × .5125 =	$ 8,200
Opportunity cost due to contribution margin forgone by dropping *K:* $240,000 × .375 =	90,000
Decrease in annual net income due to dropping *K*	$ (81,800)

13.5 **(a)** Maximize $18x + 15y$

subject to $2x + 4y = 16{,}000$ (machining)

$.25x + .2y \leq 1{,}250$ (packing)

$x, y \geq 0$

(b)

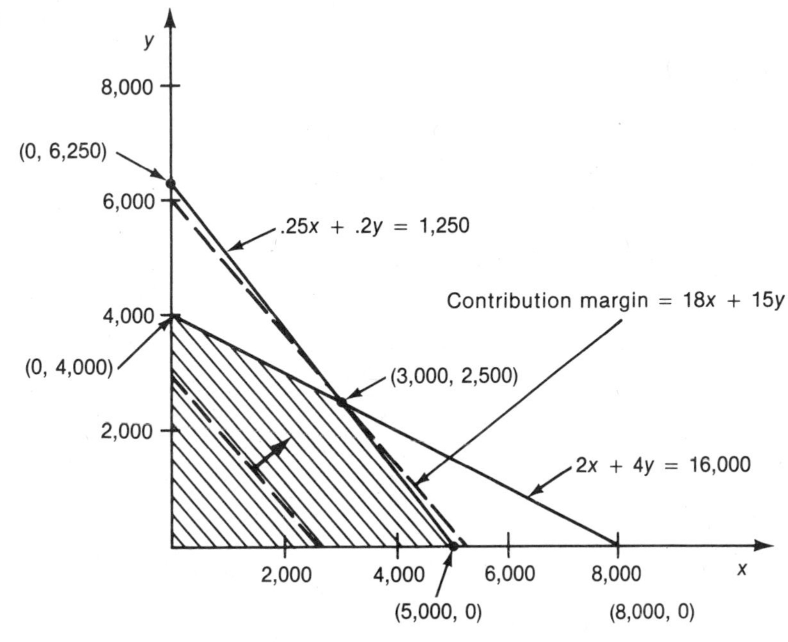

The feasible region is the shaded portion of the graph.

(c) The dashed line in the above graph is the contribution-margin line. Moving it upward as far as possible while still intersecting the feasible region leads to the optimal solution of $x = 3{,}000$ and $y = 2{,}500$. Total weekly contribution is maximized when 3,000 of *X* and 2,500 of *Y* are made and sold.

Chapter **14**

Cost Analysis and Pricing Decisions

CHAPTER OVERVIEW AND LEARNING OBJECTIVES

This chapter is concerned with the managerial decision problem of pricing the products or services that an organization offers for sale. After completing this chapter, you should understand:

1. The four major influences on pricing decisions
2. The profit-maximizing pricing model
3. How to set prices using cost-plus pricing formulas
4. How to determine prices using the time-and-material pricing method
5. The use of relevant costing in setting prices in special-order or competitive-bidding situations
6. The issues involved in the strategic pricing of new products
7. The role of activity-based costing in setting a target cost
8. How product-cost distortion can undermine a firm's pricing strategy
9. The legal restrictions on setting prices

AN OUTLINE FOR CHAPTER STUDY

A. The problem of setting prices in an organization is one of the most important and most difficult decision problems that must be resolved by management. Major influences that govern the setting of prices include:

   1. Customer demand. Discerning customer demand is a critically important and ongoing process. An organization must provide products or services to its customers at a price that they perceive is appropriate.
   2. Action of competitors. Management must keep a watchful eye on the prices charged by its competitors. When considering the reactions of competitors, as well as customers, it is very important to be sure that the product is properly defined. Defining a product too narrowly or too broadly can have a profound impact on marketing and pricing strategies.
   3. Costs. In most industries, both market forces and cost issues heavily influence prices. Prices determined by the market must also be constrained by the fact that costs must be covered in the long run. Prices based on costs are also constrained by the reactions of customers and competitors.
   4. Political, legal, and image-related issues. Laws generally prohibit an organization from discriminating against any of its customers in setting prices. Neither is it legal for firms to

collude in setting prices. Organizations must also take into account their public image and political overtones in the price-setting process.

B. Generally speaking, as the price of a product or service decreases, demand increases, and vice versa. Frequently in economics the relationships between revenue, cost, and demand are depicted by the following curves or graphs:

1. The total revenue curve gives total sales revenue as a function of quantity sold. Often revenue increases at a declining rate when quantity sold increases.
2. The demand curve (also called the average revenue curve) shows sales price as a function of quantity sold.
3. The marginal revenue curve portrays the change in total revenue that occurs when a change takes place in quantity sold.
4. The total cost curve gives total cost as a function of quantity made and sold each period. Often this curve first increases at a decreasing rate and then increases at an increasing rate when quantity produced and sold increases.
5. The marginal cost curve depicts the change in total cost that accompanies a change in quantity produced and sold.

With these various curves, one can show that profit (revenue less cost) is maximized at the quantity-sold level where marginal cost is equal to marginal revenue; that is, profit is maximized at the point where the marginal cost curve intersects the marginal revenue curve. The price corresponding to this level of units sold is called the profit-maximizing price. Finding the price by employing these curves and functions is referred to as using the profit-maximizing model.

C. The impact of price changes on sales volume is called price elasticity. Demand is elastic if price increases have a large negative impact on sales volume, and vice versa. Demand is inelastic if price changes have virtually no impact on sales quantity. Cross-elasticity pertains to the extent to which a change in a product's price affects the demand for other substitute products.

D. Some limitations of the profit-maximization model include the following:

1. An organization's demand and marginal revenue curves are difficult to discern with precision.
2. The marginal revenue–marginal cost model is not valid for all forms of market organization. In an oligopolistic market, in which a few sellers compete among themselves, this model is not appropriate.
3. It is often very difficult to measure marginal cost. To do so may be very costly.

Most managers make pricing decisions based on a combination of economic considerations and product-cost information. However, the marginal cost–marginal revenue approach to pricing provides a useful conceptual basis with which to analyze the pricing decision problem.

E. Most managers base prices on product costs to some extent. Reasons for this include the following:

1. Since most firms sell many products, managers need a quick, straightforward method for pricing, and this can be found in cost-based pricing.
2. Costs give managers a place to start in forming prices even though eventually the market may determine the final price of a product.
3. The cost of a product or service is a floor below which a price cannot be set in the long run.

F. Cost-based pricing formulas generally have the following form:

$$\text{Price} = \text{Cost} + \text{Markup percentage} \times \text{Cost}$$

Various definitions (or bases) of cost are used in this formula. They include:

1. Variable manufacturing costs. This approach bases the price only on production costs that are variable. In this case the markup percentage must be large enough to cover all other costs plus the desired profit margin.
2. Absorption manufacturing cost. Reasons given for the use of this cost are:
    - **a.** In the long run, all costs and a normal profit margin must be covered by the price.
    - **b.** It provides a justifiable price that tends to be perceived as equitable by all parties involved.

c. It gives some understanding of how competitors with like cost structures set prices.
d. Information on absorption costs is readily available from the firm's cost-accounting system.

The main disadvantage of this cost definition for pricing purposes is that it obscures the cost behavior patterns of the firm.

3. Total variable costs. This cost definition has the following advantages:

   a. Variable-cost data do not obscure the distinction between fixed and variable costs.
   b. Variable-cost data do not require allocation of common fixed costs to individual product lines.
   c. Variable-cost data are exactly the type of information managers need when facing certain decision problems such as the special-order decision problem.

   The chief disadvantage of using variable cost as the cost definition in price setting is that managers may tend to set prices too low for the firm to cover its fixed costs.

4. Total cost. A key advantage of using total cost as a cost definition is that all costs are highlighted in the price calculation.

G. Whichever definition of cost is used in the cost-based price formula, it is still necessary to determine how the markup percentage is to be computed. A common approach to determining the markup percentage is to base profit on the firm's target return on investment (ROI). The general formula for computing the markup percentage in cost-based pricing formulas is:

$$\text{Markup percentage based on given cost base} = \frac{\text{Profit needed for target ROI} + \text{Total annual cost not included in cost base}}{\text{Annual volume} \times \text{Given cost base per unit}}$$

H. The time-and-material pricing approach to setting prices involves determining one charge for labor used on a job and another charge for the materials used on that job. The labor charge includes the direct cost of the employee's time plus a charge to cover various overhead costs. The charge for materials includes the direct cost of materials together with a charge for material handling and storage. This approach to setting prices is often used in organizations such as construction companies, repair shops, and professional firms. Formulas that can be used for computing charges are as follows:

$$\text{Time charges} = \text{Hourly labor cost} + \frac{\text{Annual overhead except matl. handling and storage}}{\text{Annual labor hours}} + \text{Hourly charge to cover profit margin}$$

$$\text{Material charges} = \text{Matl. cost incurred on job} + \left(\text{Matl. cost incurred on job} \times \frac{\text{Matl. handling and storage costs}}{\text{Annual cost of materials used on all jobs}}\right)$$

I. Under competitive bidding, at least two firms submit sealed bids (prices) on products or services to a potential buyer. There is a trade-off between bidding low to get the contract and bidding high in order to make a good profit. When a firm has excess capacity, a bid that covers the incremental costs that would be incurred because of the job will contribute to the firm's fixed costs and profit. However, if the firm has no excess capacity, then the bid amount should cover not only the incremental costs of the job, but also a charge that reflects the opportunity cost of using limited capacity on that job. Other issues, such as the promotional benefits of getting the bid and the likelihood of getting the bid in the competitive environment, must also be considered in setting the price for the bid. The special-order problem discussed in the preceding chapter is very similar to the bid-pricing problem. Both situations involve the analysis of relevant costs for the order or the contract.

J. Pricing a new product is much more difficult than pricing a mature product because of uncertainties about the new product. One approach to pricing a new product is called skimming pricing; in this approach the price is set high to reap short-term profits from the product. This approach is often used for unique products. Another approach is called penetration pricing; this strategy involves setting a relatively low initial price with the hope of penetrating and quickly gaining a large share of the market. The choice between these two pricing strategies depends on the nature of the new product and involves a trade-off of volume versus price.

K. Target costing involves starting first with a price at which market research indicates a new product will sell and then computing a cost for which the product must be made to yield a desired profit margin. This cost becomes the target cost for producing the product. The firm then seeks to achieve this cost level in making the new product.

L. Activity-based costing can prove helpful in achieving a product's target cost. ABC enables product designers to break down the cost of producing a new product into its component activity costs. Then designers can seek cost improvement in the component activities to bring a new product's projected cost into line with its target cost. Additionally, ABC can help eliminate product-cost distortion because it measures the extent to which each product line drives production costs in a firm that makes a variety of products. Traditional volume-based product costing does not provide these more accurate cost measures. Traditional product costing fails to capture the cost implications of product diversity.

M. Antitrust laws which prohibit price discrimination include the Robinson-Patman Act. Different prices for different customers for the same product are unlawful unless there are justifiable reasons for these different prices. Also, it is illegal to use predatory pricing. This consists of dropping prices to broaden demand with the intent of later restricting supply and then raising the price.

KEY TERMS

Average revenue curve 721
Competitive bidding 735
Cost-plus pricing 727
Cross-elasticity 726
Demand curve (average revenue curve) 721
Marginal cost curve 724
Marginal revenue curve 721
Oligopolistic market 726
Penetration pricing 739
Predatory pricing 742
Price discrimination 741
Price elasticity 725
Price taker 720
Return-on-investment pricing 730
Skimming pricing 738
Target cost 739
Target costing 739
Time-and-material pricing 733
Total cost curve 723
Total revenue curve 721

SELF-EVALUATION QUESTIONS AND ANSWERS

True-False Questions

_____ **1.** Discerning customer demand is very important in setting prices of products.

_____ **2.** Political considerations are never relevant in setting prices.

_____ **3.** As the price of a product or service increases, demand increases, generally speaking.

_____ **4.** The demand curve is the same as the average revenue curve.

_____ **5.** The law does not prohibit companies from discriminating among their customers in setting prices.

_____ **6.** Understanding cost behavior is important in pricing decisions.

_____ **7.** In setting the price of a product, managers must be very concerned about the prices that competitors charge for the same type of product.

_____ **8.** The total revenue curve gives total sales revenue as a function of price.

_____ **9.** In the profit-maximizing price model, the profit-maximizing price corresponds to the demand level where the marginal cost curve intersects the marginal revenue curve.

_____ **10.** Measuring price elasticity is important in economics, but not in market research.

_____ **11.** In most industries, both market forces and cost considerations heavily influence prices.

_____ 12. In the long run, price must cover all costs and a normal profit margin.

_____ 13. A disadvantage of variable-cost pricing is that it does not require the allocation of common fixed costs to individual product lines.

_____ 14. The profit-maximizing pricing model is not valid for all forms of market organization.

_____ 15. Consideration of a company's public image is not relevant in setting prices.

_____ 16. Demand is elastic if a price increase has a positive impact on sales volume, and vice versa.

_____ 17. In time-and-material pricing the material charge does not include any cost for material handling and storage.

_____ 18. When a firm has no excess capacity, the bid amount in competitive bidding should include both the incremental costs of the job and a charge that reflects the opportunity cost of using limited excess capacity on that job.

_____ 19. Traditional product costing is effective in capturing the cost implications of product diversity.

Fill-in-the-Blank Questions

1. If a company's prices are totally determined by the market, the company is known as a(n) ________________.
2. The ________________ curve shows the relationship between sales price and the quantity of units sold.
3. The ________________ curve shows the change in total revenue that accompanies a change in quantity sold.
4. The ________________ curve shows the relationship between total cost and quantity produced and sold each month.
5. The ________________ curve depicts the change in total cost that accompanies a change in quantity produced and sold.
6. In the profit-maximizing pricing model, profit is maximized when ________________ equals ________________.
7. The impact of price changes on sales volume is called ________________.
8. In ________________ pricing, price equals the sum of cost and a markup.
9. ________________ refers to the extent to which a change in a product's price affects the demand for other substitute products.
10. A common approach to determining the profit margin in cost-plus pricing is to base profit on the firm's target ________________.
11. ________________ pricing involves determining a charge for labor used on a job and a charge for the materials used on that job.
12. Demand is ________________ if price changes have little or no impact on sales quantity.
13. In ________________, at least two companies submit sealed bids for a product or service to a potential buyer.
14. ________________ pricing involves setting the initial price of a new product high, so as to reap good short-term profits from that product.
15. ________________ pricing involves setting an initial price low in order to gain a large market share quickly.
16. Basing a product cost on a price determined by market research and then trying to make the product at that cost is called ________________ costing.
17. U.S. antitrust laws prohibit price ________________.
18. Cutting prices to broaden demand with the intention of subsequently restricting supply and raising these prices is called the illegal practice of ________________ pricing.

Multiple-Choice Questions

_____ 1. Consider the following two statements about the profit-maximizing pricing model:

I. Demand and marginal revenue curves are difficult to discern with precision, generally speaking.

II. Marginal cost is usually difficult to measure from data available in a firm's cost accounting system.

Which is (are) true?

(a) Only I
(b) Only II
(c) Both I and II
(d) Neither I nor II

_____ 2. Most managers base prices on product costs to some extent because

(a) most companies sell only one product.
(b) cost provides the final word in setting prices.
(c) the cost of a product is a floor below which prices cannot be set in the long run.
(d) methods of computing cost-based prices require much effort and time, so it is important to use the output of this work.

_____ 3. A firm makes and sells only one product, and its annual target ROI is 25 percent. The average invested capital is $400,000. The total cost of one unit of product is $1,250, and the firm expects to sell 500 units next year. The markup percentage of this unit next year, based on total cost and target ROI, should be:

(a) 16.00 percent.
(b) 20.00 percent.
(c) 18.00 percent.
(d) 17.58 percent.

_____ 4. Which of the following would *not* typically be used as a cost base in cost-plus pricing techniques?

(a) Variable manufacturing cost
(b) Variable selling and administrative cost
(c) Total cost
(d) Absorption manufacturing cost

_____ 5. Consider the following two statements about absorption-cost pricing:

I. The main disadvantage is that it obscures the cost-behavior pattern of the firm.

II. The information needed for this pricing method is not readily available from a firm's cost-accounting system.

Which is (are) true?

(a) Only I
(b) Only II
(c) Both I and II
(d) Neither I nor II

_____ 6. The Whitney Company uses time-and-material pricing. The Repair Department had the following data:

Labor rate per hour including benefits	$25.00
Annual labor hours	12,000
Annual overhead costs	
Material handling and storage	$48,000
Other overhead costs	$240,000
Cost of materials used per year	$800,000
Hourly charge to cover profit margin	$10.00

The time charge per hour should be

(a) $59.
(b) $55.
(c) $35.
(d) $25.

_____ **7.** Refer again to the Whitney Company in Question 6. The amount needed to be added to each dollar of material cost to obtain the material charge is
(a) $.06.
(b) $.20.
(c) $.24.
(d) $.32.

Exercises

14.1 The Pinkerton Company sells a unique product in the northeastern United States. The marketing and accounting departments have assembled the following data:

Case	Monthly Sales Demand	Unit Sales Price	Average Cost
1	50	$800	$600
2	100	700	550
3	150	600	525
4	200	500	575

Required:

(a) For each case, compute the monthly profit from this product. Base your calculations on the method used in panel (c) of Exhibits 14-1, 14-2, and 14-3 in the text.
(b) Suppose that the price of this product is to be based on the profit-maximization pricing model and only one of the four given prices is to be chosen. Which one should be selected? Why?

Solution Space for Exercise 14.1:

(a)

Case	Sales Demand	Unit Sales Price	Average Cost	Total Revenue	Total Cost	Profit
1						
2						
3						
4						

(b) ______________________________

14.2 The Ostrander Company has the following data concerning a deluxe computer table which it manufactures:

Variable manufacturing cost	$40
Applied fixed manufacturing cost	15
Variable selling and administrative cost	7
Allocated fixed selling and administrative cost	12

Required:

Develop a cost-plus pricing formula that will yield a price of $100 for this computer table for each of the following cost bases:

(a) Variable manufacturing cost
(b) Absorption manufacturing cost
(c) Total variable cost
(d) Total cost

Solution Space for Exercise 14.2:

(a) ____

____

(b) ____

____

(c) ____

____

(d) ____

____

14.3 The McClure Company has the following annual budget data for a product called a hipple that it makes and sells at its Hinesville plant:

Units sold	600
Variable costs	$186,000
Fixed costs	$174,000

The invested capital at Hinesville is $500,000. Management desires an annual ROI from the production and sale of hipples to be 15 percent.

Required:

Compute the markup percentage using each of the following cost bases in order to reflect management's desired ROI:

(a) Total cost
(b) Total variable cost

Solution Space for Exercise 14.3:

____

(a) ____

(b) ____

14.4 Clark's Computer Repairs is a small firm that repairs microcomputers and minicomputers. The firm uses time-and-material pricing. The following data have been assembled for 19x8:

Labor rate per hour including benefits	$20
Annual labor hours	8,000 hours
Yearly overhead costs	
Material handling and storage	$30,000
Other overhead costs	$125,000
Yearly cost of materials used	$200,000
Hourly charge to cover profit margin	$8

Required:

(a) Find formulas for Clark's
  (1) time charges
  (2) material charges

(b) Suppose Clark's receives a request for computer repair that requires an estimated 120 hours of labor and $8,000 of material cost. What price should be assigned to this job?

Solution Space for Exercise 14.4:

(a) (1) ______________________________

(2) ______________________________

(b) ______________________________

14.5 Reddy Industries has just received a special request from the Dolby Company in France for 5,000 gearboxes at a price of $45 each, FOB shipping point. Ordinarily, Reddy sells these gearboxes through its regular channels at $58 each. The managerial accountant at Reddy has done a careful relevant costing analysis of this situation and has found that Reddy can afford to sell these gearboxes at a unit price of $53.20 and still break even. Also, she has learned that there is sufficient production capacity to provide these 5,000 gearboxes to Dolby without interfering with production for regular customers.

Required:

Write a paragraph identifying the factors, besides price, that Reddy should consider before offering to fill the special order for Dolby.

Solution Space for Exercise 14.5:

Answers to True-False Questions

1. T
2. F Sometimes political considerations have a bearing on price setting.
3. F Generally, as the price increases, demand will decrease.
4. T
5. F Laws do prohibit price discrimination; the Robinson-Patman Act is an example of such a law.
6. T
7. T
8. F This curve gives total sales revenue as a function of quantity sold.
9. T
10. F It is also important in market research.
11. T
12. T
13. F This is an advantage, since individual product lines are not charged with arbitrarily allocated common costs.
14. T
15. F A consideration of a company's public image is very relevant in price setting.
16. F Demand is elastic if a price increase has a negative impact on sales volume.
17. F It does include a charge for material handling and storage.
18. T
19. F It fails to capture the cost implications of product diversity.

Answers to Fill-in-the-Blank Questions

1. price taker
2. demand
3. marginal revenue
4. total cost
5. marginal cost
6. marginal revenue, marginal cost
7. price elasticity
8. cost-plus
9. Cross-elasticity
10. return on investment
11. Time-and-material
12. inelastic
13. competitive bidding
14. Skimming
15. Penetration
16. target
17. discrimination
18. predatory

Answers to Multiple-Choice Questions

1. (c)
2. (c) Answers (a), (b), and (d) are untrue.
3. (a) $100,000/(500 × $1,250) = 16%.
4. (b) The answers in the other choices are all used as a cost base.
5. (a) Absorption-cost pricing data are readily available from a firm's cost-accounting system.
6. (b) $25 + $240,000/12,000 + $10 = $55.
7. (a) $48,000/$800,000 = $.06.

Solutions to Exercises

14.1 (a)

Case	Sales Demand	Unit Sales Price	Average Cost	Total Revenue	Total Cost	Profit
1	50	$800	$600	$ 40,000	$ 30,000	$ 10,000
2	100	700	550	70,000	55,000	15,000
3	150	600	525	90,000	78,750	11,250
4	200	500	575	100,000	115,000	(15,000)

(b) The price should be $700, because profit is maximized at that price.

14.2 In order to yield a price of $100, we must find the markup percentage corresponding to each cost base. Since Price = Cost + Markup percentage × Cost, we have Markup percentage = (Price − Cost)/Cost.

(a) Variable manufacturing cost per unit = $40
Markup percentage = ($100 − $40)/40 = 150%

(b) Absorption manufacturing cost per unit = $55
Markup percentage = ($100 − $55)/55 = 81.8%

(c) Total variable cost per unit = $47
Markup percentage = ($100 − $47)/47 = 112.8%

(d) Total cost per unit = $74
Markup percentage = ($100 − $74)/74 = 35.1%

14.3 Target profit = .15 × $500,000 = $75,000

(a) Markup percentage = $75,000/(600 × $600) = 20.83%

(b) Markup percentage = ($75,000 + $174,000)/(600 × $310) = 133.87%

14.4 (a) (1) Time charge = $20 + $125,000/8,000 + $8 = $43.62/hour

(2) Material charge = Material cost for job + Material cost for job × $30,000/$200,000 = Material cost for job + 15% × Material cost for job

(b) Price = (120 × $43.63) + ($8,000 × $1.15) = $14,435.60

14.5 Before agreeing to fill Dolby's special request, the management of Reddy should consider the possible impact that this sale will have on future sales to Dolby and how it might affect Reddy's future involvement in the international marketplace. Reddy should also be cognizant of the effect this special sale would have on sales to its regular customers. In addition, the management of Reddy ought to consider the possible tax implications of this sale. Since there is enough extra productive capacity for this special order, Reddy should analyze the effect of this special order on equipment maintenance.

Chapter 15

Capital Expenditure Decisions: An Introduction

CHAPTER OVERVIEW AND LEARNING OBJECTIVES

This chapter introduces a class of managerial decision-making problems called capital-budgeting problems. These problems involve the analysis of long-term investments—expenditures of capital for assets having lives of more than a year. After completing this chapter, you should understand:

1. The importance of the time value of money in capital-budgeting decisions
2. How to compute the future value and present value of cash flows occurring over time
3. The net-present-value method and the internal-rate-of-return method of evaluating investment proposals—how to use them, how to compare them, and their underlying assumptions
4. The total-cost approach and the incremental-cost approach to evaluating investment proposals
5. The nature of the capital-budgeting approval process and a postaudit
6. The conflict between discounted-cash-flow analysis for approving capital projects and accrual accounting for periodic performance evaluation
7. The process of justifying investments in advanced manufacturing technology

AN OUTLINE FOR CHAPTER STUDY

A. Capital-budgeting decisions are managerial decisions involving cash inflows and outflows for a period of more than one year. Two types of capital-budgeting decisions are as follows:

1. Accept-or-reject decisions. These are decisions where a manager must decide whether or not to undertake a given investment project.
2. Capital-rationing decisions. These are decisions where a manager must choose among several acceptable investment projects in the face of limited funds for investment purposes.

The focus of capital-budgeting decisions is on specific programs or projects.

B. The time value of money is the key concept in analyzing capital-budgeting decision problems. The idea behind the time value of money is that a dollar at some future time is worth more than a dollar right now; this is because having a dollar in your possession now means that you can invest it or let others use it for a charge or a fee. This charge or fee is called interest, and so money can earn extra value over time. In fact, not only do invested funds earn interest, the earned interest can earn more interest over time. This is called compound interest, and this concept provides the basis for most of the computations in capital-budgeting analysis. The invested amount is called the principal. For convenience, in capital-budgeting analysis a given time horizon is broken down into time periods, usually years. The rate at which interest is compounded is usually assumed to be constant in the analysis.

C. Suppose that a given amount P (the principal) is invested now at the (compound) interest rate r per year for n years. Then the value of the investment n years from now is given by the formula

$$F_n = P(1 + r)^n$$

The expression $(1 + r)^n$ is called the accumulation factor. Table I in the appendix of this chapter in the text gives values of this accumulation factor for selected values of n and r. Often it is important to know how much, call it P, must be invested now to yield an amount F_n at the annual interest rate r by the end of n years from now. The formula for finding P in this case is:

$$P = F_n(1 + r)^{-n} = \frac{F_n}{(1 + r)^n}$$

The expression $(1 + r)^{-n}$ or $1/(1 + r)^n$ is called the discount factor, and P is called the present value of the investment; in this type of problem r is referred to as the discount rate. Table III in the appendix of this chapter in the text gives values of the discount factor for selected values of n and r.

D. A series of payments over time is called an annuity. Suppose that instead of a single amount invested now (as in the previous section), a series of uniform amounts of W dollars each are invested at the end of each year for the next n years at the annual compound interest rate r. Then the value of this investment n years from now is given by the formula

$$F_n = \frac{W[(1 + r)^n - 1]}{r}$$

The expression $[(1 + r)^n - 1]/r$ is called the annuity accumulation factor. Table II in the appendix of this chapter in the text gives values of this annuity accumulation factor for various values of n and r. Now consider the opposite type of situation. Suppose that P dollars invested now will yield a series of uniform payments of W dollars each at the end of each year for the next n years at the annual interest rate r. The amount P, called the present value of the investment, can be computed from the formula

$$P = \frac{W[1 - (1 + r)^{-n}]}{r}$$

The expression $[1 - (1 + r)^{-n}]/r$ is called the annuity discount factor. Table IV in the appendix of this chapter in the text gives values of this annuity discount factor for selected values of n and r.

E. Discounted-cash-flow analysis of capital investment decisions takes into account the time value of money. Two methods of discounted-cash-flow analysis are as follows:

1. Net-present-value (NPV) method. The steps for applying this method to an investment proposal can be summarized as follows:

   a. Prepare a table showing the cash flows over the life of the investment.
   b. Compute the present value of each cash flow using a proper discount rate. (This rate is often called the hurdle rate or the minimum desired rate of return or the cost of capital.) Cash inflows should be treated as positive and cash outflows as negative. Use Table II or Table IV.
   c. Compute the algebraic sum of the present values of all flows. This is called the net present value of the investment. Another way to say this is that the net present value equals the present value of all future flows less the net initial outlay now.
   d. If the NPV is positive, accept the investment proposal on economic grounds; otherwise, do no accept it.

2. Internal-rate-of-return (IRR) method. This method consists of finding the interest rate that makes the net present value of an investment proposal zero. This interest rate is called the investment's internal rate of return or time-adjusted rate of return. The meaning of this

interest rate is that the initial outlay invested at this rate would yield all the future cash flows of this investment at their specified points in time. The internal rate of return is usually calculated by trial and error or interpolating with the annuity accumulation factors in Table IV. A computer is often employed to find the internal rate of return by a trial-and-error method. The decision rule for this method is to accept the investment proposal if the internal rate of return exceeds the organization's hurdle rate (minimum desired rate of return, cost of capital); otherwise, do not accept the investment proposal.

F. The following assumptions underlie discounted-cash-flow analysis:

1. All cash flows are treated as though they occur at the end of the year for the sake of simplicity.
2. The cash flows are treated as if they were known with certainty.
3. Each cash flow is viewed as if it were immediately reinvested at the same interest rate used in the analysis.
4. The cash flows are treated as if they are made in a perfect capital market where money is borrowed or lent at the interest rate given in the analysis.

G. Additional observations concerning discounted-cash-flow analysis are as follows:

1. The net-present-value method has two advantages over the internal-rate-of-return method:
   - **a.** It is easier to compute when a sophisticated computer or calculator is unavailable.
   - **b.** The analyst can adjust for risk considerations. Cash flows that are quite uncertain can be compensated for to some extent by using higher hurdle rates. Sometimes sensitivity analysis is used.
2. The choice of hurdle rate is a complex problem. It is determined by management based on the investment opportunity rate—the rate the firm can earn on its best alternative investments of equivalent risk. Some firms use the cost of capital as the interest rate in discounted-cash-flow analysis; the cost of capital should reflect the cost of raising capital from all the sources used by the firm.
3. Periodic depreciation charges are not cash flows, and therefore are not themselves used in discounted-cash-flow analysis. The tax implications of depreciation deductions do have an impact on discounted-cash-flow analysis. (This is considered in Chapter 16.)
4. The managerial accountant plays an important role in discounted-cash-flow analysis by helping to determine accurate cash flow projections.

H. When comparing two competing investment proposals, we are dealing with a relevant costing problem similar to those in Chapter 13, except that now we consider the time value of money. Two equivalent approaches using the net-present-value method are available in making this comparison of two competing investment proposals:

1. The total-cost approach. In this approach all the relevant cash flows over time for each alternative are considered. The net present value of each alternative is considered. Assuming that each net present value represents cost (is negative reflecting outflows), the alternative having the least negative (that is, closest to zero) net present value is the best alternative on economic grounds. This is equivalent to saying that the best alternative is the one that minimizes the net present value of the costs incurred in the investment project.
2. Incremental-cost approach. For each time period over the lives of the two investment proposals (assuming that they have equal lives), the difference between the net flows of each investment proposal is computed. These differences (computed in the same order) are then discounted at the hurdle rate to compute the net present value of the differences. Assuming that these differences are computed in the order of investment proposal 1 less investment proposal 2, proposal 1 is the best alternative if the net present value of the differences is positive; if it is negative, proposal 2 is best; if it is zero, management can be indifferent to the two proposals on economic grounds.

I. Most organizations have an elaborate approval process for proposed investment projects. Many organizations have a capital-budgeting staff whose function it is to analyze all capital-budgeting proposals. Most organizations systematically follow up on accepted investment projects to see how they turn out; this process is called a postaudit.

J. There is a conflict between discounted-cash-flow methods and accrual accounting performance-evaluation methods. Discounted-cash-flow methods put the focus on cash flows, whereas accrual accounting methods emphasize revenues and expenses including depreciation. One possible result of this conflict is that a manager may reject a positive-NPV investment proposal because it unfavorably impacts on accrual accounting–based performance measures. This conflict could be resolved to some extent by deemphasizing the accrual accounting–based performance measures.

K. Some difficulties in applying NPV methods in advanced manufacturing systems include the following:

1. The hurdle rates may be set too high.
2. Time horizons may be too short.
3. There may be a bias toward investments with shorted lives, whereas high-technology investments usually require long time horizons.
4. There is greater uncertainty about operating cash flows.
5. Some benefits of advanced manufacturing systems are difficult to quantify. Some of these benefits include greater production flexibility, shorter cycle times and reduced lead times, reduction of non-value-added costs, reduced inventory levels, lower floor-space requirements, and higher product quality.

KEY TERMS

Acceptance or rejection decision 766
Accumulation factor 768
Annuity 770
Capital-budgeting decision 765
Capital-rationing decision 766
Compound interest 768
Discount rate 770
Discounted-cash-flow analysis 773
Future value 768
Hurdle rate (or minimum desired rate of return) 773
Incremental-cost approach 784
Internal rate of return (or time-adjusted rate of return) 774
Investment opportunity rate 780
Net present value 774
Postaudit (or reappraisal) 786
Present value 769
Principal 767

SELF-EVALUATION QUESTIONS AND ANSWERS

True-False Questions

_____ **1.** It is worth more to a manager to have a dollar one year from now than it is to have it now.

_____ **2.** If \$2,000 is invested for 5 years at the annual compound interest rate of 10 percent, then at the end of 5 years this investment will be worth \$3,222.

_____ **3.** If the net present value of a single investment proposal is negative, then the investment should be accepted.

_____ **4.** The internal rate of return is the same as the hurdle rate.

_____ **5.** The reason for purchasing an asset is an expectation that it will provide benefits in the future.

_____ **6.** If the cash flows from an investment are uneven, it is not possible to calculate the investment's internal rate of return.

_____ **7.** If an investment analysis is carried out by hand, it is easier to compute a project's NPV than its IRR.

_____ **8.** Capital-budgeting problems tend to focus on specific projects or programs.

_____ **9.** If \$4,000 is to be received at the end of 5 years from now and money is worth 10 percent per year, compounded annually, the present value of this payment is \$2,843.60.

_____ **10.** If the internal rate of return of an investment exceeds the organization's cost of capital, then the investment should be rejected.

_____ **11.** An advantage of the IRR method is that the analyst can adjust for risk considerations.

_____ **12.** Discounted-cash-flow analyses treat cash flows of an investment project as though they were known with certainty.

_____ 13. The internal rate of return for an investment is the interest rate that makes the net present value of the investment equal to zero.

_____ 14. Periodic depreciation charges are cash flows.

_____ 15. Both the NPV method and the IRR method make use of a hurdle rate.

_____ 16. Discounted-cash-flow analysis assumes an imperfect capital market.

_____ 17. Most organizations have an elaborate approval process for proposed investment projects.

_____ 18. The NPV method can be applied without difficulty to advanced manufacturing systems.

Fill-in-the-Blank Questions

1. Decisions involving cash flows beyond the current year are called _______________ decisions.
2. The fundamental concept in a capital-budgeting decision analysis is the _______________.
3. _______________ is money paid for the use of an invested sum of money and previously earned interest.
4. Decisions where managers must decide which of several worthwhile projects should be adopted in the face of limited funds are called _______________ decisions.
5. If money is worth 12 percent per year, compounded annually, then $800 now is equivalent economically to the amount _______________ two years from now.
6. A series of payments is called a(n) _______________.
7. Decisions that occur when managers must decide whether or not they should undertake a given investment project are called _______________ decisions.
8. The interest rate that makes the net present value of an investment zero is called the _______________.
9. The hurdle rate used in discounted-cash-flow analysis is determined by management based on the _______________ rate.
10. The first step in any investment analysis is to determine the cash flows that are _______________ to the analysis.
11. The total-cost approach and the incremental-cost approach to comparing two competing investment proposals using discounted-cash-flow analysis yield _______________ conclusions.
12. The systematic follow-up on accepted projects to see how they turn out in the capital budgeting process is called a(n) _______________.
13. Discounted-cash-flow methods of investment decision making put the focus on _______________.
14. Accrual accounting methods of evaluating periodic performance put the focus on _______________.

Multiple-Choice Questions

_____ 1. John Harris received four annual payments of $3,000 each from an investment that was made 4 years ago. The interest rate was 18 percent. The original investment 4 years ago was
   (a) $8,070.
   (b) $12,000.
   (c) $9,810.
   (d) $2,154.

_____ 2. Which of the following is *not* a name for the interest rate used in the net-present-value method?
   (a) Hurdle rate
   (b) External rate of return
   (c) Discount rate
   (d) Cost of capital

_____ **3.** Mary Jackson invested $6,000 at the end of each year for the past 7 years, the last payment being made today. Her money earned compound interest at 14 percent per year. The value of her investment today is
(a) $25,728.
(b) $64,380.
(c) $59,640.
(d) $42,000.

_____ **4.** If $16,980 is invested now and returns annual payments of $3,000 for each of the next 12 years, the internal rate of return of this investment is
(a) 10 percent.
(b) 12 percent.
(c) 14 percent.
(d) 16 percent.

_____ **5.** For a capital investment proposal to be accepted, the expected future benefits must be sufficient for the purchaser to
I. recover the investment.
II. earn a return on the investment which is at least the cost of acquiring capital.
Which is (are) correct?
(a) Only I
(b) Only II
(c) Both I and II
(d) Neither I nor II

_____ **6.** Techniques used in practice to analyze investment proposals for which the cash-flow projections are very uncertain are
I. increasing the hurdle rate.
II. using sensitivity analysis.
Which is (are) correct?
(a) Only I
(b) Only II
(c) Both I and II
(d) Neither I nor II

_____ **7.** A cost performance reporting system used to help control projects would *not* collect information on
(a) the actual cost incurred on the project to date.
(b) the actual cost of work scheduled to date.
(c) the budgeted cost of work scheduled to date.
(d) the budgeted cost of work actually performed to date.

_____ **8.** Which of the following is *not* a difficulty in applying the net-present-value approach in a computer-integrated manufacturing investment decision?
(a) Hurdle rates may be set too low.
(b) Time horizons may be too short.
(c) There is greater uncertainty about operating cash flows.
(d) Benefits that are difficult to quantify are excluded.

Exercises

15.1 Given the following three independent sets of data:

	Set 1	Set 2	Set 3
Initial investment	$80,000	?	$22,918
Yearly cash inflow	$25,000	$14,000	$7,000
Hurdle rate	12%	20%	?
Net present value	?	$8,718	0
Life of investment in years	6	8	5

Required:

- **(a)** Find the items corresponding to the question marks in the given data sets.
- **(b)** What special name is given to the interest rate found in part (a) for data set 3?

Solution Space for Exercise 15.1:

(a) Set 1: ______________________________

____

Set 2: ______________________________

____

Set 3: ______________________________

____

(b) ______________________________

15.2 The Clifton Springs Landfill is interested in buying a new bulldozer. Two models are available that would adequately meet the needs of the landfill. Model A would cost $75,000 and have annual operating costs of $6,000. Model B would cost $90,000 and have annual operating costs of $4,000. Both models would have a useful life of 10 years and no salvage value at the end of the useful life. The landfill has an 8 percent cost of capital. An existing old bulldozer can be traded in on either model for $3,000.

Required:

Employ the net-present-value method to find out which bulldozer model should be bought using

- **(a)** the total-cost approach.
- **(b)** the incremental-cost approach.

Solution Space for Exercise 15.2:

(a) ______________________________

(b)

15.3 The Board of Education of the Summersville Central School has been told by its insurance company that the school's fire insurance premium will increase to $45,000 annually unless it replaces its existing sprinkler system, which is inadequate and not repairable. The board has ascertained that if it installs a new sprinkler system, which costs $135,600 and has a useful life of 10 years with no salvage value, the school will have to pay an annual fire insurance premium of only $21,000. The school's cost of capital is 10 percent.

Required:

(a) Determine whether the board should invest in the new sprinkler system using the internal-rate-of-return method.

(b) Compute the unrecovered investment amount at the end of the first, second, and third years of this investment. Make your calculations similar to those used in Exhibit 15-7 in the text and use the internal rate of return in your calculations.

Solution Space for Exercise 15.3:

(a)

(b)

	Year 1	Year 2	Year 3

15.4 Christopher Smallen is the director of grants at the National Ecological Foundation (NEF). In this position he is responsible for the final choices of grant proposals that have been submitted to him from an Awards Committee. There are currently two proposals, *A* and *B*, of essentially equal merit relative to all of the qualitative factors of concern, but the net present value (NPV) of the cost of Proposal *A* is $385,000 while that of Proposal *B* is $349,000. Only one of these proposals can be funded by the NEF. It is customarily the case that in a situation like this, the proposal having the smaller NPV would be selected. However, several of the costs used in developing the NPV of Proposal *A* are for expenses most likely to be paid to the Hemingway Construction Company, which is owned by Smallen's father-in-law. Smallen's father-in-law has told him, "Anytime I get business from one of your grant recipients, I want you to share in my good fortune." Smallen reasoned that since he knows that Hemingway will do "first-class" construction work, Proposal *A* will be funded.

Required:

Write a paragraph commenting on the unethical behavior of Christopher Smallen in this situation.

Solution Space for Exercise 15.4:

Answers to True-False Questions

1. F Quite the contrary! It is worth more to have a dollar now than one year from now, simply because money can earn interest over time.
2. T 2,000 × 1.61051.
3. F It should be rejected.
4. F The hurdle rate is the same as the minimum required rate of return or the cost of capital. The internal rate of return is that rate which makes the net present value equal to zero.
5. T
6. F A trial-and-error method can be used in this situation to calculate the internal rate of return.
7. T
8. T
9. F $4,000 × .621 = $2,484.
10. F The investment should be accepted.
11. F This is a direct advantage of the net-present-value method, not the IRR method.
12. T
13. T
14. F Depreciation charges themselves are not cash flows.
15. T
16. F It assumes a perfect capital market.
17. T
18. F A list of difficulties can be found in Section K of the outline for this chapter.

Answers to Fill-in-the-Blank Questions

1. capital-budgeting
2. time value of money
3. Compound interest
4. capital-rationing
5. $1,003.20 = $800 × 1.254
6. annuity
7. acceptance-or-rejection
8. internal rate of return (time-adjusted rate of return)
9. investment opportunity
10. relevant
11. equivalent
12. postaudit (reappraisal)
13. cash flows
14. accounting revenues and expenses

Answers to Multiple-Choice Questions

1. (a) $3,000 × 2.69 = $8,070.
2. (b)
3. (b) $6,000 × 10.73 = $64,380.
4. (c) $16,980/$3,000 = 5.66. From Table IV in Chapter 15 in the text, we see that the appropriate interest rate is 14 percent.
5. (c)
6. (c)
7. (b)
8. (a) The difficulty is that hurdle rates may be set too high.

Solutions to Exercises

15.1 **(a)** Set 1: $n = 6$ and $r = 12$ percent; from Table IV we obtain the annuity discount factor of 4.111. The net present value = $25,000 × 4.111 – $80,000 = $22,775.

Set 2: $n = 8$ and $r = 20$ percent; from Table IV the annuity discount factor is 3.837. Let P be the initial investment amount. Then $14,000 × 3.837 – P = $8,718, and so P = 45,000.

Set 3: $n = 5$ and r is to be determined. The annuity discount factor = 22,918/7,000 = 3.274. From Table IV with $n = 5$, we see that an annuity discount factor of 3.274 corresponds to $r = 16$ percent. No interpolation is needed in this case.

(b) Internal rate of return or time-adjusted rate of return.

15.2 **(a)** Total-cost approach:

	Model A	Model B
Trade-in value of old bulldozer now	$ 3,000	$ 3,000
Cost of new bulldozer now	(75,000)	(90,000)
Annual operating cost for 10 years	(6,000)	(4,000)

For this application $n = 10$ and $r = 8$ percent; from Table IV the annuity discount factor is 6.710.

Model A: NPV = –$6,000 × 6.710 – ($75,000 – $3,000) = $(112,260)

Model B: NPV = –$4,000 × 6.710 – ($90,000 – $3,000) = $(113,840)

Thus, Model A should be chosen on economic grounds; notice that the $3,000 salvage value of the old bulldozer is irrelevant.

(b) Incremental-cost approach:

Differences will be in the form: Model B less Model A.

	Difference
Trade-in value of old bulldozer now	$ 0
Cost of new bulldozer now	(15,000)
Annual operating costs for 10 years	2,000

As in part (a), the annuity discount factor is 6.710.

NPV of differences: $2,000 × 6.710 − $15,000 = $(1,580)

Hence, Model A should be chosen on economic grounds. Notice that $(113,840) − $(112,260) = $(1,580), showing that the total-cost approach and the incremental-cost approach give equivalent results.

15.3 **(a)** Here $n = 10$ and the annuity discount factor based on the given data is $135,600/($45,000 − $21,000) = 5.65. From Table IV with $n = 10$, this annuity discount factor corresponds to $r = 12$ percent (no interpolation needed), which is the internal rate of return. Since 12% > 10% (the cost of capital), the sprinkler system should be installed.

(b)

	Year 1	Year 2	Year 3
Unrecovered investment at the beginning of the year	$135,600	$127,872	$119,217
Cost savings during the year	24,000	24,000	24,000
Return on unrecovered investment	16,272	15,345	14,306
Recovery of investment during the year	7,728	8,655	9,694
Unrecovered investment at the end of the year	127,872	119,217	109,523

Note: For $r = 12\%$ and $n = 3$, the Table III factor is .712 and the Table IV factor is 2.402. As a check, observe that $109,523 × .712 + $24,000 × 2.402 = $135,628 (off from $135,600 due to rounding).

15.4 Smallen is digressing from the customary procedure in granting awards for reasons that are suspect. His professional behavior is unethical because he is not avoiding an actual or apparent conflict of interest. On top of this, it is reprehensible that Smallen should be influenced by the potential "kickbacks" he might receive from grant recipients' business received by Hemingway; this violates the Standards of Ethical Conduct for Managerial Accountants, which asserts that "management accountants have a responsibility to refuse any gift, favor or hospitality that would influence or would appear to influence their actions."

Chapter **16**

Further Aspects of Capital Expenditure Decisions

CHAPTER OVERVIEW AND LEARNING OBJECTIVES

This chapter extends the discounted-cash-flow analysis discussed in the previous chapter by considering tax implications. Also, the pros and cons of some other criteria used in capital-budgeting decisions are presented. When you have finished this chapter, you should understand:

1. The impact of income taxes on capital-budgeting decisions in profit-oriented firms
2. How to find after-tax flows in investment analysis and how to compute an asset's depreciation tax shield
3. The use of the accelerated cost recovery system (ACRS) to compute an asset's depreciation schedule for tax purposes
4. How to use discounted-cash-flow analysis to evaluate investment proposals, giving full consideration to income tax issues
5. The difficulties in ranking investment proposals and the use of the profitability index
6. How to evaluate capital investment projects using the payback method and the accounting rate of return
7. The impact of inflation on capital-budgeting analysis (after studying the appendix)

AN OUTLINE FOR CHAPTER STUDY

A. Any aspect of an investment project that affects revenue, expenses, gains, or losses will generally affect a company's income tax liability. Payments for a tax liability are cash flows and thus must be considered in any discounted-cash-flow analysis. The after-tax cash flow is the cash flow that results after all tax implications have been taken into account. After-tax cash flows for items that affect income can be computed from the following formulas:

   1. Incremental sales revenue × (1 – tax rate) = after-tax cash inflow
   2. Incremental cash expense × (1 – tax rate) = after-tax cash outflow
   3. Tax-deductible noncash expense × tax rate = reduced cash outflow from taxes

   The reduced cash outflow from taxes in item 3 behaves just like a cash inflow for capital-budgeting purposes; depreciation expense is an example of a tax-deductible noncash expense. It should be noted that the cash flow resulting from the purchase of an asset does not affect income and thus does not have any direct tax consequences.

B. An accelerated depreciation method is any method under which an asset is depreciated more quickly in the early part of its life than it would be under straight-line depreciation. Examples include the double-declining-balance method and the sum-of-the-years'-digits method. Current tax law does not require that the same method be used for both tax purposes and external reporting purposes. Current tax law, under its modified accelerated cost recovery system (MACRS) program, permits two methods of depreciation for tax purposes.

1. The use of MACRS tables based on the double-declining-balance method. For information on asset classification, see Exhibit 16-3 in the text. The MACRS depreciation percentages are given in Exhibit 16-4 in the text.
2. The optional straight-line method. This is not the conventional straight-line method. This tax method assumes that assets are placed in service halfway through the tax year; hence only one-half a year's ordinary straight-line depreciation is allowed in the first year the asset is placed in service. The other half year of depreciation is taken in the second tax year of the asset's service. This pattern continues. Thus, an asset having a depreciable life of 5 years for tax purposes will actually have one-half year's tax depreciation in the sixth year under this method.

C. Further observations concerning tax depreciation as it pertains to capital investment analysis are as follows:

1. It is assumed that the cash flow from tax savings due to depreciation occurs in the same year as other taxable cash flows, even though the taxes may actually be paid the following year.
2. The number of years of depreciation specified by the tax code is usually not the same as an asset's useful life.
3. In computing an asset's depreciation basis, no salvage value of the asset is considered. That is, the full cost of a depreciable asset is depreciated under MACRS rules over the taxable life of the asset. Any salvage value is treated as a taxable inflow for capital-budgeting analysis purposes.

D. The book value of an asset is the acquisition cost of the asset less the accumulated tax depreciation on the asset. If an asset is sold for more than its book value, there is a taxable gain on the disposal. If an asset is sold for less than its book value, there is a tax deduction due to the loss on disposal. Notice that the gain or loss itself is not a cash flow, but the tax saving from the loss is a cash inflow; likewise, the tax on the gain is a cash outflow.

E. Working capital is the excess of current assets over current liabilities. Any investment project that requires an increase in working capital, such as more inventory, must have that working capital treated as a cash flow for capital-budgeting analysis. If a project requires working capital, its value is treated as a cash outflow at the beginning of the project's life. When it is released at the end of the project's life, it is treated as a cash inflow at that time.

F. No valid method exists for ranking independent investment projects with positive net present values for all types of situations. One measure sometimes used by managers to rank investment proposals is the profitability index. The profitability index is defined as:

Present value of future cash flows/Initial investment

Notice that when NPV is greater than 0, the profitability index exceeds 1; if NPV equals 0, the profitability index is 1; and if NPV is less than 0, the profitability index is less than 1. The advantage of the profitability index over NPV in ranking investment projects is that it puts the projects onto a comparable footing (the initial investment amount), whereas NPV does not.

G. The payback period of an investment project is the time it will take the after-tax cash inflows to recoup the initial investment (that is, the length of time needed for the flows to accumulate to the initial investment). It is defined as:

Initial investment/Annual after-tax cash inflows

Some observations about the payback-period method are as follows:

1. No adjustment is made for the time value of money.
2. It ignores any salvage value of the investment at the end of the project's useful life.
3. It fails to consider the project's profitability beyond the payback period.
4. It is simple to use and easy to compute.

5. It puts the focus on liquidity. (Note that NPV and IRR put the focus on profitability.)
6. The method will also work with uneven cash flows; in this case the payback period must be found by looking at the cash flows incrementally (on a year-by-year basis).
7. This method provides a tool for rough screening of investment proposals; it should be used in conjunction with discounted cash-flow analysis.

H. The accounting-rate-of-return method emphasizes the incremental accounting income that results from a project. The accounting rate of return is defined as:

$$\frac{\text{Average incremental revenue} - \text{Average incremental expenses (including depreciation and income taxes)}}{\text{Initial investment}}$$

Instead of dividing by the initial investment, some managers prefer to divide by the average investment (the average accounting book value over the project's life). Some points concerning the accounting rate of return are as follows:

1. It does not consider the time value of money.
2. Its use provides a simple tool for screening investment proposals.
3. Other names for the accounting rate of return are simple rate of return, rate of return on assets, and unadjusted rate of return.
4. Despite its shortcomings, the accounting rate of return is still used in practice—some managers use it because they believe that it parallels financial-accounting statements.

I. Activity-based costing generally improves the ability of a cost analyst to estimate the cash flows associated with a project; this is especially important in evaluating an investment in advanced manufacturing equipment.

J. (Appendix) Inflation can be incorporated into discounted cash-flow analysis in two possible ways. The two approaches are distinguished by the use of either nominal or real interest rates and dollars. Before considering these approaches, the following terms are needed:

1. The real interest rate is the underlying interest rate; it includes compensation to investors for the time value of money and the risk of investment.
2. The nominal interest rate is the real interest rate plus an additional premium to compensate investors for inflation.
3. A cash flow measured in nominal dollars is the actual cash flow that occurs.
4. A cash flow measured in real dollars reflects an adjustment for the dollar's purchasing power.

The two approaches to capital budgeting under inflation are as follows:

1. Use cash flows measured in nominal dollars and a nominal interest rate to find the nominal discount rate.
2. Use cash flows measured in real dollars and a real interest rate to find the real discount rate.

Either of these approaches will provide a correct analysis, provided that it is applied consistently.

KEY TERMS

Accounting-rate-of-return method 831
After-tax cash flow 821
Depreciation tax shield 814
Modified Accelerated Cost Recovery System (MACRS) 816
Payback period 828
Profitability index (or excess present value index) 827
Working capital 822

KEY TERMS: APPENDIX

Nominal dollars 836
Nominal interest rate 836
Real dollars 836
Real interest rate 836

SELF-EVALUATION QUESTIONS AND ANSWERS

True-False Questions

_____ 1. If the tax rate is 40 percent and taxable sales revenue is $8,000, then the corresponding after-tax cash inflow is $3,200.

_____ 2. Some cash flows do not appear on the income statement.

_____ 3. It is usually disadvantageous for a business to take tax deductions as early as allowable under the tax law.

_____ 4. Current tax law requires that the same depreciation method be used for both tax purposes and external reporting purposes.

_____ 5. Income tax payments must be considered in any discounted cash-flow analysis.

_____ 6. The number of years of depreciation specified by the tax code is the same as an asset's useful life.

_____ 7. If the tax rate is 40 percent and tax-deductible cash expenses amount to $12,000, then the after-tax cash outflow is $7,200.

_____ 8. The cash flow resulting from the purchase of an asset affects income but has no direct tax consequences.

_____ 9. Under MACRS depreciation computations, an asset's salvage value is not subtracted in computing the asset's depreciation basis.

_____ 10. If tax-deductible depreciation expense is $6,000 and the tax rate is 40 percent, the corresponding reduced cash outflow is $3,600.

_____ 11. Working-capital increases needed to support an investment project should not be included in discounted-cash-flow analysis.

_____ 12. In general, no valid method exists for ranking independent investment projects with positive net present values.

_____ 13. If the NPV of an investment is negative, the profitability index will also be negative.

_____ 14. The payback-period method puts the focus on the profitability of the investment.

_____ 15. The payback method cannot be used on investment projects with uneven cash flows.

_____ 16. If the payback method is used in capital-budgeting analysis, it should be used in conjunction with discounted-cash-flow analysis.

_____ 17. The payback method is widely used in practice.

_____ 18. (Appendix) Using cash flows measured in real dollars and a nominal interest rate to determine the nominal discount rate provides a correct capital-budgeting analysis.

_____ 19. Evidence from management accounting practice suggests that the most widely used investment evaluation technique is NPV.

_____ 20. (Appendix) A correct capital-budgeting analysis consists of using cash flows measured in real dollars and a real interest rate to determine the real discount rate.

Fill-in-the-Blank Questions

1. A(n) ________________ is the cash flow expected after all tax implications have been considered.
2. The reduction in income taxes due to depreciation expense is called a(n) ________________.
3. The main concept underlying discounted-cash-flow analysis is the ________________.
4. A(n) ________________ method is any method under which an asset is depreciated more quickly in the early part of its life than it would be using straight-line depreciation.
5. The ________________ of an asset is defined as the asset's acquisition cost minus the accumulated depreciation on the asset.
6. The MACRS optional straight-line depreciation method assumes that assets are placed into service ________________ through the tax year.
7. The present value of future cash flows from a project divided by the initial investment is called the ________________.
8. When an asset is sold for more than its current book value, a(n) ________________ is recorded.
9. The ________________ of an investment project is the time needed for the after-tax cash inflows from the project to accumulate to an amount that covers the original investment.
10. The ________________ method puts the focus on the incremental accounting income that results from a project.
11. When an asset is sold for less than its current book value, a(n) ________________ is recorded.

12. (Appendix) The ________________ is the underlying interest rate, which includes compensation to investors for the time value of money and the risk of investment.

13. (Appendix) A cash flow measured in ________________ dollars is the actual cash flow we observe.

14. (Appendix) The ________________ is a rate which includes the real interest rate plus an additional premium to compensate investors for inflation.

15. (Appendix) A cash flow measured in ________________ reflects an adjustment for the dollar's purchasing power.

Multiple-Choice Questions

_____ **1.** Consider the following two statements:
I. If the NPV of an investment project is positive, the profitability index is less than 1.
II. If the NPV of an investment is 0, the profitability index equals 1.
Which is (are) true?
(a) Only I
(b) Only II
(c) Both I and II
(d) Neither I nor II

_____ **2.** The Parsley Company is considering the purchase of a machine costing $8,424 which will provide the annual cost saving of $5,200. The tax rate is 40 percent. The payback period in years for this investment proposal is
(a) 1.62.
(b) 1.9.
(c) 2.25.
(d) 2.7.

_____ **3.** Which of the following is *not* a disadvantage of the payback method?
(a) It ignores the salvage value of the investment.
(b) It does not use after-tax cash flows.
(c) It ignores the time value of money.
(d) It fails to consider a project's profitability beyond the payback period.

_____ **4.** The Weaver Company has just sold a truck for $7,500. The truck presently has a book value of $10,200. The tax rate is 40 percent. The cash flow resulting from the tax implications of the loss on disposal of the truck is
(a) $1,080 inflow.
(b) $1,080 outflow.
(c) $1,620 inflow.
(d) $1,620 outflow.

_____ **5.** Consider the following two statements about the accounting-rate-of-return method:
I. The method does not consider the time value of money.
II. The method provides a simple way of screening investment proposals.
Which is (are) true?
(a) Only I
(b) Only II
(c) Both I and II
(d) Neither I and II

_____ **6.** An investment project has a net present value of $9,700. The initial outlay for the investment is $48,500. The profitability index for this investment is
(a) 1.2.
(b) 5.0.
(c) 0.2.
(d) impossible to determine from the information given.

_____ 7. The Corley Company has just sold a computer for $2,700. The book value of the computer at the time of sale is $1,200. The tax rate is 40 percent. The cash flow resulting from the tax implications of the gain on disposal of the computer is
(a) $600 inflow.
(b) $600 outflow.
(c) $900 inflow.
(d) $900 outflow.

Exercises

(*Note:* The MACRS tables in Exhibit 16-4 in the text are needed for some of these exercises.)

16.1 The Luther Company has recently bought industrial tools amounting to $78,000. This investment falls into the 3-year property class under the MACRS. The tax rate is 40 percent and the company's after-tax cost of capital is 14 percent.

Required:

(a) Compute the total present value of all the cash flows resulting from the depreciation tax shield of this investment assuming that depreciation is computed using the MACRS table percentages.
(b) Repeat part (a) assuming that depreciation is computed using the optional straight-line method.
(c) Which of the two methods in parts (a) and (b) makes the biggest contribution to the NPV calculation?

Solution Space for Exercise 16.1:

(a)

Year	MACRS %	Depreciation Deduction	Depreciation Tax Shield	Table III Factor	Present Value of Tax Shield

(b)

Year	Depreciation Deduction	Depreciation Tax Shield	Table III Factor	Present Value of Tax Shield

(c) ____

____

____

16.2 The Jewett Company has just purchased a new copy machine for $64,000. This machine is in the 5-year MACRS property class and will be depreciated using MACRS table percentages. The useful life of this machine is 6 years, and it will be worthless at the end of 6 years. The company anticipates that the annual revenue from this machine will be $45,000 and that annual expenses, excluding depreciation and taxes, will be $12,000. The tax rate is 40 percent.

Required:

(a) Prepare a schedule similar to Exhibit 16-10 in the text and then compute the average annual income.

(b) Use the information in part (a) to determine the accounting rate of return based on the initial investment in the denominator.

Solution Space for Exercise 16.2:

(a)

Year	Sales Revenue	Operating Expenses	MACRS Depreciation	Income Before Taxes	Income Taxes	Net Income

____

(b) ____

____

16.3 (*Note:* Ignore income taxes in solving this problem.) The Van Dorn Community Library is considering the purchase of a bookmobile truck costing $83,000. This truck is expected to produce annual cash operating inflows of $23,000. The truck will have a useful life of 5 years and will have a salvage value of $6,000 at the end of 5 years. The library's cost of capital is 12 percent.

Required:

(a) Find the profitability index of this investment. Should the bookmobile be bought?

(b) Suppose that the bookmobile will need extra working capital of $9,000 if it is purchased. This working capital would be released at the end of the bookmobile's useful life. Under these circumstances, what is the net present value of this investment? Should the bookmobile be bought in this case?

Solution Space for Exercise 16.3:

(a)

(b)

16.4 The Tryon Company makes a product called a nump in its Stubenville plant. It is contemplating the purchase of two robots for its Assembly Department which would revolutionize the production methods in a department that is presently doing its work manually. In order to keep pace with its competition in an age of high-tech production, the management of Tryon believes it is necessary to give serious consideration to the possibility of buying these two robots. In order to help management make a well-informed decision about these robots, the company accountant has gathered the following data:

Purchase cost of the two robots now	$793,200
Cost of physical installation of the robots	42,900
Other costs related to robot installation	8,500
Incremental yearly cost in maintenance and energy costs	96,100
Additional yearly costs of MIS and computer support	85,300
Salvage value of both robots in 8 years	12,000
Useful life of both robots	8 years

These robots are in the 7-year MACRS property class and would be depreciated using MACRS tables for tax purposes. Tryon's tax rate is 40 percent, and its after-tax cost of capital is 18 percent.

One of the concerns troubling management is that if in fact these two robots are purchased, 16 laborers currently in the Assembly Department will have to be laid off. At Tryon laborers work 2,000 hours per year at an average wage of $12.45. There is another firm located 8 miles from Tryon that has indicated it probably would be willing to offer these laborers somewhat similar employment in the event they were discharged from Tryon. The average wage of these laborers will be stable over the next 8 years.

Required:

(a) Find the net present value of the two robots.
(b) Find the profitability index of this investment.
(c) Should the robots be purchased on economic grounds?

Solution Space for Exercise 16.4:

Computation of annual operating cash flows:

Computation of present value of depreciation tax shield:

(a)

(b) ____

____

(c) ____

____

Answers to True-False Questions

1. F It is $8,000 × (1 − .4) = $4,800.
2. T
3. F It is usually advantageous to take tax deductions as early as possible.
4. F The law allows different methods for tax purposes and external reporting purposes.
5. T
6. F The number of years specified by the tax code is usually different from an asset's useful life.
7. T
8. F The cash flow resulting from the purchase of an asset does not immediately affect income.
9. T
10. F It is $6,000 × .4 = $2,400.
11. F They should be included in the analysis.
12. T
13. F It will be less than 1 and hence could be positive.
14. F It puts the focus on liquidity.
15. F It can be used with uneven cash flows.
16. T
17. T
18. F For a correct analysis, nominal dollars should be used with a nominal interest rate.
19. F The illustration from management-accounting practice in the text at the end of the chapter indicates that the payback method is most widely used.
20. T

Answers to Fill-in-the-Blank Questions

1. after-tax cash flow
2. depreciation tax shield
3. time value of money
4. accelerated
5. book value
6. halfway
7. profitability index
8. gain on disposal
9. payback period
10. accounting-rate-of-return
11. loss on disposal
12. real interest rate
13. nominal
14. nominal interest rate
15. real dollars

Answers to Multiple-Choice Questions

1. (b) If NPV is positive, the profitability index exceeds 1.
2. (d) $8,424/($5,200 × .6) = 2.7 years.
3. (b) The payback method does use after-tax cash flows.
4. (a) ($10,200 − $7,500) × .4 = $1,080. Since there is a loss, this is an inflow.
5. (c)
6. (a) Present value of future flows = $48,500 + $9,700 = $58,200; profitability index = $58,200/$48,500 = 1.2.
7. (b) ($2,700 − $1,200) × .4 = $600. Since there is a gain, this is an outflow.

Solutions to Exercises

16.1 (a) Cost of tools = $78,000; 3-year MACRS property class.

Year	MACRS %	Depreciation Deduction	Depreciation Tax Shield	Table III Factor	Present Value of Tax Shield
1	33.33	$25,997	$10,399	.877	$ 9,120
2	44.45	34,671	13,868	.769	10,664
3	14.81	11,552	4,621	.675	3,119
4	7.41	5,780	2,312	.592	1,369
		$78,000			$24,272

Total present value = $24,272

(b) Straight-line depreciation = $78,000/3 = $26,000

Year	Depreciation Deduction	Depreciation Tax Shield	Table III Factor	Present Value of Tax Shield
1	$13,000	$ 5,200	.877	$ 4,560
2	26,000	10,400	.769	7,998
3	26,000	10,400	.675	7,020
4	13,000	5,200	.592	3,078
	$78,000			$22,656

Total present value = $22,656

(c) The MACRS table percentage method makes the biggest contribution to the NPV calculation, since it gives the largest present value of tax-shield inflows.

16.2 **(a)** Asset cost = $64,000

Year	Sales Revenue	Operating Expenses*	MACRS Depreciation	Income Before Taxes	Income Taxes	Net Income
1	$45,000	$12,000	$12,800	$20,200	$ 8,080	$12,120
2	45,000	12,000	20,480	12,520	5,008	7,512
3	45,000	12,000	12,288	20,712	8,285	12,427
4	45,000	12,000	7,373	25,627	10,251	15,376
5	45,000	12,000	7,373	25,627	10,251	15,376
6	45,000	12,000	3,686	29,314	11,726	17,588
			$64,000			$80,399

*Excluding depreciation and taxes.

Average annual income = $80,399/6 = $13,400

(b) Accounting rate of return = $13,400/$64,000 = 20.94%

16.3 **(a)**

Item	Dollar Amount	Present Value Factor	Present Value of Flow
Initial cost (now)	$(83,000)	1	$(83,000)
Annual cash operating inflows	23,000	3.605	82,915
Salvage value (year 5)	6,000	.567	3,402
Net present value			3,317

Profitability index = ($82,915 + $3,402)/$83,000 = 1.040. The bookmobile should be bought since the profitability index exceeds 1. (Also, NPV > 0.)

(b)

Item	Dollar Amount	Present Value Factor	Present Value of Flow
Initial cost (now)	$(83,000)	1	$(83,000)
Working capital needed (now)	(9,000)	1	(9,000)
Annual cash operating inflows	23,000	3.605	82,915
Salvage value (year 5)	6,000	.567	3,402
Working capital released (year 5)	9,000	.567	5,103
Net present value			$(580)

Since NPV < 0 in this case, the bookmobile should not be purchased on economic grounds.

16.4 Computation of annual operating cash flows:

Saving in direct labor costs	2,000 × $12.45 × 16 = $398,400
Incremental maintenance and energy costs	(96,100)
Cost of MIS and computer support	(85,300)
Annual cash operating inflows	$217,000

Total initial cost = $844,600

Computation of present value of depreciation tax shield:

Year	MACRS %	Depreciation	Tax Shield	PV Factor	Present Value
1	14.29	$120,693	$48,277	.847	$ 40,891
2	24.49	206,843	82,737	.718	59,405
3	17.49	147,721	59,088	.609	35,985
4	12.49	105,491	42,196	.516	21,773
5	8.93	75,423	30,169	.437	13,184
6	8.92	75,337	30,135	.370	11,150
7	8.93	75,423	30,169	.314	9,473
8	4.46	37,669	15,068	.266	4,008
		$844,600			$195,869

(a)

Item	Dollar Amount	Present Value Factor	Present Value of Flow
Purchase cost (now)	$(793,200)	1	$(793,200)
Physical installation (now)	(42,900)	1	(42,900)
Other costs (now)	(8,500)	1	(8,500)
Annual cash operating inflows	217,000	4.078	884,926
Total depreciation tax shield	—	—	195,869
Salvage value (year 8)	12,000	.266	3,192
Net present value			$ 239,387

(b) Profitability index = ($844,600 + $239,387)/$844,600 = 1.283

(c) Yes, since NPV > 0; also, profitability index > 1.

Chapter 17

Cost Allocation: A Closer Look

CHAPTER OVERVIEW AND LEARNING OBJECTIVES

Back in Chapter 11 you learned about the three steps in cost allocation. They are cost distribution, service-department cost allocation, and cost application. The second of these steps, service-department cost allocation, is a main focus of this present chapter. Also, you will learn about joint cost allocation. After completing the chapter you should understand:

1. The direct method and the step-down method of service-department cost allocation
2. The dual-cost allocation method for service departments
3. The difference between two-stage cost allocation with departmental overhead rates and activity-based costing (ABC)
4. How to use the physical-units method, relative-sales-value method, and net-realizable-value method of joint cost allocation
5. The purposes for which joint cost allocation is useful and those for which it is not

AN OUTLINE FOR CHAPTER STUDY

A. A service department is a segment of an organization that is not involved directly in producing the organization's goods or services; it offers support to those departments in which direct production does take place. In order to determine the cost of goods or services, all service department costs must be allocated to the production departments which generate the goods or services. Two methods of service-department cost allocation that are used in practice are the direct method and the step-down method.

B. The direct method consists of allocating the costs of the service departments directly to the producing departments without giving any consideration to the fact that service departments may give service to one another as well as to the producing departments. The portion of each service department's costs that are allocated to each producing department is determined by the relative proportion of the service department's output that is consumed by or is attributable to each producing department.

C. The step-down method gives partial recognition to service departments' serving each other. In this method the managerial accountant first selects a sequence of service departments in which to allocate service department costs. A common approach to sequencing the service departments is to choose as the first in the sequence the service department that serves the largest number of other service departments; the last in the sequence would be the department that serves the smallest number of other service departments. It is not always possible to determine a sequence in this fashion, but it is often possible to approximate such a sequence. The main point is that for this method the service departments must be ordered in some manner. Once a service department's costs are allocated to remaining service departments and the producing departments, no costs are ever allocated back to it. This process continues until all service department costs have been allocated; this explains why the method is called the "step-down" method. If a different sequence of service departments is chosen, the allocations received by the producing departments will be different. The best way to comprehend this method fully is to examine carefully the example in Exhibit 17-4 in the text.

D. The allocation schemes of the previous two sections do not distinguish between fixed and variable costs. This can result in an unfair cost allocation among the producing departments. One approach to overcoming this problem is to use the dual-allocation method. Under this method variable costs are allocated on the basis of short-run usage of the service department's output; fixed costs are allocated to producing departments on the basis of long-run average usage of the service department's output. The dual-allocation approach can be used with either the direct method or the step-down method. In order to implement this approach, fairly accurate projections of the long-run average usage of each service department by each producing department are needed. The higher a producing department's manager estimates long-run average usage to be, the greater will be the fixed-cost allocation of service department cost; this could encourage managers to unrealistically underestimate their long-run average usage.

E. When service department costs are allocated to producing departments, budgeted service department cost should be used. The allocation of actual service department costs could result in unfairly passing along the cost of service department inefficiencies to the producing departments. The appropriate approach in allocating service department costs is as follows:

1. Compute variances between actual and budgeted service department costs.
2. Use these variances to help control service department costs.
3. Close out the variances of service department costs against period income.
4. Allocate the budgeted service department costs to the producing departments.

F. Service-department cost allocations are still used in the new manufacturing environment of just-in-time and computer-integrated manufacturing systems. The extent of these allocations is decreasing, since in high-tech manufacturing environments more production costs are traceable directly to product lines. In an activity-based costing (ABC) system the breakdown of costs by activity is more refined than a breakdown by departments as is done in traditional service-department cost allocation. In ABC the costs of various activities are assigned to activity cost pools; these costs are then assigned to products or services. The ABC approach generally provides more accurate costs of a firm's products or services.

G. A joint production process is one where, as common raw material is converted, there is a point where at least two products (called joint products) become identifiable. The point where these products become identifiable is called the split-off point. The costs of production incurred up to the split-off point are called joint costs. It is necessary to allocate these joint costs to joint products for inventory valuation and income determination. Three methods used in the practice of allocating these joint costs are as follows:

1. Physical-units method. This method allocates joint costs to products formed at split-off on the basis of some physical characteristic such as weight.
2. Relative-sales method. This method allocates the joint costs to joint products on the basis of the relative sales value of each joint product at the split-off point.
3. Net-realizable-value method. This approach employs the net realizable value of the joint products at split-off as a basis for the allocation of the joint costs. Net realizable value is defined as the sales value of a product after further processing beyond split-off less the separable costs incurred after the split-off point. The net realizable value of a product can be viewed as a surrogate for a nonexistent sales price at split-off. Some joint products are not marketable at split-off.

Of these three methods, the physical-units method is the least preferable, because it is not based on any economic measure. It should be noted that joint costs of production are not relative to the decision problem of whether to sell joint products at split-off or process them further. This decision problem was studied in Chapter 13.

H. A joint product with a very low sales value relative to other joint products is called a by-product. A common procedure of accounting for by-products is to subtract a by-product's net realizable value from the joint cost of production, and then allocate the remaining joint cost to the main joint products.

I. (Appendix) The reciprocal-services cost allocation method is an alternative method to the direct method and the step-down method of allocating service department costs to producing departments. It is more accurate than the direct method and the step-down method in that it gives full recognition to the interaction of service departments with one another. It is the theoretically correct method of service-department cost allocation. When used in combination with the dual-allocation method, fixed and variable costs are allocated separately by the reciprocal-services method.

KEY TERMS

By-product 878
Direct method 867
Dual cost allocation 871
Joint production process 876
Joint products 876
Net realizable value 877
Net-realizable-value method 877
Physical-units method 877
Reciprocal service 869
Reciprocal-services method 869
Relative-sales-value method 877
Service department 864
Split-off point 876
Step-down method 867

SELF-EVALUATION QUESTIONS AND ANSWERS

True-False Questions

_____ **1.** Service departments are unimportant in nonmanufacturing organizations.

_____ **2.** In order to determine the cost of goods in an organization, all legitimate service department costs must be allocated to producing departments where these goods are made.

_____ **3.** The direct method does not ignore the fact that some service departments provide services to other service departments.

_____ **4.** Department size would not be a proper allocation base for allocating service department costs to producing departments.

_____ **5.** The primary purpose of cost allocation is to ensure that all costs incurred by the firm ultimately are assigned to its products or services.

_____ **6.** Cost allocations under the step-down method are the same regardless of how the service departments are sequenced in the allocation process.

_____ **7.** When fixed and variable costs are not distinguished in a service-department cost allocation method, unfair cost allocations can result among the producing departments.

_____ **8.** The dual-allocation method can be used in conjunction with both the direct method and the step-down method.

_____ **9.** When allocating service department costs to producing departments, actual service department costs should be used.

_____ **10.** Service-department cost allocations are used more extensively in advanced manufacturing systems than in traditional manufacturing systems.

_____ **11.** Joint cost allocations are necessary for inventory valuation and income determination.

_____ **12.** All joint products are salable at split-off.

_____ **13.** The breakdown of costs by activity in an ABC system is much finer than a breakdown by departments in traditional cost allocation.

_____ **14.** (Appendix) The reciprocal-services cost allocation method fully accounts for the mutual provision of services among all the service departments.

_____ **15.** (Appendix) The reciprocal-services cost allocation method cannot be used in conjunction with the dual-allocation approach.

Fill-in-the-Blank Questions

1. A(n) ________________ is a unit in an organization that is not involved directly in producing the organization's goods and services.
2. Under the ________________ method, each service department's costs are allocated only among the producing departments.
3. The ________________ method of service-department cost allocation gives partial recognition of the fact that some service departments render services to other service departments.
4. The mutual provision of service among service departments is called ________________ services.
5. Under the dual-allocation method, variable costs are allocated on the basis of ________________ usage of the service department's output.
6. Under the dual-allocation method, fixed costs are allocated on the basis of ________________ usage of the service department's output.
7. A joint production process results in at least two products called ________________.
8. The common costs incurred in a joint production process before split-off are called ________________.
9. The ________________ of a final product made by a joint production process is its sales value after further processing less any separable costs incurred after the split-off point.
10. The ________________ method of joint cost allocation is based on the relative sales value of each joint product at the split-off point.
11. A joint product with a small sales value relative to that of other joint products is called a(n) ________________.

Multiple-Choice Questions

____ 1. Which of the following is *not* a proper step in allocating service department costs to producing departments?
- (a) Computing variances between budgeted and actual service department costs
- (b) Using variances to help control service department costs
- (c) Closing out service department costs against the period's income
- (d) Allocating the service department's actual costs to the producing departments

____ 2. Consider the following two statements about joint-cost allocation methods:
- I. The physical-units method is not based on economic characteristics of the joint products.
- II. These methods are useful in managerial decision problems about selling joint products at split-off instead of further processing them before sale.

Which is (are) true?
- (a) Only I
- (b) Only II
- (c) Both I and II
- (d) Neither I nor II

____ 3. A common practice in accounting for a by-product of a joint production process is to
- (a) add the cost of the by-product to the joint cost before allocating the joint cost.
- (b) subtract the net realizable value of the by-product from the joint cost before allocating the joint cost.
- (c) subtract the cost of the by-product from the joint cost before allocating the joint cost.
- (d) add the net realizable value of the by-product to the joint cost before allocating the joint cost.

____ 4. A service department has costs of $15,000. Producing Department X uses 35 percent of the service department's output, and Producing Department Y uses the rest of the service department's output. Under the direct method, the portion of the service department's cost allocated to Producing Department Y is
- (a) $5,250.
- (b) $6,750.
- (c) $9,750.
- (d) $11,250.

Exercises

17.1 Sommer's Realty is a large real estate firm that has two revenue-producing departments: Residential and Commercial. It also has two service departments, Personnel and Computing. The usage of the service departments' output last year was as follows:

	Provider of Service	
User of Service	**Personnel**	**Computing**
Personnel	—	10%
Computing	15%	—
Residential	40%	30%
Commercial	45%	60%

The budgeted costs last year for the service departments were as follows:

Personnel	$138,000
Computing	195,000

Required:

(a) Allocate the costs of the service departments to the revenue-generating departments by the direct method.

(b) Allocate the costs of the service departments to the revenue-generating departments by the step-down method, allocating personnel costs first and then computing costs.

Solution Space for Exercise 17.1:

(a)

(b)

17.2 The Ramsey Company has three producing departments—Fabricating, Assembly, and Finishing. The company has one service department—Energy. The following data are available for March:

Department	Energy Used (in kWh)	Long-Run Monthly Average Usage (in kWh)
Fabricating	15,000	18,000
Assembly	12,000	6,000
Finishing	3,000	6,000

Costs of Energy Department:

	Actual	Budgeted
Variable	$15,000	$12,000
Fixed	5,400	6,000

Required:

(a) Compute the total cost variance for the Energy Department.
(b) Use the dual-allocation method to allocate the budgeted energy costs to the producing departments. Find the total allocated amount for each producing department.

Solution Space for Exercise 17.2:

(a) ______________________________

(b)

17.3 The Armstrong Company produces products X-200 and Z-450 from a joint production process. Each of these products can be sold at split-off or processed further. Costs of processing further are all variable and are traceable directly to the individual products. In 19x3 the joint costs of production were $40,000 and both products were processed beyond split-off. Additional data for 19x3 are as follows:

			Further Processing Data	
Product	**Units Made**	**Sales Value at Split-off**	**Sales Value**	**Separable Costs**
X-200	5,000	$18,750	$32,500	$8,750
Z-450	3,000	21,000	27,000	6,000

Required:

Allocate the joint costs of production to the joint products and find the total unit cost of each product using

(a) The physical-units method based on volume of production
(b) The relative-sales-value method
(c) The net-realizable-value method

Solution Space for Exercise 17.3:

(a)

(b)

(c)

17.4 (Appendix) Sun Valley Hospital is a small hospital which renders health care and performs X rays on its patients. All other services needed for patients are performed at nearby independent facilities. The hospital has two service departments—Maintenance and Administration. Budget data for July are as follows:

	Provider of Service		Budgeted
Department	**Maintenance**	**Administration**	**Costs**
Maintenance	—	15%	$50,000
Administration	10%	—	70,000
Health Care	80%	80%	90,000
X ray	10%	5%	10,000

Required:

(a) Find the final total costs (both indirect and direct) of the Health Care and X ray departments using the reciprocal-services cost-allocation method.

(b) Suppose that a certain health care procedure has direct costs of $12.00 for labor and $21.00 for supplies. Find an appropriate total cost for this procedure which includes a charge for the allocated indirect costs of the service departments.

Solution Space for Exercise 17.4:

(a)

(b)

Answers to True-False Questions

1. F They are also very important segments in nonmanufacturing organizations such as hospitals.
2. T
3. F It does ignore the fact that some service departments serve other service departments.
4. F Department size could possibly be a proper allocation base.
5. T
6. F They are different, depending on how the service departments are sequenced.
7. T
8. T
9. F Budgeted service department costs should be used.
10. F They are used less.
11. T
12. F Some joint products are marketable only after further processing.
13. T
14. T
15. F It can be used in conjunction with the dual-allocation method.

Answers to Fill-in-the-Blank Questions

1. service department
2. direct
3. step-down
4. reciprocal
5. short-run
6. long-run average
7. joint products
8. joint costs
9. net realizable value
10. relative-sales-value
11. by-product

Answers to Multiple-Choice Questions

1. (d) The budgeted costs should be allocated to the producing departments.
2. (a) Joint-cost allocation methods are irrelevant for the sell-or-process-further decision problem.
3. (b) The other choices are all false.
4. (c) $15,000 × .65 = $9,750.

Solutions to Exercises

17.1 (a)

		Revenue-Generating Departments			
	Cost to	Residential		Commercial	
Service Department	Be Allocated	Fraction	Amount	Fraction	Amount
Personnel	$138,000	40/85	$ 64,941	45/85	$ 73,059
Computing	195,000	1/3	65,000	2/3	130,000
			$129,941		$203,059

(b)

	Service Departments		Producing Departments	
	Personnel	Computing	Residential	Commercial
Costs prior to allocation	$138,000	$195,000		
Allocation of personnel costs	$138,000	20,700 (15%)	$ 55,200 (40%)	$ 62,100 (45%)
Allocation of computing costs		$215,700	71,900 (1/3)	143,800 (2/3)
Total allocated costs			$127,100	$205,900

17.2 (a) Total cost variance = $20,400 – $18,000 = $2,400 unfavorable

(b)

Cost	Amount to Be	Producing Departments		
Type	Allocated	Fabricating	Assembly	Finishing
Variable	$12,000	$6,000 (15/30)	$4,800 (12/30)	$1,200 (3/30)
Fixed	6,000	3,600 (18/30)	1,200 (6/30)	1,200 (6/30)
Totals	$18,000	$9,600	$6,000	$2,400

17.3 **(a)** Physical-units method:

Product	Units Made	Relative Proportion	Allocated Joint Cost	Separable Costs	Total Cost	Unit Cost
X-200	5,000	5/8	$25,000	$8,750	$33,750	$6.75
Z-450	3,000	3/8	15,000	6,000	21,000	7.00
	8,000					

(b) Relative-sales-value method:

Product	Units Made	Sales Value at Split-off	Relative Proportion	Allocated Joint Cost	Separable Cost	Total Cost	Unit Cost
X-200	5,000	$18,750	.4717	$18,868	$8,750	$27,618	$5.52
Z-450	3,000	21,000	.5283	21,132	6,000	27,132	9.04
		$39,750					

(c) Net-realizable-value method:

Product	Units Made	Sales Value after Further Processing	Separable Costs	Net Realizable Value	Relative Proportion	Allocated Cost	Total Cost	Unit Cost
X-200	5,000	$32,500	$8,750	$23,750	.5307	$21,228	$29,978	$6.00
Z-450	3,000	27,000	6,000	21,000	.4693	18,772	24,772	8.26
				$44,750				

17.4 **(a)** Let M and A be the redistributed costs of Maintenance and Administration, respectively, after receiving each other's cost allocations. Then:

$M = 50{,}000 + 0.15A$

$A = 70{,}000 + 0.10M$

Solving these equations simultaneously, we obtain $M = \$61{,}421.10$ and $A = \$76{,}142.10$.

Total final cost of Health Care = $90,000 + 0.80($61,421.10) + 0.80($76,142.10) = $200,051

Total final cost of X ray = $10,000 + 0.10($61,421.10) + 0.05($76,142.10) = $19,949

(b) Portion of Health Care's final cost that is indirect (from service department allocations) is $200,051 − $90,000 = $110,051.

Rate for indirect costs of Health Care = $110,051/$90,000 = 1.2228 = 122.28%

Cost of given Health Care procedure:

Direct costs		
Labor	$12.00	
Materials	21.00	$33.00
Indirect costs: 1.2228 × $33		40.35
Total cost for procedure		$73.35

Chapter **18**

Analyzing Financial Statements

CHAPTER OVERVIEW AND LEARNING OBJECTIVES

In this chapter you study the various ways in which accountants and others analyze financial information revealed by the balance sheet, the income statement, and the retained earnings statement. After completing this chapter, you should understand:

1. The objectives of financial statement analysis
2. How to use horizontal analysis, trend analysis, vertical analysis, and ratio analysis
3. The importance of comparisons and trends in financial statement analysis
4. How to prepare and interpret common-size financial statements
5. How to compute the various financial ratios discussed in the chapter

AN OUTLINE FOR CHAPTER STUDY

A. Financial statements are the primary vehicle for managers to communicate the financial condition of their organization to outside parties. The four primary financial statements are as follows:

1. Balance sheet. This statement gives the organization's financial position at a specific point in time.
2. Income statement. This statement reports the income for the period between two balance sheet dates.
3. Retained earnings statement. This statement shows how income and dividends for the period have changed the organization's retained earnings.
4. Statement of cash flows. This statement shows how cash was obtained during the period and how it was used.

These statements are based on historical accounting information.

B. The objective of financial statement analysis is to use historical accounting data to help predict how the organization will fare in the future. In financial statement analysis every financial measure should be compared across time and across other companies to be meaningful. Comparing financial data with industry norms also provides important information about the firm being analyzed. Sources of information for financial statement analysis besides published financial statements can be found in publications such as *The Wall Street Journal, BusinessWeek,* and *Forbes.* Financial advisory services are available from such organizations as Dun and Bradstreet, Standard and Poor's, and Dow Jones.

C. Comparative financial statements and change data make it possible for analysts to do a horizontal analysis, which is an analysis of the year-to-year change in each financial statement item. The purpose of horizontal analysis is to determine:

1. How each financial statement item changed
2. Why each financial statement item changed
3. Whether the changes in financial statement items are favorable or unfavorable

D. When financial statements are compared for at least three years, the method is called trend analysis. Trends can be given in both dollar and percentage form by designating the first year in the sequence as the base year; amounts after the first year are shown as a percentage of the base-year amount.

E. Vertical analysis consists of analyzing the relationships among various financial items on a particular financial statement for a given period or point in time (not across time as is done in horizontal and trend analysis). The items on the financial statement are expressed as a percentage of some base item on that statement. For the balance sheet the base item is total assets; for the income statement the base item is sales. Financial statements prepared in terms of percentages of a base amount are called common-size statements. This type of analysis provides insight into the relative importance or magnitude of various items in the financial statements. This facilitates comparing a firm's financial condition and performance from year to year.

F. Ratio analysis consists of forming various ratios of financial statement items that give a certain message or portray a certain picture about the relationship of the items in the ratio. These various ratios may seem endless, but each one has an important observation about the financial condition or performance of the organization. In the sections that follow, ratios will be categorized according to the financial statement to which they mainly relate. A summary of the key financial ratios is given in Exhibit 18-9 in the text; you should have it available for ready reference.

G. Working capital is current assets less current liabilities. A reasonable amount of working capital is needed to ensure that short-term obligations are paid on time and unforeseen circumstances and opportunities can be covered without difficulty. The following measures pertain primarily to the balance sheet.

1. The current ratio is current assets divided by current liabilities. This ratio gives a measure of a firm's ability to meet its short-term obligations. It gives the working-capital position in ratio form.
2. The acid-test ratio (or quick ratio) is defined as quick assets divided by current liabilities. Quick assets are current assets less inventory; these assets can be converted into cash more quickly than inventory can. This ratio gives a sharper measure than the current ratio in indicating a firm's ability to meet its short-term debts.
3. The accounts receivable turnover is credit sales divided by the average accounts receivable balance. This ratio is used to evaluate the effectiveness of a firm's credit terms and collection policies; the higher the ratio value, the greater the effectiveness.
4. The average collection period is 365 days divided by accounts receivable turnover. It measures the average number of days needed to collect accounts receivable.
5. Inventory turnover is the ratio of the cost of goods sold to the average balance in inventory. This ratio provides a measure of the appropriateness of a firm's inventory level. It indicates how many times the firm's inventory has been sold during the year.
6. The average number of days per inventory turnover is defined as 365 days divided by inventory turnover. This measure indicates the average time needed to sell inventory one time.
7. Some companies compute the book value of each type of security held. This measure gives an indication of the firm's assets available to back up its debt and ownership obligations.
8. The debt-equity ratio is defined as total liabilities divided by total stockholders' equity. It gives a measure of the relationship between a firm's resources provided by debt and those provided through ownership. The greater this ratio is, the more risky the company is as an investment. This ratio is an example of what is called a capitalization ratio.

H. Operating income is a key item on an income statement, since it measures the operating results of the firm for the period in dollars. This measure does not involve financing and tax considerations. The following measures are related mainly to the income statement.

1. Interest coverage is the ratio of operating income to interest expense. This ratio measures the firm's ability to pay its obligated bond interest.
2. Coverage of dividends on preferred stock is defined as net income divided by stated dividends on preferred stock. This measure indicates the extent to which a firm's net income is sufficient to pay stated dividends on preferred stock.
3. Earnings per share is net income available to common-stock holders divided by the number of shares of outstanding common stock. This measure relates a company's earnings to its common stock. Sometimes a company will experience gains or losses outside the ordinary realm of business—for example, losses due to fire. Earnings per share is computed exclusive of the effect of any such extraordinary gains or losses and their related tax effect.
4. Fully diluted earnings per share is defined as net income available to common-stock holders divided by the number of shares of outstanding common stock, assuming full conversion of all convertible securities. Convertible securities are those securities that can be converted to a specified number of shares of common stock.
5. The price-earnings ratio is market price per share divided by earnings per share. Some investors use this ratio to help determine the appropriate price for a company's stock.
6. Return on assets is the ratio of net income plus interest expense (net of its tax effect) to average total assets. This ratio indicates how effectively management has discharged its responsibility in generating income for the owners.
7. Return on equity is defined as net income available to common-stock holders divided by average common-stock holders' equity. This measure relates income available to common-stock holders (income after preferred dividends have been subtracted from net income) to equity held by common-stock holders.
8. Return on sales is net income divided by sales. This measure gives the fraction of each sales dollar that results in net income.
9. Financial leverage is the name given to the situation where a small increase in income yields a proportionately large increase in return to common-stock holders. This is made possible by having a relatively large proportion of financing through debt or preferred stock which pays interest or dividends at a fixed rate; when income increases, bond interest and preferred stock dividends stay constant.

I. Net income increases retained earnings and dividends decrease retained earnings. The following measures pertain mainly to the statement of retained earnings.

1. The dividend payout ratio is defined as dividends per share of common stock divided by earnings per share. This ratio indicates the proportion of earnings per share that is paid to the common-stock holders in the form of dividends.
2. The dividend yield ratio is defined as dividends per share of common stock divided by the market price per share. This measure relates dividends to stock price.

J. Final observations about financial statement analysis are as follows:

1. Footnotes to financial statements offer important insights about the financial condition and performance of an organization. They should be viewed as an integral part of the financial statements.
2. Financial ratios serve only as an attention-getting device. Sometimes they raise more questions than they answer, and more in-depth research about an organization may be needed.
3. Some limitations of financial statement analysis include:

   a. Financial statements are based on historical data, which might not be indicative of the future.
   b. Price levels are constantly changing and may not be reflected by historical costs in financial statements.
   c. Comparisons across companies may be difficult to make.

KEY TERMS

Common-size financial statements 901
Comparative financial statements 908
Financial leverage 913
Horizontal analysis 898
Quick assets 905
Trend analysis 900
Vertical analysis 901
Working capital 903

Also see the various ratios defined in Exhibit 18-9 in the text.

SELF-EVALUATION QUESTIONS AND ANSWERS

True-False Questions

_____ 1. Financial statements are based on historical accounting information.

_____ 2. The balance sheet presents an organization's financial position over a given period of time.

_____ 3. The most important point about financial statement analysis is that every financial statement should be compared at one point in time and across other companies to be meaningful.

_____ 4. A reasonable amount of working capital should be available to ensure that short-term obligations can be paid on time.

_____ 5. Financial statements provide the primary means whereby managers communicate about the financial condition of their firm to outside parties.

_____ 6. Comparing key financial data with industry norms generally has no value in financial statement analysis.

_____ 7. The statement of cash flows shows how income was earned and dividends were paid over a given period.

_____ 8. Published financial statements provide the primary source of data about any organization's financial condition and performance.

_____ 9. The current ratio does not tell the whole story of a company's ability to meet its short-term obligations.

_____ 10. The objective of financial statement analysis is to use historical accounting data to help predict how a firm will fare in the future.

_____ 11. Quick assets divided by current liabilities equals the acid-test ratio.

_____ 12. Accounts receivable turnover measures the average number of days needed to collect accounts receivable.

_____ 13. Some analysts compute the book value of each of a company's securities as a measure of the assets available to back up the company's debt and ownership obligations.

_____ 14. In general, the lower the debt-equity ratio, the more risky the company is as an investment.

_____ 15. Interest coverage equals operating income divided by interest expense.

_____ 16. Inventory turnover measures the average time needed to sell inventory over time.

_____ 17. Coverage of dividends on preferred stock is defined as the ratio of operating income to stated dividends on preferred stock.

_____ 18. Accepted accounting practice requires that earnings per share be computed exclusive of the effect of any extraordinary gains or losses and their related tax effect.

_____ 19. High financial leverage carries with it the possibility of great return and low risk.

_____ 20. Published financial statements are almost always accompanied by footnotes.

_____ 21. Financial ratios serve only as an attention-getting device.

Fill-in-the-Blank Questions

1. The ________________ reports the income for the period between two balance sheet dates.
2. ________________ is an analysis of the year-to-year change in each financial statement item.
3. Financial statements prepared in terms of percentages of a base amount are called ________________.
4. ________________ focuses on the relationships among various financial items on a given financial statement.
5. Current assets less current liabilities is defined as ________________.
6. The ________________ presents an organization's financial position at a point in time.

7. When the comparison of financial statement data covers at least three years, the technique is called ________________.

8. The ________________ shows how income and dividends for the period have changed the organization's retained earnings.

9. Current assets divided by current liabilities equals the ________________.

10. ________________ are defined as current assets less inventory.

11. A(n) ________________ is the proportion of the face value of a particular type of security to the company's total equity.

12. A key measure that relates a company's earnings to its common stock is the firm's ________________.

13. The ________________ measures the relationship between the firm's resources provided through debt and those provided through ownership.

14. Securities that can be converted into a specified number of shares of common stock are called ________________.

15. The ________________ is defined as market price per share divided by earnings per share.

16. The percentage that net income is of sales is called the ________________.

17. ________________ refers to the situation where a relatively small increase in income can elicit a proportionately larger increase in return to the common-stock holders.

Multiple-Choice Questions

_____ 1. Which of the following is *not* a primary financial statement?
(a) Balance sheet
(b) Statement of working capital
(c) Statement of cash flows
(d) Income statement

_____ 2. Which of the following is used to assess the effectiveness of a firm's credit terms and collection policies?
(a) Accounts receivable turnover
(b) Average sales period
(c) Average days per inventory turnover
(d) Inventory turnover

_____ 3. Which of the following measures how effectively management has discharged the responsibility of generating income for the owners?
(a) Earnings per share
(b) Fully diluted earnings per share
(c) Return on assets
(d) Return on sales

_____ 4. Which of the following is *not* an analytical tool used in financial statement analysis?
(a) Horizontal analysis
(b) Vertical analysis
(c) Oblique analysis
(d) Trend analysis

_____ 5. The ratio that relates dividends and stock price is
(a) the dividend yield ratio.
(b) the dividend payout ratio.
(c) the dividend per share ratio.
(d) the dividend-earnings ratio.

_____ 6. Which of the following is *not* a limitation inherent in financial statement analysis?
(a) Financial statements are based on historical accounting data.
(b) Comparing financial statements across companies is sometimes difficult.
(c) Historical-cost values provide the basis for accounting valuation, even though price levels are constantly changing.
(d) Financial ratios are difficult to compute.

Exercises

18.1 The Phelps Company had the following data for a period of four consecutive years:

	19x5	19x4	19x3	19x2
Current assets	$296,000	$342,000	$382,200	$424,320
Inventory	127,650	184,300	235,200	285,600
Current liabilities	185,000	190,000	196,000	204,000

Required:

(a) Express the given trend data in terms of percentages with 19x2 as the base year.
(b) Construct a table that gives the trend in Phelp's current ratio and quick ratio for the given four-year period.
(c) Discuss the significance of the trend data. What conclusions about the given trend data can you draw?

Solution Space for Exercise 18.1:

(a)

(b)

(c)

18.2 The Alston Company had the following financial statement data:

THE ALSTON COMPANY
Balance Sheet Data

	12/31/x8	12/31/x7
Cash	$ 48,000	$ 63,000
Accounts receivable (net)	196,000	208,000
Inventories	219,000	247,000
Property, plant, and equipment	620,000	550,000
Accumulated depreciation	(250,000)	(180,000)
Total assets	$833,000	$888,000
Current liabilities	$285,00	$230,000
Stockholders' equity	548,000	658,000
Total liabilities and stockholders' equity	$833,000	$888,000

Required:

(a) Express the comparative balance sheet in common-size format.
(b) Explain why common-size statements are useful in financial statement analysis.

Solution Space for Exercise 18.2:

(a)

Common-Size Balance Sheet Data

(b) ____

____

____

____

18.3 The Kingsley Company had the following data for 19x2:

THE KINGSLEY COMPANY
Balance Sheet Data
As of 12/31/x2

Assets		**Liabilities and Stockholders' Equity**	
Cash	$ 27,000	Accounts payable	$ 28,350
Accounts receivable	54,000	Accrued liabilities	37,800
Inventory	47,250	Long-term obligations	91,800
Plant and equipment	432,000	Common stock	124,200
Accumulated depreciation	(162,000)	Retained earnings	116,100
Total assets	$398,250	Total liabilities and stockholders' equity	$398,250

THE KINGSLEY COMPANY
Income Statement
For the Year 19x2

Sales	$396,800
Cost of goods sold	(173,600)
Gross margin	$223,200
Operating expenses:	
Depreciation	(29,760)
Miscellaneous	(106,640)
Operating income	$ 86,800
Interest expense	(7,440)
Income before taxes	$ 79,360
Income taxes at 30%	23,808
Net income	$ 55,552

Kingsley has 49,680 shares of common stock outstanding. Common stock is priced at $6 per share. Dividends were $1.20 per share. Accounts receivable had a balance on 12/31/x1 of $63,400. All sales in 19x2 were credit sales. The Inventory account balance on 12/31/x1 was $43,000. Total assets at the end of 19x1 amounted to $385,400. The 12/31/x1 balance in the Common Stock account was the same as at the end of 19x2.

Required:

Compute each of the following ratios:

(a) Accounts receivable turnover
(b) Inventory turnover
(c) Quick ratio
(d) Current ratio
(e) Debt-equity ratio
(f) Average collection period

(g) Average number of days per inventory turnover
(h) Earnings per share
(i) Interest coverage
(j) Price-earnings ratio
(k) Return on assets
(l) Return on equity
(m) Return on sales
(n) Dividend payout ratio
(o) Dividend yield ratio

Solution Space for Exercise 18.3:

(a) ______________________________

(b) ______________________________

(c) ______________________________

(d) ______________________________

(e) ______________________________

(f) ______________________________

(g) ______________________________

(h) ______________________________

(i) ______________________________

(j) ______________________________

(k) ______________________________

(l) ______________________________

(m) ______________________________

(n) ______________________________

(o) ______________________________

18.4 The Ginsberg Company makes and sells fancy candy. The following audited data were extracted from the accounting records by Sarah Miles, the company accountant, to be used by her to compute some key ratios for the president, Mark Ginsberg:

	12/31/x8	12/31/x7
Cash	$15,000	$92,000
Accounts receivable (net)	$55,000	$144,000
Inventory	$85,000	$163,000
Marketable securities	$32,000	$8,000
Accounts payable	$78,000	$124,000
Other short-term payables	$17,000	$27,000

	19x8	19x7
Annual cash sales	$1,750,000	$1,482,000
Annual credit sales	$650,000	$738,000
Cost of goods sold for the year	$1,160,000	$1,331,000

With these data Sarah computed key ratios and provided the president with the following information:

1. The acid-test ratio as of 12/31/x8 is 1.968. This ratio is a measure of short-term liquidity because it compares the amount of resources provided by creditors to the resources provided by stockholders.
2. The inventory turnover ratio for 19x8 is 10.73. This ratio is an indicator of the number of times Ginsberg sells its average inventory level during the year. A high inventory turnover usually indicates excessive inventory or outdated candy in stock.

Required:

Prepare a memo to the president which comments on the correctness of the information provided by Sarah Miles and the ethical implications of the work she did in preparing the information for the president.

Solution Space for Exercise 18.4:

MEMORANDUM

To: Mr. Mark Ginsberg

From: ____________________

Date: ____________________

Subject: Comments on Sarah Miles' info concerning key financial ratios

Answers to True-False Questions

1. T
2. F The balance sheet gives the financial position at a specific point in time.
3. F Financial statements should be compared across time and across other similar companies.
4. T
5. T
6. F Company financial data with industry norms has considerable value in financial statement analysis.
7. F The statement of cash flows shows how cash was obtained during the period and how it was used.
8. T
9. T
10. T
11. T
12. F Accounts receivable turnover measures the effectiveness of a firm's credit and collection policies.
13. T
14. F The higher the debt-equity ratio, the more risky the company is as an investment.
15. T
16. F Inventory turnover measures the appropriateness of a firm's inventory level.
17. F It is defined as net income divided by stated dividends on preferred stock.
18. T
19. F High financial leverage carries with it the possibility of great return, but it also entails high risk.
20. T
21. T

Answers to Fill-in-the-Blank Questions

1. income statement
2. Horizontal analysis
3. common-size statements
4. Vertical analysis
5. working capital
6. balance sheet
7. trend analysis
8. retained earnings statement
9. current ratio
10. Quick assets
11. capitalization ratio
12. earnings per share
13. debt-equity ratio
14. convertible securities
15. price-earnings ratio
16. return on sales
17. Financial leverage

Answers to Multiple-Choice Questions

1. (b) The statement of working capital is not today regarded as a primary financial statement.
2. (a)
3. (c)
4. (c) There is no such thing as oblique analysis.
5. (a)
6. (d) Financial ratios are generally easy to compute.

Solutions to Exercises

18.1 (a)

	19x5	19x4	19x3	19x2
Current assets	70%	81%	90%	100%
Inventory	45%	65%	82%	100%
Current liabilities	91%	93%	96%	100%

(b)

	19x5	19x4	19x3	19x2
Current ratio	1.60	1.80	1.95	2.08
Quick ratio	0.91	0.83	0.75	0.68

(c) Trend data enable the analyst to compare financial statement items over time to see if any data patterns are observed. From part (b) we see that the current ratio over time is decreasing, suggesting that Phelps's ability to meet its short-term obligations is declining. However, we note that the quick ratio is increasing over time; this ratio gives a better picture of Phelps's ability to meet its short-term debts than does the current ratio. The conclusion is that Phelps's liquidity picture is getting better over time but still needs much improvement since the quick ratio in 19x5 is still below 1.

18.2 (a)

Common-Size Balance Sheet Data

	12/31/x8	1/1/x8
Cash	6	7
Accounts receivable (net)	24	23
Inventories	26	28
Property, plant, and equipment	74	62
Accumulated depreciation	(30)	(20)
Total assets	100	100
Current liabilities	34	26
Stockholders' equity	66	74
Total liabilities and stockholders' equity	100	100

(b) Common-size statements enable the analyst to discern changes in a company's financial condition from year to year. When financial statements are common size, they are on the same footing, and so it is easy to compare like financial statement items.

18.3 (a) Accounts receivable turnover = $396,800/[.5 × ($63,400 + $54,000)] = 6.76
(b) Inventory turnover = $173,600/[.5 × ($43,000 + $47,250)] = 3.85
(c) Quick ratio = ($27,000 + $54,000)/($28,350 + $37,800) = 1.22
(d) Current ratio = ($27,000 + $54,000 + $47,250)/($28,350 + $37,800) = 1.94
(e) Debt-equity ratio = ($28,350 + $37,800 + $91,800)/($124,200 + $116,100) = 0.66
(f) Average collection period = 365/6.76 = 54.0 days
(g) Average number of days per inventory turnover = 365/3.85 = 94.8 days
(h) Earnings per share = $55,552/49,680 = $1.12 per share
(i) Interest coverage = $86,800/$7,440 = 11.67
(j) Price-earnings ratio = $6/$1.12 = 5.357
(k) Return on assets = ($55,552 + $7,440 × 0.7)/($385,400 + $398,250)/2 = 15.5%
(l) Return on equity = $55,552/$240,300 = 23.1%
(m) Return on sales = $55,552/$396,800 = 14%
(n) Dividend payout ratio = $1.20/$1.12 = 1.07
(o) Dividend yield ratio = $1.20/$6 = 0.20

18.4 The information provided to you by Sarah Miles is incorrect in several respects. First, her computation of the acid-test ratio as of 12/31/x8 should be 1.094; what she reported is actually the current ratio. While both of these ratios measure short-term liquidity, the acid-test ratio is a measure of more immediate liquidity in that it indicates Ginsberg's ability to pay its immediate debts from cash or near-cash assets. Sarah's explanation of the meaning of the acid-test ratio is also wrong; her explanation actually describes the meaning of the debt-to-equity ratio.

Second, her computation of the 19x8 inventory turnover ratio is in error; it should be 9.33 instead of 10.73. Apparently she used the 19x7 cost of goods sold amount instead of the 19x8 amount. Further, her comment about a high inventory turnover rate's being indicative of excessive inventory or outdated candy is wrong; a low, not a high, inventory turnover rate would indicate this.

According to the Standards of Ethical Conduct for Management Accountants, Sarah has a responsibility to maintain an appropriate level of professional competence and to prepare an appropriate analysis of relevant and reliable information. It seems clear that Sarah has failed to meet these standards in this situation.

Chapter **19**

Preparing the Statement of Cash Flows

CHAPTER OVERVIEW AND LEARNING OBJECTIVES

In this final chapter of the text you will learn about the statement of cash flows. This is a major financial statement, as are the balance sheet and income statement. You will learn how this statement is prepared and how it is used by managers, investors, and financial analysts. After completing this chapter, you should understand:

1. The evolution of the statement of cash flows
2. The purpose of the statement of cash flows
3. The types of cash flows in each part of the three sections of the statement of cash flows
4. How to use the indirect method, the direct method, and the T-account approach in preparing the statement of cash flows
5. How to prepare a schedule disclosing direct-exchange transactions
6. How the statement of cash flows is used by a firm's managers and by other interested parties

AN OUTLINE FOR CHAPTER STUDY

A. The statement of cash flows has evolved over the past 30 years into what now is a major financial statement. Nowadays, it is to be prepared in a fashion that conforms to Financial Accounting Standards Board (FASB) Standard No. 95. This standard came out in 1987, and its requirements for the statement of cash flows will be developed in this chapter.

B. The chief purpose of the statement of cash flows is to provide information about the sources and uses of a firm's cash during a given time period. According to FASB Standard No. 95, the statement of cash flows should provide users with insights about the following:

1. The firm's ability to generate positive future net cash flows
2. The firm's ability to meet its financial obligations and pay dividends
3. The future need of the firm for external financing
4. The reasons for the difference between net income and net cash flows related to operating activities
5. The effects of the firm's cash and noncash investing and financing activities.

C. Cash equivalents are highly liquid investments that may easily be converted into a known amount of cash and are near to their maturity dates. The statement of cash flows is designed to show financial statement users why cash and cash equivalents changed as they did over a given period of time.

D. The organization of the statement of cash flows has been specified by the FASB. The statement has three sections which reveal cash flows that come about as a result of the following three activities:

1. Operating activities. These are events and transactions that relate to the provision of goods and services. Transactions that enter into the determination of net income are generally classified as operating activities. This section of the statement shows cash flows from the production and sale of goods and services. It also includes cash receipts from interest on securities and cash disbursements to pay taxes or to pay interest on the firm's debt.
2. Investing activities. The activities for this section involve granting or collecting loans, acquiring or disposing of investments, and buying or selling productive, long-term assets. It is important to note that these activities include changes in the principal amount of loans, but not the interest earned on these loans. (The interest is included in the section on operating activities.)
3. Financing activities. The activities for the last section are transactions involving the firm's debt or equity capital. Included in this section of the statement are cash receipts from the issuance of debt or the sale of the firm's own capital stock. It should be observed that this section does not include cash disbursements to pay interest on the firm's debt. (Interest payments are included in the section for operating activities.)

Exhibit 19-1 in the text provides a nice summary of the various activities reported in the statement of cash flows. You should have this exhibit readily available for reference purposes.

E. There are three sources of data in preparing the statement of cash flows. They are:

1. The income statement
2. Comparative balance sheets
3. Other selected transactions of the firm

There are two alternative methods used in preparing the operating activities section of the statement of cash flows. They are the direct method and indirect method; these methods are summarized in the next two sections.

F. The indirect method (or the reconciliation method) of preparing the operating activities section of the statement of cash flows involves beginning with the accrual accounting-based income statement and then adjusting the net income amount to a cash basis. The end result of these adjustments yields the cash flows from operating activities. Typical adjustments to accrual accounting-based net income for a merchandising firm include the following:

1. Add to (subtract from) net income a decrease (an increase) in accounts receivable.
2. Add to (subtract from) net income a decrease (an increase) in merchandise inventory.
3. Add to (subtract from) net income an increase (a decrease) in accounts payable.
4. Add to (subtract from) net income a decrease (an increase) in prepaid expenses.
5. Add to (subtract from) net income an increase (a decrease) in accrued liabilities.
6. Add to (subtract from) net income an increase (a decrease) in deferred income taxes.
7. Add to net income depreciation expense, depletion expense, and amortization expense.

G. Under the direct method a cash-basis income statement is constructed. The income statement items are included in the cash flow statement in the operating activities section. Examples of how accrual accounting net income items for a merchandising firm are adjusted to give the corresponding cash-basis income statement items are given below:

1.	Cash receipts from customers:	
	Accrual accounting revenue	$$$
	Add: Decrease in accounts receivable	$$$
	Subtract: Decrease in deferred revenue	$$$
	Cash collected from customers	$$$
2.	Cash payments to suppliers of merchandise:	
	Accrual accounting cost of goods sold	$$$
	Add: Increase in merchandise inventory	$$$
	Subtract: Increase in accounts payable	$$$
	Cash payments to merchandise suppliers	$$$

3. Cash payments to employees:

Accrual accounting wages expense	$$$
Add: Decrease in accrued wages payable	$$$
Cash payments to employees	$$$

4. Cash payments for income taxes:

Accrual accounting income tax expense	$$$
Add: Decrease in deferred taxes	$$$
Cash payments for income taxes	$$$

5. Cash payments for insurance and property taxes:

Accrual accounting insurance and property tax expense	$$$
Add: Increase in prepaid expenses	$$$
Cash payments for insurance and property taxes	$$$

H. The second section of the cash flow statement focuses on investment activities. This section includes the following types of items:

1. Cash receipts from the sale of securities such as stock in other organizations or bonds (not including cash equivalents)
2. Cash receipts from the sale of buildings, land, and equipment
3. Cash disbursements for the procurement of securities that are not cash equivalents
4. Cash disbursements for the purchase of buildings, land, and equipment

I. The third section of the statement of cash flows emphasizes financing activities. This section contains items such as the following:

1. Cash receipts from the issuance of notes, bonds, and other debt instruments
2. Cash receipts from the issuance of stock
3. Cash disbursements for the liquidation of notes, bonds, and other types of debt
4. Cash disbursements for dividends

J. Sometimes T-accounts are used to help in the preparation of the cash flow statement. The procedure for using T-accounts is as follows:

1. Prepare the T-accounts.
2. Enter the account balances.
3. Analyze the cash flows from operating activities. Make all T-account entries that pertain to changes in cash and cash equivalents.
4. Analyze the cash flows from investing activities. Make all T-account entries that relate to changes in cash and cash equivalents.
5. Analyze the cash flows from financing activities. Place in the T-accounts all the entries that involve a change in cash or cash equivalents.

When these steps are completed, the Cash and Cash Equivalents T-account will contain all the information needed to prepare the statement of cash flows.

K. It is common practice when preparing the investing activities and financing activities sections of the statement of cash flows to report gross transaction amounts (all the individual component amounts that relate to a cash flow) rather than just the net amount for that cash flow. However, net amounts are used in the operating activities section.

L. When a firm has a substantive investing or financing activity that does not involve a cash flow, this is called a direct-exchange transaction. Such transactions are not included in the body of a cash flow statement but should be disclosed in a separate schedule accompanying the statement.

M. Both managers of firms and those outside the firm who are interested in the activities of the firm use the cash flow statement as a convenient way to reconcile net income with cash flows. The cash flow statement helps managers determine the firm's dividend policy and needs for borrowing. The statement of cash flows also provides information to managers about the ability of the firm to invest in facilities and equipment. Investors, creditors, and financial analysts use the cash flow statement to help predict a firm's future performance.

KEY TERMS

Cash equivalents 941
Direct exchange (or noncash) transaction 966
Direct method 943
Financing activities 941
Indirect method (or reconciliation method) 943
Investing activities 941
Operating activities 941
Statement of cash flows 939

SELF-EVALUATION QUESTIONS AND ANSWERS

True-False Questions

F 1. In 1987 the Securities and Exchange Commission issued a standard which requires that the statement of cash flows be prepared in a specified manner.

T 2. The cash flow statement focuses on the total of a firm's cash and cash equivalents.

T 3. Today most managers, investors, and financial analysts regard the cash flow statement to be as important as a firm's balance sheet or income statement.

F 4. The financing activities section of the cash flow statement should include the cash flows needed to pay the interest on the company's debt.

T 5. The reconciliation method of preparing the operating activities section of the cash flow statement is the same as the indirect method.

F 6. The investing activities section of the cash flow statement should include cash receipts from any interest-bearing securities owned by the firm.

F 7. Sources of information used in preparing the statement of cash flows include a firm's balance sheet, but not the income statement prepared on an accrual-accounting basis.

F 8. Significant direct-exchange transactions are included in the body of the statement of cash flows.

T 9. The statement of cash flows provides useful information for both managers and interested parties outside the organization.

T 10. The practice of reporting gross transaction amounts instead of net amounts in the investing and financing portions of the cash flow statement is regarded by accountants as the proper method of presentation.

F 11. The cash flow statement does not provide information about the ability of a firm to invest in facilities, equipment, or expanded operations.

T 12. In the statement of cash flows, investment activities would include cash inflows from the collection of loans.

F 13. Paying off a loan is an example of a cash outflow that would be included in the investment activities section of the cash flow statement.

T 14. The cash flow statement should provide users of financial statements insight concerning the future needs of a firm for external financing.

F 15. Returns on interest-bearing securities is an example of cash outflows that would appear in the operating activities section of the cash flow statement.

F 16. Depletion and amortization are examples of cash expenses.

T 17. After using the T-account approach to assist in preparing the cash flow statement, all the information needed to prepare that statement is summarized in the Cash and Cash Equivalents account.

F 18. In the statement of cash flows, cash inflows from the sale of productive, long-lived assets would be included in the financial activities section.

F 19. In order to obtain the amount of cash collected from customers, an increase in deferred revenue should be subtracted from accrual accounting-based total revenue for a given period.

T 20. Cash outflows resulting from the production of goods or services would appear in the operating activities section of the statement of cash flows.

Fill-in-the-Blank Questions

1. In the cash flow statement, operating activities include all activities related to the provision of goods and services.
2. The collection of loans is an illustration of a(n) investing activity in the statement of cash flows.

3. Cash equivalents are highly liquid investments that may easily be converted into a known amount of cash and are near to their maturity dates.

4. Cash payments of dividends to stockholders are an example of a(n) financing activity in the cash flow statement.

5. Under the direct method of preparing the operating activities section of the cash flow statement, income statement items are listed on the cash flow statement, adjusted to a cash basis.

6. Investing activities are defined as extending or collecting loans, acquiring or disposing of investments, and buying or selling productive long-term assets.

7. The cash payment of taxes to the government is an example of a(n) Operating activity in the cash flow statement.

8. Cash outflows for interest payments are included in the Operating activities section of the statement of cash flows.

9. The indirect method of preparing the operating activities section of the cash flow statement uses the net income figure and then adjusts it from an accrual basis to a cash basis.

10. Financing activities are the cash flow transactions involving debt or equity capital, such as receipts from issuance of debt or the sale of the company's own capital stock.

11. In the indirect method of preparing the operating activities section of the cash flow statement, depreciation expense is added to net income as an adjustment to net income.

12. A transaction which does not involve cash is called a(n) direct exchange transaction.

Multiple-Choice Questions

C 1. According to FASB Standard No. 95, the statement of cash flows should provide financial statement users insight about all of the following *except*:
(a) the firm's ability to generate future positive net cash flows.
(b) the firm's ability to pay its debts and pay dividends.
(c) the reasons for the difference between net income and the net cash flows related to financing activities.
(d) the future needs of the firm for external financing.

A 2. Consider the two statements that follow concerning adjustments to net income under the indirect method of preparing the operating activities section of the cash flow statement.
I. An increase in prepaid expenses should be subtracted from net income.
II. An increase in accounts payable should be subtracted from net income.
Which is (are) correct?
(a) Only I
(b) Only II
(c) Both I and II
(d) Neither I nor II

B 3. Which of the following is *not* a section of a statement of cash flows as specified by the FASB?
(a) Operating activities
(b) Accounting activities
(c) Financing activities
(d) Investing activities

B 4. Which of the following would appear in the financing activities section of the statement of cash flows?
(a) Purchase of stock in another company
(b) Payment of dividends
(c) Purchase of equipment
(d) Sale of land

B 5. Consider the following two statements about adjustments to net income under the indirect method of preparing the operating activities section of the cash flow statement.

I. A decrease in accounts receivable should be subtracted from net income.

II. An increase in merchandise inventory should be subtracted from net income.

Which is (are) true?

(a) Only I

(b) Only II

(c) Both I and II

(d) Neither I nor II

Exercises

19.1 The Welbourn Company had the following transactions last year:

1. Paid deferred income taxes of $18,350.
2. Issued Welbourn common stock in exchange for a building valued at $84,000 and land valued at $23,000.
3. Purchased production materials costing $52,600 for cash.
4. Purchased an automated machine for the assembly department for $400,000 cash.
5. Recorded depreciation expense of $48,000.
6. Sold a fully depreciated machine in the assembly department for $12,000. The machine had a cost of $154,000 when initially purchased.
7. Paid cash dividends of $34,100.
8. Sold stock in a pharmaceutical company for $95,400 cash, the same amount that was initially paid for the stock.
9. Recorded amortization expense of $17,800.
10. Received $14,000 cash for deferred revenue.
11. Paid off an income tax liability from two years ago amounting to $65,900.

Required:

Prepare a table with the headings indicated below that will classify each of the given transactions.

Transaction Number	Activity Type*	Effect on Cash**	In Body of Cash Flow Statement (Y/N)?

* Operating, investing, or financing.

** Increase, decrease, or no change.

Assume that the direct method is used in preparing the cash flow statement.

Solution Space for Exercise 19.1:

#	Operating	Investing	Financing	Effect on Cash	CF Statement
1	18,350			D	Y
2				NC	N
3	52,600			D	Y
4		400,000		D	Y
5				NC	N
6		12000		I	Y
7			34,100	D	Y
8		95,400		I	Y

#	Oper.	Inv.	Fin	Effect/Cash	SOCF
9				NC	No
10	14,000			Incr.	Yes
11	65,900			D	Yes

19.2 The Gardner Company had the following changes in balance sheet accounts last year:

1. Wages payable—increase of $15,300
2. Prepaid expenses—increase of $8,920
3. Mortgages payable—decrease of $48,200
4. Accumulated depreciation—increase of $63,000
5. Accounts receivable—increase of $25,700
6. Merchandise inventory—decrease of $11,400
7. Deferred taxes—decrease of $30,500
8. Patents—decrease of $7,000
9. Equipment—increase of $105,000
10. Deferred revenue—increase of $14,000
11. Accounts payable—decrease of $19,800

Required:

For each of the given balance sheet account changes, do the following, assuming that the indirect method is used for operating activities:

(a) Indicate the section of the cash flow statement where the change will be reported.
(b) Show how the change will be reported on the cash flow statement.

Solution Space for Exercise 19.2:

Item	Section of Statement	How Change Is Reported
1	Operating	added to Net Income
2	Operating	subtr from Net Income
3	Investing	Outflow
4	Operating	added to Net Income
5	Oper.	subtr from Net Income
6	Oper	add to Net Income
7	Oper	subtr from Net Income
8	Oper.	add to Net Income
9	Investing	Cash outflow
10	Oper.	Added to Net Income
11	Oper	subtr from NI

19.3 The Rourke Company, a merchandising firm in Troy, has provided the following financial statements for 19x3:

THE ROURKE COMPANY
Income Statement
For the Year Ended 12/31/x3

Sales	$342,000
Cost of goods sold	191,500
Gross margin	$150,500
Operating expenses	86,300
Operating income	$ 64,200
Interest expense	19,260
Net income	$ 44,940

THE ROURKE COMPANY
Comparative Balance Sheets
As of 12/31/x2 and 12/31/x3

Assets	**19x3**	**19x2**
Cash	$ 72,980	$ 16,580
Accounts receivable	88,560	47,560
Inventory	107,800	72,130
Prepaid expenses	3,280	4,100
Land	82,000	57,400
Buildings	403,000	328,000
Accumulated depreciation	(83,640)	(56,580)
Total assets	$673,980	$469,190
Liabilities and Owners' Equity		
Accounts payable	$ 83,160	$ 9.440
Accrued liabilities	14,730	11,600
Bonds payable (due in 19x9)	75,000	—
Common stock	423,000	394,000
Retained earnings	78,090	54,150
Total liabilities and owners' equity	$673,980	$469,190

The following data pertain to the financial activities of Rourke during 19x3:

1. Included in operating expenses is depreciation expense of $27,060.
2. Dividends amounting to $21,000 were declared and paid in cash.
3. New land was purchased for $24,600 cash.
4. A new building was purchased for $75,000. Six-year bonds were issued to cover this building purchase.
5. The company received $29,000 cash for the sale of common stock.
6. The interest expense was paid in cash.

Required:

(a) Prepare a statement of cash flows for 19x3 using the indirect method for the operating activities section of the statement.
(b) Prepare T-accounts to show the changes in Cash and Cash Equivalents for 19x3.
(c) Prepare a 19x3 cash flow statement using the direct method.

Solution Space for Exercise 19.3:

(a)

THE ROURKE COMPANY
Statement of Cash Flows
For the Year Ended December 31, 19x3

Net Income		44,940
Adj to Net Income		
Depreciation Exp	27,060	
Increase in A/R	(41,000)	
Increase in Inventory	(35,670)	
Decrease in pp expenses	820	
Increase in A/P	73,720	
Increase in Accrued Liab	3130	
Total Adj. to Net Income		28,060
Net CF from Operating		73,000
CF from Investing		
Outflow for Land	(24600)	
Total CF from Investing		(24,600)
CF from financing		
Sale of Common Stock	29,000	
Outflow for dividends	(21,000)	
Net CF from Financing		8,000
Net Increase in Cash + CE		54,600
Beg bal of Cash + CE		16,580
Ending bal of Cash + CE		72,980
Investing + Financing Not		
affected by Cash		
Purchase of Building by		
issuance of 6yr bonds		75,000

(b)

Cash and Cash Equivalents

Accounts Receivable

Inventory

Accounts Payable

Prepaid Expenses

Accrued Liabilities

Land

Common Stock

Buildings

Retained Earnings

Accumulated Depreciation

Bonds Payable

(c)

THE ROURKE COMPANY
Statement of Cash Flows
For the Year Ended December 31, 19x3

19.4 You work in the Consulting Division of an accounting firm and have been approached by Janice Webber, president of Mahar Enterprises, for an explanation of why a "statement of cash flows" is important and how it could be of benefit to her. Janice points out, "For years I have been reading and analyzing our company balance sheets and income statements and that seems good enough for me."

Required:

Prepare a memo to Janice Webber explaining clearly and concisely why a statement of cash flows is important and how she could benefit from such a statement.

Solution Space for Exercise 19.4:

MEMORANDUM

To: Ms. Janice Webber

From: ______________________

Date: ______________________

Subject: The importance and usefulness of a statement of cash flows

1) Firms ability to generate positive future cash flows
2) firms ability to meet financial obligations + pay dividends
3) future need of firm for external financing
4) effects of Both cash + not cash investing + financing activities

Answers to True-False Questions

1. F The Financial Accounting Standards Board issued the standard.
2. T
3. T
4. F The cash used to pay the interest on a company's debt should be included in the operating activities section of the cash flow statement.
5. T
6. F Cash receipts from interest-bearing securities should be included in the operating activities section of the cash flow statement.
7. F The accrual accounting income statement is also used to prepare the cash flow statement.
8. F These transactions should be in a schedule that accompanies the body of the cash flow statement.
9. T
10. T
11. F It does provide information about the ability of a firm to invest in facilities.
12. T
13. F Paying off a loan would be included in the financing activities section of the cash flow statement.
14. T
15. F Returns on interest-bearing securities are an example of a cash inflow (not outflow) that would be included in the operating activities section of the cash flow statement.
16. F Depletion and amortization are noncash expenses.
17. T
18. F Cash inflows from the sale of productive, long-lived assets would be included in the investing activities section of the cash flow statement.
19. F An increase in deferred revenue should be added to accrual accounting revenue.
20. T

Answers to Fill-in-the-Blank Questions

1. operating
2. investing
3. Cash equivalents
4. financing
5. direct
6. Investing
7. operating
8. operating
9. indirect
10. Financing
11. added to
12. direct-exchange (noncash)

Answers to Multiple-Choice Questions

1. (c)
2. (a) An increase in accounts payable should be added to net income.
3. (b)
4. (b) The items in (a), (c), and (d) are included in the investing activities section of the cash flow statement.
5. (b) A decrease in accounts receivable should be added to net income.

Solutions to Exercises

19.1

Transaction Number	Activity Type: Operating	Investing	Financing	Effect on Cash	In Body of Cash Flow Statement?
1	×			Decrease	Y
2				No change	N
3	×			Decrease	Y
4		×		Decrease	Y
5				No change	N
6		×		Increase	Y
7			×	Decrease	Y
8		×		Increase	Y
9				No change	N
10	×			Increase	Y
11	×			Decrease	Y

19.2

Item	Section of Statement	How Change Is Reported
1	Operating	Addition to net income
2	Operating	Subtraction from net income
3	Financing	Cash outflow
4	Operating	Addition to net income
5	Operating	Subtraction from net income
6	Operating	Addition to net income
7	Operating	Subtraction from net income
8	Operating	Addition to net income
9	Investing	Cash outflow
10	Operating	Addition to net income
11	Operating	Subtraction from net income

19.3 **(a)** Indirect method:

THE ROURKE COMPANY
Statement of Cash Flows
For the Year Ended December 31, 19x3

Cash flows from operating activities		
Net income		$ 44,940
Adjustments to net income to determine cash provided by operations:		
Depreciation expense	$ 27,060	
Decrease in prepaid expenses	820	
Increase in accrued liabilities	3,130	
Increase in inventory	(35,670)	
Increase in accounts payable	73,720	
Increase in accounts receivable	(41,000)	
Total adjustments		28,060
Net cash flow from operating activities		$ 73,000
Cash flows from investing activities		
Purchase of land		(24,600)
Cash flows from financing activities		
Payment of dividends	$(21,000)	
Sale of common stock	29,000	
Net cash received from financing activities		8,000
Net increase in cash and cash equivalents		$ 56,400
Beginning balance of cash and cash equivalents		16,580
Ending balance of cash and cash equivalents		$ 72,980
Investing and financing activities not affecting cash:		
Purchase of new building by issuance of 6-year bonds		$ 75,000

(b)

Cash and Cash Equivalents

Net income	$44,940	Inventory	$35,670
Depr.	27,060	Accts. rec.	41,000
Prepd. exp.	820		
Accru. liab.	3,130		
Accts. pay.	73,720		
Net cash from oper.	73,000		
		Land	24,600
Sale of stock	29,000	Dividends	21,000
Incr. in cash and equiv.	56,400		

Accounts Receivable

Beg. bal.	$47,560		
	41,000		
End. bal.	$88,560		

Inventory

Beg. bal.	$ 72,130		
	35,670		
End. bal.	$107,800		

Accounts Payable

		Beg. bal.	$ 9,440
			73,720
		End. bal.	$83,160

Prepaid Expenses

Beg. bal.	$4,100		$820
End. bal.	$3,280		

Accrued Liabilities

		Beg. bal.	$11,600
			3,130
		End. bal.	$14,730

Land

Beg. bal.	$57,400		
	24,600		
End. bal.	$82,000		

Common Stock

		Beg. bal.	$394,000
			29,000
		End. bal.	$423,000

Buildings

Beg. bal.	$328,000		
	75,000	(No effect on cash)	
End. bal.	$403,000		

Retained Earnings

	$21,000	Beg. bal.	$54,150
			44,940
		End. bal.	$78,090

Accumulated Depreciation

		Beg. bal.	$56,580
			27,060
		End. bal.	$83,640

Bonds Payable

(No effect on cash)			$75,000
		End. bal.	$75,000

(c) Direct method:

THE ROURKE COMPANY
Statement of Cash Flows
For the Year Ended December 31, 19x3

Cash flows from operating activities:		
Cash received from customers: $342,000 – $41,000 =		$301,000
Cash payments		
For merchandise: $191,500 + $35,670 – $73,720 =	$153,450	
For operating expenses: $86,300 – $27,060 – $820 – $3,130 =	55,290	
For interest expense	19,260	
Total cash payments		228,000
Net cash flow from operations		$ 73,000
Cash flows from investing activities:		
Purchase of land		(24,600)
Cash flows from financing activities:		
Payment of dividends	($21,000)	
Sale of common stock	29,000	
Net cash received from financing activities		8,000
Net increase in cash and cash equivalents		$ 56,400
Beginning balance of cash and cash equivalents		16,580
Ending balance of cash and cash equivalents		$ 72,980
Investing and financing activities not affecting cash:		
Purchase of new building by issuance of 6-year bonds		$ 75,000

19.4 While you feel that your reading and analyses of balance sheets and income statements have been sufficient for you in the past, you should understand that the statement of cash flows brings together information from income statements and balance sheets that is virtually impossible to obtain easily without the cash flow statement.

The statement of cash flows will give you insights into Mahar's ability to generate positive future net cash flows and to meet its financial obligations. It will reveal Mahar's future needs for external financing and give information on why Mahar's net income from operations is different from its cash flows from operations. All of this information provided by the statement of cash flows can be useful for planning future operating, financial, and investing activities at Mahar. What's more, outside parties may need to know how Mahar is generating and using cash; this type of information would be useful to future lenders to and investors in Mahar Enterprises.

I trust this information is helpful to you in seeing why the cash flow statement is so important.

Notes

Notes

Notes